VILLAGE INFER

WITCHES' ADVOCATES

**IBERIAN ENCOUNTER
AND EXCHANGE
475–1755 | Vol. 5**

SERIES EDITORS
Erin Kathleen Rowe
Michael A. Ryan
The Pennsylvania State University
Press

The Iberian Peninsula has
historically been an area of the
world that fostered encounters and
exchanges among peoples from
different societies. For centuries,
Iberia acted as a nexus for the
circulation of ideas, people, objects,
and technology around the pre-
modern western Mediterranean,
Atlantic, and eventually, the Pacific.
Iberian Encounter and Exchange,
475–1755, combines a broad
thematic scope with the territorial
limits of the Iberian Peninsula and
its global contacts. In doing so,
works in this series will juxtapose
previously disparate areas of study
and challenge scholars to rethink
the role of encounter and exchange
in the formation of the modern
world.

ADVISORY BOARD
Paul H. Freedman
Richard Kagan
Marie Kelleher
Ricardo Padrón
Teofilo F. Ruiz
Marta V. Vicente

OTHER TITLES IN THIS SERIES
Thomas W. Barton, *Contested
Treasure: Jews and Authority in the
Crown of Aragon*

Mercedes García-Arenal and Gerard
Wiegers, eds., *Polemical Encounters:
Christians, Jews, and Muslims in
Iberia and Beyond*

Nicholas R. Jones, *Staging* Habla de
negros: *Radical Performances of the
African Diaspora in Early Modern
Spain*

Freddy Cristóbal Domínguez,
*Radicals in Exile: English Catholic
Books During the Reign of Phillip II*

VILLAGE INFERNOS AND WITCHES' ADVOCATES

WITCH-HUNTING IN NAVARRE, 1608–1614

LU ANN HOMZA

THE PENNSYLVANIA STATE UNIVERSITY PRESS
UNIVERSITY PARK, PENNSYLVANIA

Library of Congress Cataloging-in-Publication Data

Names: Homza, Lu Ann, 1958– author.
Title: Village infernos and witches' advocates : witch-hunting in Navarre, 1608–1614 / Lu Ann Homza.
Other titles: Iberian encounter and exchange, 475–1755 ; vol. 5.
Description: University Park, Pennsylvania : The Pennsylvania State University Press, [2022] | Series: Iberian encounter and exchange, 475–1755 ; vol. 5 | Includes bibliographical references and index.
Summary: "A revisionist account of the Spanish witch-hunt that took place in northern Navarre from 1608 to 1614. Combines new readings of the Inquisitional evidence with archival finds from non-Inquisitional sources, including local secular and religious courts, and from notarial and census records"—Provided by publisher.
Identifiers: LCCN 2021047879 | ISBN 9780271091815 (cloth) | ISBN 9780271091822 (paper)
Subjects: LCSH: Witch hunting—Spain—Navarre—History—17th century. | Inquisition—Spain—Navarre—History—17th century. | Witchcraft—Spain—Navarre—History—17th century.
Classification: LCC BF1584.S7 H66 2022 | DDC 203/.32094652—dc23
LC record available at https://lccn.loc.gov/2021047879

The Pennsylvania State University Press is a member of the Association of University Presses.

It is the policy of The Pennsylvania State University Press to use acid-free paper. Publications on uncoated stock satisfy the minimum requirements of American National Standard for Information Sciences—Permanence of Paper for Printed Library Material, ANSI Z39.48–1992.

Contents

Acknowledgments

This project has taken a startlingly long time to complete because the sources wouldn't stop coming. Like my predecessors who studied this witch hunt, I too began with materials from the Spanish Inquisition and focused on Inquisitor Alonso de Salazar Frías. My original ambition was to understand Salazar as a Catholic lawyer and inquisitor in seventeenth-century Spain: whereas earlier scholars had highlighted his possible links to modernity, my initial aim was to restore him to his early modern environment. Everyone knew that the inquisition's trial records of the witch-defendants in this persecution had been lost when Napoleon's forces burned down the relevant inquisition tribunal in 1808. We all believed that the most important primary sources were contained in an enormous dossier of inquisition materials in Madrid's Archivo Histórico Nacional, which famed researcher Gustav Henningsen had discovered in 1967. Thanks to James Amelang, María José del Rio, Erin K. Rowe, Alison P. Weber, and Richard L. Kagan, I was able to present some initial findings at Madrid's Universidad Autónoma, the University of Virginia, and Johns Hopkins University. I was heartened by the encouragement I received in those settings.

Then, I took a train to Pamplona, and the archives there changed the scope of this study. In that wonderful city, I found innumerable records tied to this witch hunt in two legal jurisdictions beyond the Spanish Inquisition: namely, the royal, secular court system, as well as the episcopal court overseen by Pamplona's bishop. Notarial documents also held fascinating texts that reflected the witch hunt's progress and effects. Extraordinary experts direct the two main archives in Pamplona. They are invested in the highest scholarly goals, happy to welcome researchers, and generous by default. It is such a pleasure to thank them here for their support; I treasure them as colleagues. In the Archivo Diocesano de Pamplona (ADP), I am beyond grateful for the insights and friendship of archivists Don José Luis Sales Tirapu and Teresa Alzugaray. In the Archivo Real y General de Navarra (AGN), archivist Peio J. Monteano Sorbet has been a constant resource for demography, Basque phrases, community norms, and basically everything relating to early modern Navarre. Peio read this manuscript from start to finish to help me manage the gap between early modern orthography and modern Basque spellings that readers today would recognize. Félix Segura Urra, Miriam Etxeberria, and Berta Elcano of the AGN have consistently encouraged my work. Professor Jesús M. Usunáriz Garayoa kindly facilitated my introduction to the Universidad de Navarra. Pamplona friends Pilar López de Goicoechea and Mary Zacher have enthusiastically supported this project from the beginning.

Much of the research for this book occurred while I was the dean for educational policy at William & Mary, and Kate Conley, then Dean of Arts and Sciences, supported the project in every conceivable way. Karin Wulf has expressed faith in my work for years; Teresa Longo has been a long-term ally. Ron Schechter applauded archival finds. Tuska Beneš read an early version of the introduction, with helpful suggestions. Nicholas Popper read the entire study and told me with only a hint of irony that I had to say what the evidence meant. Thanks to Elizabeth Wright, Benjamin Ehlers, Daniel Wasserman-Soler, and Daniel Bornstein, I shared later research results at the University of Georgia, Alma College, and Washington University in St. Louis. Audiences there reinforced the sense that I was on a good track, which helped counterbalance the experience of having work rejected by three journals in a row. Jan Machielsen has generously shared his research on Pierre de Lancre and has looked over mine; he is a comrade, as is everyone else named in these acknowledgments.

Kimberly Lynn laughed with me over my inquisitors' idiosyncrasies and helped me locate crucial legal theory about revocations of confessions before Spanish inquisitors. Celeste I. McNamara postponed her own book revisions to read drafted sections of this study: she offered forceful commentary and pushed me to deepen my arguments. Amanda L. Scott provided constant precious feedback, frequently at a moment's notice, and urged me on. These women set research standards that I have tried hard to follow.

Another important intellectual community for this project is an undergraduate one. Thanks to the support of Professor Emeritus of Government Joel Schwartz, former director of the Roy R. Charles Center for Academic Excellence at William & Mary, I began to take small groups of our undergraduates to Pamplona for archival research in 2009. These trips were only possible because of financial assistance from the Mellon Foundation and William & Mary's honors program. Students spent a semester with me in independent study, learning how to read early modern Spanish handwriting; we then typically traveled over to Spain over spring break. The students' goal was to find legal manuscripts in the AGN or ADP that they could read. They transcribed sections from those manuscripts, and then worked up research papers on particular topics after they returned to campus in Williamsburg, Virginia. Not surprisingly, archivists and staff at the AGN and ADP were invariably encouraging as my students entered archives and handled manuscripts for the first time. While the undergraduates were poring over trials for cloud conjuring, tobacco smuggling, theft, clerics addicted to clockmaking, intent to murder, and so on, I was reading materials about witches. We shared our discoveries every evening and formed a wonderful intellectual bond over early modern Navarre. It was such fun. In chronological order from 2009 to 2019, my thanks to Eric Schmaltz, Kim Dailey, Amanda L. Scott, Aaron Gregory, Meredith Howard, Hanna Langstein, Katie Brown, Ashley Hughes, Julie Silverman, Crosby Enright, Tracey Johnson, Jack Middough, Jessie Dzura, Sagra Alvarado, Morgan Silvers, Jessie Barkin, Maureen Harrison, Mary Andino, Emma Kessel, Molly Duke, Jessica Bimstein, Alex Wingate, Logan Bishop, Leideen Escobar-Hernández, Ansley Levine, Cassie Davenport, and Olivia Vande Woude.

Thank you to Eleanor Goodman, my editor at Penn State University Press, as well as Erin K. Rowe and Michael A. Ryan, the series editors for Iberian Encounter and Exchange, 475–1755, for your interest in this project. My thanks as well to managing editor Laura Reed-Morrisson for her diligent support.

Family support for this investigation has been abundant. Among that network, I am grateful for my equestrian community at Stonehouse Stables in Toano, Virginia. Coaches and friends there have asked questions about the project, understood when I've gone abroad, adjusted training when this project made me distracted, and have taken good care of me and my horses, Land Shark and Springdale. Much appreciation to Tara Mathews Best, E. C. Best, Susan Cornett, Jessica Craig, Aly Haynes-Travers, Karen Hogue, Buddy Janovsky, Isabella Janovsky, Stephanie McCallister, Bill Reiff, Laura Rodríguez, Stacey Schneider, Laura Cornett Wang, and Sydney Wilson. In my immediate domestic circle, Chris and Wendy have cheered me on for years. My father, Daniel, and stepmother, Linda, have followed the archival stories with enthusiasm. Lisa Esposito has been present throughout, in the most crucial sense. Tom is my beloved partner in all things historical and beyond. I am so lucky to have you.

This book is dedicated to my father. He has always encouraged these adventures.

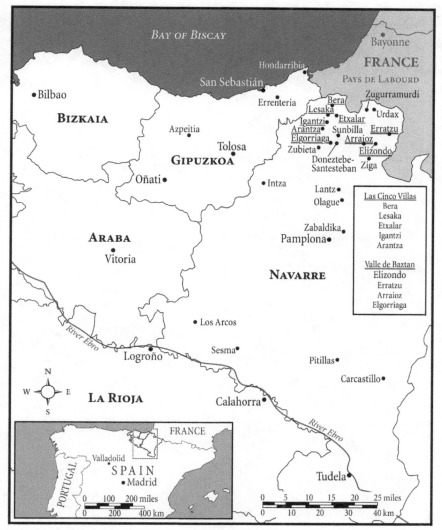

Key witch-hunting sites, 1608–14

INTRODUCTION

The Events

In December 1608, a young woman named María de Ximildegui returned to the village of Zugarramurdi, in northern Navarre, after working across the French border in the Pays de Labourd. María announced to Zugarramurdi's residents that she had belonged to a witches' coven while living in the French Pyrenees; she also asserted that she had attended diabolical gatherings in Zugarramurdi itself.[1] Though now reconverted to Christianity, María remembered the witches she had seen and began to name them. Within four weeks, at least ten men and women, ranging in age from twenty to eighty, confessed to witchcraft in Zugarramurdi's parish church and begged their neighbors' pardon for having committed harmful magic. Those events soon were reported to the tribunal of the Spanish Inquisition in the city of Logroño: Logroño lay outside Navarrese territory, but its inquisitors were responsible for monitoring heresy there.[2] Within two months, or by February 1609, Logroño's inquisitors had seized four alleged ringleaders of the Devil's sect, and they had imprisoned six more individuals who had confessed to witchcraft in Zugarramurdi but then tried to retract their admissions. The inquisitors refused to believe their recantations and started investigations instead.[3]

In the wake of rising accusations, one of Logroño's inquisitors, Juan de Valle Alvarado, went into the field in the second half of 1609 with an edict of faith, which broadcast the inquisition's interest in finding witches and their accomplices. While on visitation, Valle heard three hundred adults confess to witchcraft and sent seventeen of them to the tribunal for trial. By November 1610, in a public ceremony of sentencing called an *auto de fe*, or "act of faith," the inquisition tribunal handed out punishments to thirty-one defendants who had been convicted of the heresy of witchcraft.[4] Eleven of the thirty-one were burned at the stake because they refused to confess and repent; five of those eleven were burned in effigy because they had died in prison during their trials. The other twenty defendants—who had confessed their guilt and repented—were reconciled to the Catholic Church and given penances of imprisonment and exile.[5]

The witches sentenced in November 1610 had described astonishing events while they were under interrogation. Their deeds were read aloud during the auto de fe; a printed pamphlet about them appeared within weeks.[6] The witch suspects said they had deliberately turned away from Christianity in order to worship the Devil. They reported that the Devil had arranged a diabolical apprenticeship, with each stage having its own responsibilities. For example, child-witches were put in charge of guarding toads that the older witches used to make poison. Adult witches sought to wreak as much physical harm as they could and thus damaged crops, raised storms, and poisoned neighbors. The Devil always wanted to recruit more people into his service, so older witches tricked adults into attending his meetings or kidnapped children for the same purpose.[7]

Heresy

From the viewpoint of the Spanish Inquisition and early modern Christianity, Protestant as well as Catholic, the witches of Zugarramurdi were actively engaging in heresy. Heresy has been a concern within Christianity for as long as Christianity has existed. The term comes from the Greek word *hairesis*, which meant "choice" in the ancient world. After Paul the Apostle's encounters with religious dissidents in the first century CE, hairesis gradually came to be associated with religious errors voiced stubbornly and publicly.

It bears emphasizing that heresy was not doubt. Furthermore, heresy could only be defined in opposition to orthodoxy, for Christians had to express what was acceptable before they could tag what was in error. Because the Christian New Testament was not formally codified until the Council of Carthage pronounced its content in 397 CE, and because Christianity's theology and rituals changed over time, the characteristics of heresy altered, too. The earliest heresies in Christianity pertained to Jesus's relationship to God (Arianism); the relative power of God and the Devil (Manicheism); the impact of a priest's ethics on the power of the sacraments he administered (Donatism); and the existence of original sin and free will (Pelagianism). In the twelfth and thirteenth centuries in western Europe, new heresies were labeled as such on account of stubborn public statements about the holiness of poverty (Waldensianism) or apparent belief in a dualistic universe that pitted good against evil (Catharism).[8] In the sixteenth century, followers of Martin Luther, Ulrich Zwingli, and John Calvin were categorized as heretics by Catholic popes because of their insistence, among other things, that the Bible was the only true touchstone for Christianity.

As for the heresy of witchcraft, modern historians now know that the complete stereotype of the European witch came together in the early fifteenth century.[9] When baptized members of early modern Christian communities chose to follow the Devil, they were turning their reverence, trust, and obedience toward God's enemy and violating their baptismal vows: they were deemed heretics as a result. In Navarre in 1608, María de Ximildegui's statements and witch suspects' confessions seemed to make it clear that villagers had joined the Devil's congregation. The Spanish Inquisition—founded to combat heresy—consequently stepped in.

The Spanish Inquisition

From its origins in 1478, the Spanish Inquisition was an institution that blended religious duties and political loyalties. Inquisitors owed their ability to investigate heresy to the papacy, but they were put into office by Spanish kings, and if they had to choose between pope and monarch, they almost always sided with the latter.[10] This does not mean that inquisitors' religious objectives were a cover for political strategies. There was no separation between church and state in early modern Europe. Spanish sovereigns always cared deeply about Catholic orthodoxy; inquisitors knew that their primary responsibility, like that of their medieval predecessors, was to guard the Catholic faith. By 1609, *how* they should protect Catholicism had been laid out in detail.[11] Inquisitors were only supposed to prosecute baptized Christians, because it took a rejection of baptismal vows to make a heretic. The extent of the apostasy should have been persistent and public; in early modern Spain, it could also be implicit. Inquisitors could read heresy into various actions, such as avoiding Mass, following Jewish dietary laws, disputing the virgin birth of Jesus, endorsing sexual intercourse between unmarried, consenting adults, or swearing while gambling.

When such actions came to their attention, inquisitors pursued defendants in various ways. Sometimes, inquisitors (and their employees) could remain relatively passive, for it was not unusual for individuals to denounce themselves for religious errors and beg for forgiveness. If self-denunciations were not in play, witnesses to a potential heresy could appear voluntarily or be solicited by an inquisition tribunal. Once enough testimony had been collected to make proof seem secure, the prosecutor would present an indictment to the inquisitors and request an arrest. The suspect would then be seized and brought to the tribunal for trial. The charges would be read before the defendant, who had to respond immediately and orally to the accusations. Crucially, identifying details about witnesses would be kept secret from defendants in all communications with them, because the Spanish Inquisition, like its medieval counterpart, worried about vengeance from the families of accused heretics. That rule of secrecy was supposed to apply to everyone employed by the tribunal as well as everyone who appeared before it. Witnesses, too, had to swear oaths not to divulge what they said or what they might have learned while testifying.

If an inquisition defendant declined to confess after hearing the charges, inquisitors and their prosecutor proceeded to trial. A silent or stubborn defendant would be presented with a written statement of prosecution testimony, from which specifics again had been expunged to preserve the rule of secrecy. People on trial could try to fight back by guessing the identity of the prosecutor's witnesses and then attacking the motives of those who might have testified against them. This sort of defense strategy typically included the naming of mortal enemies, whose depositions, if they existed, should have been nullified if capital enmity was sufficiently proven. A defendant also could present character witnesses for support as well as people who could contradict the prosecution's evidence. In the end, though, it was rare for inquisitors not to prove their cases.

As for punishment, if a defendant quickly admitted sins and named accomplices, the sentence typically involved readmittance to the Catholic Church through a process of social humiliation and religious reeducation. It bears emphasizing that inquisitors and their theorists had a religious goal behind their legal process, which was to win convicted heretics back to the Catholic Church. Physical discipline was supposed to be applied for spiritual ends.[12] The guilty could be "reconciled" to the church in private ceremonies with the inquisitors and then commanded to carry out penances in the world: they might be required to sponsor a certain number of Masses, to fast, or to recite particular prayers on specific days. The guilty also could endure hearing their crime and punishment read aloud before a large audience in an auto de fe. Autos de fe were grand events for individual tribunals: they required a great deal of planning, as well as enough convicted and reconciled heretics to make the ceremony worthwhile. Autos de fe usually involved a wide range of sentences for a significant variety of offenders. The convicted could be required to wear a penitential garment, called a *sambenito*, whenever they left the house. They could be exiled or condemned to a period of incarceration in a monastery. They also could be sentenced to "perpetual prison"—which was never actually perpetual—with the prison being owned and monitored by the inquisition tribunal. Individuals who were convicted of heresy but did not confess in a timely manner also could be reconciled to the church, though with a much more severe sentence, such as time in the royal galleys. Meanwhile, defiant suspects, and people who had relapsed a second time into heresy, were supposed to be released to secular justices— called "relaxation to the secular arm"—and burned at the stake.

The inquisitors in Logroño who took charge of the witches' investigation in 1609 knew they might face competition from other legal authorities. They could expect interest from Pamplona's bishop, since bishops traditionally monitored their dioceses for religious errors of all kinds; bishops had their own court system, which was called the episcopal legal jurisdiction. Because the Devil helped his followers practice harmful magic (called *maleficium*) against people and property, the secular court system, based in Pamplona, also paid serious attention to suspected witches.[13] Witchcraft in early modern Navarre thus could potentially draw the attention of three legal jurisdictions: inquisitorial, episcopal, and secular. The fact that multiple court systems were interested in the heresy and crime of witchcraft generally held for Catholic environments across early modern Europe.

The Inquisitors' Visitations

This particular witch persecution in Navarre was both wide-ranging and dramatic. In 1609, witchcraft accusations not only spread rapidly beyond the village of Zugarramurdi but also continued even after the inquisition's public auto de fe in November 1610. Denunciations moved west to a cluster of five hamlets, called Las Cinco Villas, on the Spanish-French border. Accusations also spread east and south, to an area known as the Valle de Baztan. They occurred even farther afield in Olague, a short distance from Pamplona, as well as in San Sebastián, in the Basque province of Gipuzkoa. To make matters worse, children almost immediately began to play a crucial role in the accusations. Not only were they victims of the witches' harmful magic, but also hundreds insisted that witches were taking them to the Devil's gatherings against their will. Parents became desperate; village officials wrote to the inquisitors in Logroño; the bishop of Pamplona traveled throughout his diocese to investigate. Eventually, the governing royal council of the Spanish Inquisition, which was called the Suprema and located in Madrid, decided that an inquisitor would have to go back into the field to resolve the situation. At this point, the Logroño tribunal had three inquisitors. Alonso Becerra Holguín had toured the district in 1601; Juan de Valle Alvarado had done the same in 1609. The trip in 1611 thus fell to Alonso de Salazar Frías, who was the tribunal's junior member.

Salazar left on visitation on May 22, 1611, and did not return until January 10, 1612. While on the road, he resolved 1,802 cases of witchcraft. He absolved 1,384 children "as a precaution" (ad cautelam): in accordance with canon law, he defined "children" as under age twelve for girls and under age fourteen for boys. He also absolved 41 adults for having incurred a light suspicion of heresy (abjuración de levi) and reconciled 290 people for the heresy of witchcraft: 190 members of the latter group were under age twenty. Salazar heard 81 children and adults revoke confessions to witchcraft; he also heard 6 people tell him they had relapsed into that heresy.[14]

Once Salazar returned to the inquisition tribunal in Logroño, he refused to follow standard protocol, which dictated that he first should have shared his case notes with his colleagues, inquisitors Becerra and Valle, after which all three would have voted on the guilt of individual suspects. Instead, Salazar locked himself in his office and rebuffed consultation.[15] He declined to follow the usual process because he had decided he had something radical to say. In the report he ultimately sent to the Suprema, on March 24, 1612, he argued that given what he had seen and heard on visitation, the Logroño tribunal lacked sufficient proof to put current and future witch suspects on trial. There were too many contradictions in the witches' statements. There also was a near-total lack of physical evidence that devil worship and evil magic had actually happened. While he was away, Salazar learned how local bribery, coercion, and even torture had produced witchcraft confessions. All these findings gave him pause. His fellow inquisitors were outraged by his position; their conflict continued for a full year and half, with documents

6

flying back and forth to the Suprema. Eventually, in 1614, that council invited Salazar to Madrid.

Revised Instructions

Once there, in consultation with his superiors, Salazar expanded and codified the rules for the inquisition's prosecution of witches. The new rules stressed ascertaining the difference between reality and illusion, verifying intent, discouraging forced confessions, inviting other explanations for catastrophic events, and allowing the revocation of witchcraft admissions made under oath. Finally, the new instructions stated that the witch defendants who had been executed or penanced in the November 1610 auto de fe would have their sentences lifted: they would not lose their property, wear penitential garments, or see their descendants labeled infamous. They could leave the monasteries or convents in which they were secluded and return to Navarre from exile. The new instructions were endorsed in 1614 and sent to every inquisition tribunal in Spanish imperial territory.[16] As a result, modern scholars have believed that the Spanish Inquisition basically never prosecuted witches again.[17]

Modern Appraisals

The Spanish Inquisition hardly ever admitted error or exonerated the dead, and the way this witch hunt ended has astonished historians for centuries. Earlier experts agreed that what mattered most about the episode was its revelation of a skeptical, rational outlook where it was least expected, namely, in a Spanish inquisitor, Salazar, who seemed to confront and overturn superstitious beliefs, and thereby appeared to be ahead of his time.[18] Spain has been associated with anti-modern tendencies and values ever since Dutch and British Protestants created the Black Legend of Spanish atrocities in the sixteenth century.[19] Finding a Spaniard, and an inquisitor, who appeared to dismiss witches as an invention of the imagination allowed the country figuratively to jump ahead of supposedly more progressive countries that experienced severe witch-hunting, such as Germany. In sum, Inquisitor Salazar stood out for his proto-modernity.[20] The story of his battle to reverse false charges of witchcraft became a matter of national pride and a way in which Spanish exceptionalism had positive rather than negative connotations.[21]

New Evidence

Earlier scholars of the Zugarramurdi witch hunt knew that significant evidence about it could not be recovered. For example, none of the witches' trial records survived because Napoleon's troops burned down the Logroño inquisition tribunal as they invaded Spain in 1808. Key researchers—ethnographer and folklorist Gustav Henningsen, along with anthropologist Julio Caro Baroja—consequently believed they had to rely upon the surviving documents that Logroño's inquisitors happened to send to Madrid as well as the papers that the Suprema sent to the inquisitors and preserved as copies. In fact, it was Henningsen who discovered an enormous dossier of such materials in Madrid's Archivo Histórico Nacional (AHN) in 1967.[22] Because he and Caro Baroja assumed the Spanish Inquisition was supremely authoritative during this witch hunt, they did not look beyond its records for other possible sources.

Not seeking out other materials was a mistake. It turns out that critical sources about the witch hunt are held in Pamplona's archives as well as Madrid's. Notaries in Navarre always recorded important village events, while the episcopal and secular court systems in Navarre had long-standing interests in witchcraft prosecutions. Navarrese notarial records and trials in other legal jurisdictions constitute a stunning new body of evidence for this witch hunt, one that is much closer to the ground than what most of the inquisition's holdings can offer. For example, notarial records reveal not only an accused witch's property holdings but peace contracts forced upon neighbors who had bludgeoned others with verbal and physical abuse during the witch hunt. Meanwhile, census registers demonstrate that multiple villages were depopulated as the witch hunt came to an end.

Even more remarkably, sources produced and stored in Navarre demonstrate that the Spanish Inquisition was not the only legal authority in play during the persecution, and Salazar was not the only witch's advocate.[23] Some accused witches decided to seek redress for their dishonor through other legal jurisdictions, even as inquisitors were trying in vain to manage the investigation. Those litigating witches won multiple cases against their accusers in the secular and episcopal courtrooms of Navarre's viceroy and Pamplona's bishop. Other secular prosecutions likewise had this witch hunt as their foundation, even though the catalogued titles of the trials never mention "witch": these prosecutions arose from defamation, intent to murder, aggression with a rock, insults shouted out a window, and dereliction of duty by village constables.[24] Two such trials were only found by Pamplona's archivists in 2014 and 2018: they come from the village of Olague, and their manuscripts contain dozens of statements by self-identified child-witches ranging in age from five to fifteen. Some of these materials are unique in European history; some of the trial manuscripts run to hundreds of folios; until my investigations, none had been studied in any detail.[25] These notarial documents, censuses, and trials are located in the Archivo Real y General de Navarra (AGN) and the Archivo Diocesano de Pamplona (ADP). Many of the surviving inquisition texts about this witch hunt are incomprehensible without these newly discovered sources.

Previous research on this witch persecution was overwhelmingly grounded in descriptions and observations by inquisitors and thus written according to the perceptions of intellectual elites. In contrast, Pamplona's archives reveal what happened from the points of view of the children, women, and men who suffered from, engaged in, and witnessed the miseries of witch-hunting.[26] Their testimonies expose the emotional logic, legal reasoning, and religious and social values of a whole range of hitherto unknown and unheard actors, a number of whom spoke to Inquisitor Salazar when he was in the field.[27] Their depositions reveal the environment that Salazar discovered when he left Logroño and help us understand how he came to his epistemological break. Salazar was not so much ahead of his time in his reasoning as he was capable of being persuaded by emotionally compelling stories of what people said they had endured. He came to doubt not whether witchcraft was possible in theory but whether his tribunal was proceeding against witch suspects with sufficient proof. Notably, too, Salazar did not solve the witch problem on his own. The archives reveal that personnel from the inquisitorial, secular, and episcopal justice systems deliberately collaborated with each other to rectify the miscarriages of justice that the witch hunt entailed, despite those systems' competing sense of privilege.

Witchcraft Scholarship

This book brings this witch hunt in line with fundamental advances made over the last forty years in the study of early modern witchcraft and early modern inquisitions. For much of the twentieth century, scholars who studied witch trials in western Europe from 1500 to 1700 had to answer questions about whether witches had really existed and whether there was any point to exploring them. They had to confront the thesis of Margaret Murray, who asserted in 1921 that women categorized as witches were simply misunderstood members of a pagan fertility cult.[28] They were challenged to explain how witch-craft accusations and prosecutions fit into a progressive vision of European history as moving toward reason and science; one scholar posited that only illiterate peasants in mountain hamlets took witch beliefs seriously.[29]

Then, in the 1960s and 1970s, European historians began to notice mod-ern anthropologists' work on witchcraft in Africa.[30] Anthropologists did not endorse the notion that witches and sorcerers were real, but they did seek to discover what witch beliefs meant and how they worked for the societies that had them. Some English scholars emulated the anthropologists' methods and mapped early modern witchcraft along functional systems; other Euro-pean historians recognized the value of the social science or anthropological approach but hesitated to apply it to their research areas.[31] Nonetheless, every historian of early modern witchcraft in Europe, Britain, or America realized that anthropologists were attempting to understand the phenomenon on its own terms and were inspired accordingly. Questions about truth and reality became irrelevant; instead, scholars began to pay attention to the process— the how and the why—of accusations.

As their studies went on, historians recognized the impossibility of coming to single, overarching causes for large-scale persecutions. They also became aware of the ways in which early modern witchcraft required mul-tilayered research.[32] The phenomena of worshipping the Devil and using diabolical help to carry out harmful magic did not truly occur, but trying to explain beliefs that they did necessarily involved attention to intellectual, religious, gender, social, political, and economic issues rooted in specific environments. Modern scholars found that European witch beliefs were shared across lines of class, sex, and profession, including between elite and popular culture.[33] They discovered that witch accusations often thrived on anxiety about fertility and depended upon authorities taking seriously the complaints of women.[34] Once, historians had imagined that prosecuting witches benefitted central governments, but with time, they also realized that central governments often tried to stop witch-hunting because it had such profoundly negative social effects.[35] All of these angles added to our understanding of the processes and outcomes of witchcraft accusations.

Inquisition Scholarship

Practically concurrently, another scholarly revolution in the study of early modern Europe began in November 1975, when Spanish dictator Francisco

Franco died after ruling Spain since 1939. Once Franco was gone, historians could begin to explore the Spanish Inquisition in an uncensored environment.[36] Studies exploded about the inquisition's structure, processes, and victims. Researchers made efforts to publish transcriptions and collections of primary sources.[37] They learned how the inquisition survived financially. They discovered that clusters of targets seemed to appear at particular chronological moments, which allowed them to suggest phases of inquisitorial activity.[38] Historians also studied specific inquisition tribunals, which revealed interactions among inquisitors, staff, and urban or rural populations.[39] Forty-five years ago, scholars were sure the Spanish Inquisition functioned like a machine; now, we know how uncoordinated and fractious it could be. The best recent work on the Spanish Inquisition in the Spanish Empire focuses on the ways in which particular environments affected practice and highlights the range of priorities that inquisitors could bring to their offices.[40]

Revisions

Significantly, Henningsen and Caro Baroja completed their archival work on this witch hunt as these scholarly revolutions about witch-hunting and the Spanish Inquisition were underway, but they did not take advantage of them.[41] Their research did not allow them to see potential gaps between theory and practice when it came to inquisitors' actions in seventeenth-century Navarre; Henningsen was not sufficiently familiar with early modern Catholicism to appreciate the role that religious fervor could play in the persecution. While both scholars believed the Spanish Inquisition was in charge, inquisitors in Logroño never had a direct line of control over Navarrese villagers, because they lived miles away and depended upon their locally embedded employees to achieve anything. Pamplona's archival sources demonstrate that those inquisition employees bent procedures and norms in the field and actually encouraged vigilante justice. Meanwhile, Navarrese villagers were not only willing to attack their neighbors in extralegal ways but were also legally astute and thoroughly familiar with litigation. Like their peers elsewhere in pre-modern Europe, they used the court systems for private ends when they attempted to recover their honor and exact revenge after suffering witchcraft accusations.[42] As for the question of whether inquisitors, bishops, and other intellectual elites dictated witch beliefs to Navarre's illiterate populace, people there did not need tutorials in the fundamental theology of Christianity, and Navarrese culture had long-standing, terrifying traditions about what witches could do. The interactions between elite and popular culture in this persecution were mutual rather than top-down.

Contributions

This book adds in multiple ways to our understanding of early modern European history. It confirms the benefit of studying various legal jurisdictions where witchcraft is concerned but also adds new twists to findings about witches in other locales. For example, one acclaimed scholar of witchcraft has found that German citizens in Rothenburg were dissuaded from labeling neighbors as witches because city magistrates were very willing to prosecute the accusers for slander.[43] While adults in Navarre could find themselves on trial for defamation over the slur of witch, it turns out that Navarrese *children* were the perfect vehicle for such allegations because they could not be sued for libel. Other scholars recently have highlighted the importance of emotions to the process of witch-hunting. My evidence also demonstrates that emotions were crucial, but with a significant difference: in this persecution, witches were seldom angry themselves; instead, this witch hunt was fundamentally a children's event driven by parental terror and rage.[44] Their dread was as much religious as practical, and a sense of spiritual combat galvanized entire villages. Finally, modern historians have taught us to notice sex, age, and socioeconomic status in witch-hunting, but the Navarrese findings capsize our presumptions in these regards. Men were accused when they had no genealogical links to other witch suspects. Allegations were hurled at fertile female teenagers, pregnant women, new mothers, and the wealthy. This witch hunt did not target poor crones.[45]

In examining the processes of witchcraft accusations and confessions, this study contributes to our grasp of religion, society, family, and gender in the early seventeenth century. And when it comes to the "why" of accusations and confessions, Navarrese evidence illustrates an endless combination of possibilities. Subsistence crises in Navarre were routine.[46] Children in this witch hunt could be bribed into allegations through gifts as meager as a single chestnut; adults could be induced into accusations through gifts of clothing. Some parents encouraged their offspring to accuse neighbors or even family members in an attempt to evade a debt or end a marriage. Yet religious motives also were obvious. Many parents interrogated their children for weeks, came to believe their children were serving the Devil, and highlighted their own spiritual despair at their offspring's fate. Certain youngsters and adults seem to have absorbed so thoroughly the label of "witch" that it became part of their identity: they repeatedly told relatives and neighbors how much they wanted to leave the Devil's service but were unable to do so; they called themselves "the bewitched" of such-and-such a place. Their testimonies speak to current scholarly debates about witchcraft and the development of subjectivity.[47] Did witch suspects put psychic content into their confessions, or did the process of confessing create a sense of self-identity? Moreover, was the witch's identity fixed, or subject to change? The evidence from Navarre indicates that these should not be framed as either/or questions, for all these possibilities were present.

Beyond witchcraft, this book adds to our grasp of the Spanish Inquisition, community responsibilities for children, and popular access to the law. If recent studies have highlighted the importance of placing inquisitors in their intellectual and social contexts, the material here charts the effects of distance, poverty, rebellion, and bad management on inquisitorial practice. My work restores Inquisitor Salazar to his legal, religious, and administrative environment; it reveals that the conflicts between him and his colleagues were more nuanced as well as more multifaceted than we had imagined. Thanks to new archival discoveries, this study adds children's voices to the mix, while simultaneously pondering what those children can tell us about adult senses of obligation.[48] Finally, the only reason many of my findings are even possible is because illiterate villagers turned to legal systems for help. Their astute use of the law to fix dishonor and achieve vengeance—as well as their occasional, dreadful legal mistakes—is breathtaking. Their example, as well as the inquisitors', speaks to larger questions about the reach of centralized authorities in what amounted to a hinterland in the Iberian Peninsula.

Organization

This study consists of five chapters, organized topically with an eye to chronology. Chapter 1, "Trauma," is grounded in legal sources that relay the opinions and experiences of illiterate, Basque-speaking men, women, and children. It describes community interactions as witches were suspected, denounced, harassed, and tortured. It highlights some of the difficulties encountered by Spanish inquisitors as they attempted to manage the rising number of accusations. Those inquisitors' absence from the field created a vacuum that was filled by their employees, with horrific consequences.

Finally, chapter 1 charts the analogous fates for accused witches in the inquisition tribunal and accused witches who remained at home.

Chapter 2, "Spiritual and Social Combat," demonstrates that allegations of witchcraft could develop out of parental fear, religious fervor, and social tensions. There is no doubt that a portion of the witchcraft accusations here occurred out of hatred and vengeance, and Pamplona's archival holdings present such motives in detail for the first time. Yet the same holdings also corroborate that the terror and dismay of parents were powerful motivators in the accusation process, and the rhetoric of religious warfare permeated everyone's speech. The language of this witch hunt was firmly indebted to the Catholicism forged at the Council of Trent.

Chapter 3, "Legal Struggles, Legal Errors," explains how the inquisitors made their decisions as the persecution continued. Scholars usually presume the Spanish Inquisition was a thoroughly centralized and efficient authority. Yet in this instance, the sources demonstrate a fractured structure, with both micromanagement and disconnections between the Suprema in Madrid and the tribunal in Logroño. The standards of proof and legal preferences that were supposed to guide inquisitorial procedure came apart from 1609 to 1612; Logroño's inquisitors became positively obstinate when faced with legal threats from the secular and episcopal courts in Pamplona. The inquisitors' legal errors had a parallel in the legal decisions made by certain accused witches in the village of Olague. There, a gang of children accused multiple adults of taking them to the Devil's gatherings. Adult neighbors acted upon the children's allegations by insulting and physically attacking three of the witch suspects. Those suspects in turn hurled public insults of their own against the adults who had assaulted them, even though they should have known the legal consequences for slander. The witch suspects were taken to court, and while they attempted to mount countersuits, they were extremely poor. The legal outcome for them was ruinous.

Chapter 4, "Collaboration, Obedience, Resistance" focuses on 1611, when all three legal jurisdictions began to make some headway in ending the witch hunt and yet were blocked by various actors, from certain inquisitors in Logroño to witch torturers in Navarre. There were striking collaborations that year among the leaders of Spain's religious institutions: for example, the inquisitor-general and the bishop of Pamplona started to liaise, with the bishop's advice being funneled back secretly to the Logroño tribunal. Concurrently, the same bishop and the secular court instigated trials against clerics and villagers who had tormented their neighbors over suspicions of witchcraft. Finally, Inquisitor Salazar left in May 1611 with an edict of grace, which allowed him to begin immediately reconciling confessed witches to the Catholic Church. He ultimately heard revocations of forced or induced admissions to witchcraft. Yet the two inquisitors who stayed in Logroño swore that the secular and episcopal courts were doing the Devil's work and ultimately insisted that Salazar's visitation was a failure. At the same time, legal victories by maltreated witch suspects, who collaborated in order to succeed, did not translate seamlessly into punishment for their attackers, because the latter fiercely resisted the penalties handed down to them. These collaborations and conflicts enhance our grasp of why the end of this witch hunt took so much time to achieve.

Chapter 5, "Transgressions and Solutions," is devoted to the period from 1612 to 1614, when Inquisitors Becerra, Valle, and Salazar were willing to publicize their rifts, in increasingly profound ways, to the Suprema. Our awareness that they came to disagree fiercely about the witches they were prosecuting is not new: forty years ago, Henningsen made their dissent with one another the centerpiece of his monumental study, *The Witches' Advocate*. What is original in chapter 5 is attention to barely studied archival documents, as well as scrutiny of new materials only discovered in 2020. Some of these sources illuminate the inquisitors' legal reasoning and legal combat as they battled for the right to be heard and believed by their superiors. Other documents reveal telling incompetence, both in terms of law and administration, on the part of the Logroño tribunal. This section presents startling evidence that the crucial notaries *del secreto* of the tribunal, whose duty was to transcribe trial testimony, were rogue agents whom the inquisitors, including Salazar, declined to control. Awareness of the notaries' delinquency undoubtedly contributed to the Suprema's 1614 decision to suspend witchcraft cases in Navarre as well as to acquit people punished for witchcraft in the auto de fe of 1610.

Finally, the epilogue lays out the most important results of this new investigation. Children and teenagers drove this witch hunt. The persecution emphasized pastoral concerns and religious combat. It made local life topsy-turvy. Yet Navarrese villagers, despite speaking only Basque and being illiterate, were nimble users of the courts and knew how to seek vengeance through the law. Spanish inquisitors, on the other hand, allowed their various chains of command to crumble and neglected well-known legal standards when it came to the collection and evaluation of proof. The leadership of the Spanish Inquisition exonerated the witches when evidence of coercion and malfeasance became too obvious to ignore. As for Inquisitor Salazar, he was alternately flexible and adamant when it came to his job's legal privileges and processes.

Ambitions

Village Infernos and Witches' Advocates seeks to expand our grasp of the distribution, timing, actors, processes, complications, and consequences of this most famous witch hunt. It works from the principle, demonstrated repeatedly by the sources, that there could be breaches and alterations as orders were given in Madrid, received in Logroño, and enacted in Navarre. It offers a portrait of dysfunctional inquisitors whose decisions and actions actually botched the processes their tribunal was bound to uphold. On the village level, this investigation uncovers the emotional and social tumult in communities besieged by witchcraft accusations. Finally, this inquiry restores religion to an episode abounding in it and sheds light on historical actors who are often nearly impossible to hear. My hope is that the book will increase our understanding of inquisitorial practice, community norms, relationships between children and adults, and this particular witch hunt in early seventeenth-century Navarre. The study may also startle readers with the wonders that can lie in historical archives, even though the very construction of archives expunges and silences so many human beings.[49]

Courts, Sources, and Money

The three legal jurisdictions that played a role in this witch hunt had certain features in common. Guilt was always presumed. Ideal witnesses for both the prosecution and the defense were men over the age of twenty-five, but because witchcraft was an exceptionally atrocious crime (*crimen exceptum*), less-than-ideal witnesses could be called to testify, such as other people accused of heresy or children under the age of fourteen for boys and twelve for girls.[50] Testimony was written down and was supposed to be ratified by the deponent before it could be used in court: that testimony was collected by deputized notaries who went into the villages to hear from witnesses.

Once they reached court, defendants had lawyers: in the inquisitorial and episcopal courts, those lawyers were employees of the inquisition and bishop, which did not mean that they did their job half-heartedly. Defendants and their families were supposed to pay for their upkeep while they were in jail and prosecutions were underway, though inquisition tribunals would always feed poor prisoners if the latter had no other recourse. The royal court in Pamplona conducted investigations to see if particular prisoners were truly so poor that they warranted free food, which could result in several weeks of starvation before a decision was reached. The episcopal system too had a jail, which was referred to as the bishop's tower. Duration of cases in all three jurisdictions could occasionally last for years, though quicker trials were the norm. The prosecutors in the secular, episcopal, and inquisitorial courts always wanted a confession, which was known as the "queen of proofs" (*regina probationum*). Full proof also could be obtained via two eyewitnesses to the same event. A sequence of eyewitnesses to different events only amounted to partial proof, and partial proofs should not have been enough to convict. The secular and inquisitorial jurisdictions would conduct torture in pursuit of a confession, which the defendant had to ratify after the torture had ceased. For the inquisitorial system, torture had an interrogatory purpose, not a punitive one, and no confession was as valuable as a spontaneous one.

As for differences, the royal secular court in Pamplona only heard cases that could not be fixed in the villages: the latter had what were called courts of "first instance," in which local justices heard complaints about crimes and offenses and sought to resolve them. The secular court required defendants to pay for their court processes, unlike the episcopal and inquisitorial varieties. The secular jurisdiction could condemn people to death or exile. The episcopal jurisdiction never handed out death sentences. The inquisitorial jurisdiction could issue rulings of death (rare) or exile (not rare), or sentence defendants to various penances that were intended to expiate the defendants' guilt for their religious errors. Penances were the most common sentences from inquisitors everywhere in the Spanish Empire. Proven capital enmity—wishing someone was dead—should have nullified witnesses in all three jurisdictions. Finally, the Spanish Inquisition and Spanish bishops, like their Catholic counterparts elsewhere, were supposed to prosecute only baptized Christians. Inquisitors were supposed to target heresy, while bishops were engaged with a broad range of clerical and lay offenses in the religious sphere. Meanwhile, the secular jurisdiction could prosecute anyone for a wide variety of harmful physical and verbal acts, ranging from counterfeiting currency to murder to theft to slander and beyond.

Trials in the secular, episcopal, and inquisitorial jurisdictions had their proceedings copied down by notaries, who undoubtedly took notes in real time and then filled in the substance later. These court cases exist only in manuscript form, and the content of the manuscripts does not necessarily proceed in chronological order. Pamplona's AGN and ADP contain the secular and episcopal trials used in this book. The ADP possesses a magnificent catalogue of its holdings, with indices, which was compiled over thirty years by its former archivist, Don José Luis Sales Tirapu. The ADP's trials are organized according to the notaries who transcribed them: each trial has been given a file, and each file is put into boxes that contain twenty to forty files in all. The boxes of files can overlap by date, since they were governed by the individual notary's ongoing work. Researchers have to search via trial/file, versus box, and it can be challenging to search via locality.

As for inquisition documentation, we lack all the inquisition trials for this witch hunt as well as trial transcripts for the Logroño tribunal's prosecutions of other heresies. But we do have books of correspondence sent from Logroño to Madrid, and vice versa—this correspondence too is in manuscript form—as well as a gigantic file (*legajo*) of assorted documents about this witch hunt and other inquisitorial concerns of the tribunal. That file contains some nine hundred folios of material, only a tiny portion of which is in chronological order. It is no wonder that it took Henningsen six years to read its contents.[51]

Finally, notarial records from Pamplona's AGN have provided crucial evidence for this study. Notaries copied down legal agreements by the millions in medieval and early modern Europe, and literally thousands of these documents exist for early modern Navarre. They are always in manuscript form. In the AGN, they are bundled individually in large boxes, without indices or lists of their contents, though each individual document within the boxes has been numbered. Often full of surprises, notarial records usually require detective work.

All translations are my own unless otherwise noted. With the much-appreciated help of senior archivist Peio J. Monteano Sorbet at the AGN, I have done my best to bring the names of Navarrese villages and villagers into line with modern Basque orthography. Exceptions are the city of San Sebastián, because its Castilian name is so well known, and María de Ximildegui, because she is a pivotal character in the witch hunt and because Henningsen rendered her surname in that way. It is important to note that the village of Olague in modern Basque does not carry a dieresis, but the surname "Olagüe" might, which is why both spellings will appear in this book.

The reader will encounter multiple terms for money here. The *maravedí* held the lowest value. The silver coin used in Navarre was the *real*, worth 34 maravedis. Though the *ducado*, or ducat, was a gold coin whose value fluctuated in this time frame, it always was more valuable than the silver real and was worth 375 maravedis.

I

TRAUMA

Fear, Emotion, and Physical Suffering

Modern historians have spent literally decades attempting to understand how and why witchcraft accusations and witchcraft confessions took place in early modern Europe. We know that real witches and effective harmful magic did not exist.[1] Our historical subjects did not agree. Bridging the gap between our cognition and theirs always has been challenging. The best current scholarship on European witchcraft has tried to solve the problem by probing the social, psychological, and religious conflicts of individual communities. It has posited that clashes among neighbors and apprehensions about fertility produced a situation in which multiple levels of society could complain about witches, and every level of society took seriously such complaints. The most successful investigations of European witchcraft have argued that the phenomenon involved a union of elite and popular religious concepts about eternal warfare between the Devil and God, as well as fears that families might not endure over time. Such studies have made witchcraft accusations make sense to modern readers.

Most contemporary researchers have discarded the paradigm that hysterical peasants drove witchcraft accusations through their ignorance and lack of control over their physical environment. Most historians are also wary of focusing on purely functional reasons for witch-hunting because they do not wish to shrink the emotional environment that led adults and children to label others or to confess themselves.[2] Similarly, when we decide that witch beliefs were normative and witchcraft accusations were routine, we risk downplaying the devastating effects that witchcraft allegations could provoke. Two recent studies of witchcraft in early modern Spain have asserted that accusations were not inherently sensational or disruptive but merely part of the fabric of early modern life.[3] Understandably, when victims appear to be relatively few, as was the case in Spain, modern historians often invoke a rule of scale, which in turn lessens the severity of the problem. Yet I suspect we come closer to the social reality by emphasizing instead that witchcraft allegations always had dire results for someone, including, occasionally, the accusers.

For example, one elderly woman had both her arms broken during court-sanctioned torture in a secular witchcraft prosecution and then was exiled.[4] Later, the same woman violated her sentence of banishment because she could find no access to food. Three related girls, aged eight, thirteen, and sixteen, starved after being jailed in Pamplona for witchcraft in 1595.[5] Accused of witchcraft in the same 1595 persecution, Martín Barazarte ultimately was whipped and banished for six years for revoking his confession.[6] Barazarte made such an impression on his neighbors and acquaintances that they could repeat exactly what had happened to him fifteen years later.[7] María Martín de Olagüe, a widow in her thirties, jumped out the window of her mother's house when accusers confronted her. She eventually died in prison; her mother, also accused, was exiled, with responsibility for María Martín's children. Witnesses attested that the grandmother and orphans would likely die if they were forced to leave, since they would have no familial support. In the village of Olague, Pedroco, age eight, named his father and mother as witches in 1611; while he was coerced into that allegation, and later explained and revoked his accusation before secular authorities, he could not save his father, who died in prison or during exile.[8] None of these events was routine for the people who suffered them or for their families.

The Power of Public Speech

The suffering that went with witchcraft accusations did not have to be purely physical. Calling someone a witch in public was a profound social affront, and it fell under the legal category of slander (*injurias*).[9] Slander always involved insults that were publicly uttered by one person against another, and people in early modern Navarre routinely sued each other for the damage in Pamplona's royal secular court.[10] Three details cemented whether the spoken insult was harmful: if it was said in public; if it was said before witnesses; if it was said in a loud voice.[11] Charges of injurias could arise from calling someone a traitor, thief, cuckold, or pimp.[12] Defamation prosecutions could be prompted by insults about religious and racial ancestry, such as epithets of *converso*, *judío*, or *agote*.[13] Some insults were gender-specific: for example, "traitor" and "cuckold" were only applied to men, and "whore" only to women. The epithet of "witch" was gender-neutral.[14]

Public insults had shattering effects in Navarre in the early modern period. Verbal affronts on the street, in church, or any other open space crippled personal and familial honor, and this was true no matter the speaker, recipient, audience, or circumstances. An insult became that much more ruinous if it were repeated. Having the wider community echo or talk about the slander, even if it was false, reinforced the injury, as did uttering more than one epithet at a time.[15] Thus, when two men began to dispute the value of a coin in a tavern in 1611, one loudly called the other "a rascal pilgrim, dirty scoundrel, and a witch," and then repeated those words various times, a detail that eyewitnesses were careful to supply.[16] Notably, the victims of slurs did not have the ability to annul insults through their own speech. Instead, the only remedy for a verbal affront in public was an immediate public apology from the defamer. If the targets of slander were not content with the apology, or if no apology was forthcoming, they could take the offenders before their local judiciary. If a village court of first instance could not solve the problem, victims would readily move to the next legal phase and see their enemies indicted in the royal secular court in Pamplona. Filing charges allowed those who had been defamed to dishonor and inconvenience their slanderers in a corresponding way. All legal systems in this period presumed guilt rather than innocence. Being indicted thus placed blame, and the charges were public knowledge. Being indicted also involved significant time and expense because the secular legal system did not pay for mounting a defense.

Children, Slander, and Guilt

Throughout the early modern period, children always had a special role in Navarre as the primary victims of witches, but in this witch hunt, they also contributed in a radical way to accusations. The insult "witch" carried the same social effects whether it was uttered by boys and girls, teenagers, or adults. Yet only adults appear ever to have been prosecuted by the secular legal jurisdiction for public insults.[17] From 1608 to 1614, adults who levied the slur of "witch" against adults could be taken, and were taken, to court, where they were made to pay for their offense with meaningful punishments.[18] Yet in the same persecution, children and teenagers who accused peers and adults of witchcraft were not charged with slander, and there was no legal mechanism to stop them from continuing to accuse. When it came to the slur of witchcraft, the secular legal system granted children a singular space for action. It also appears as though "witch" was the only epithet that Navarrese children ever uttered against adults.

Children had significant legal and practical exemptions in other ways as well. In this particular witch hunt, the only legal jurisdiction that prosecuted witch suspects was the Spanish Inquisition, but the inquisitors involved never put girls twelve and under, and boys fourteen and under, on trial for witchcraft because canon law dictated that while they had the use of reason, they still needed protection. (In fact, the revised instructions for Spanish inquisitors in 1561 dictated that any defendant under the age of twenty-five required a *procurador*, or special legal representative.) Instead, the inquisitors, as well as Navarrese adults, viewed such children as innocent victims, not least because they inevitably said they had been kidnapped by witches and taken to the Devil's gatherings, called *akelarres* in Basque. While they carried dishonor into their families through being contaminated by the Devil and his followers—and such dishonor occurred even if the children had not explicitly apostatized—their relatives and communities were far more concerned about rescuing them than punishing them. Significantly, even when girls under twelve and boys under fourteen confessed to taking still younger children to the akelarres, which occurred often, they were not prosecuted as witches by inquisitors or subjected to village ostracism and abuse. Adults bemoaned these children's spiritual states, but nothing else happened to them, due to their combination of youth and a presumed lack of intention.[19]

Notably, within their local communities, teenagers over the ages of twelve and fourteen who told their families that they too were kidnapped and taken to the Devil's gatherings also were seen as victims and were not abused by neighbors. It was almost as if these teens could put themselves into a de facto category of innocence through their first narratives: if they had been taken to the Devil's akelarre against their will, they were fundamentally blameless. On the other hand, males and females over the age of fourteen and twelve, respectively, *could* be subjected to community hostilities if they were seen at an akelarre but neglected to voice any statements about having been forcibly transported there. Such young people failed to get ahead of the story and could suffer accordingly. Numerous older teenagers would confess to witchcraft before inquisitors in this witch hunt and later reveal that they had done so because they had suffered familial or community violence.

The Challenges of Legal Evidence

This chapter focuses on the ways in which accused witches in this persecution suffered and died and how their accusers justified their actions. Its evidence is grounded in a variety of sources: correspondence and documentation from Spanish inquisitors; trials conducted in Pamplona's courts against the torturers of witch suspects; and other prosecutions for assault, attempted murder, and defamation that were rooted in this witch hunt. The documentation assessed here features statements from accusers of witches, accused witches, bystanders, and legal and religious authorities. Ultimately, this evidence offers a different perspective on events that up to now have only been studied from the inquisitors' point of view. The depositions of ordinary Navarrese villagers expand tremendously our understanding of the emotional, social, and religious universe in which this witch hunt occurred and allow us to glimpse the ordeals that suffused it.

Because so much of the evidence in this chapter comes from legal proceedings, some comments on its credibility are warranted. Scholars have long debated whether legal documents can transmit the voices of the dead. Plaintiffs, defendants, and witnesses were describing events based on memory. Their recollections were elicited by questions and then confined in narratives governed by legal conventions. In most of the testimony examined here, witnesses were deposing in Basque, with court interpreters acting as translators, and that mediation raises even more questions about the reliability of the surviving manuscripts.[20] Furthermore, one scholar of German witch trials has recently warned that any emotions we think we might see in trial transcripts were produced and standardized by torment, to the point that all we can hear are the voices of judges, scribes, and professional torturers.[21] It would be unwise, then, to treat legal sources as "ego documents" that provide transparent windows on the past.[22]

Still, deponents in courts were not inevitably confined to what interrogators expected or wanted to hear.[23] Witnesses answered questions according to their own inclinations; their statements could reveal a personal point of view despite the fact that they were being entered into a legal record according to legal formalities.[24] Because depositions in the secular, episcopal, and inquisitorial legal systems had to be ratified before they could become legally valid, witnesses made initial statements and then eventually heard their testimony read back to them. They ultimately could alter or confirm what they originally had said.[25] Sometimes they added details or corrected errors, but the notaries taking down testimony never limited how much deponents could talk. The narrative negotiations among legal authorities, defendants, and plaintiffs— questions, answers, expansions, corrections, ratifications—allowed illiterate villagers to voice their opinions and feelings and decide what details to offer.[26]

These conditions held true whether children or adults were testifying. Of course, anyone could have been coached outside of court on what to say inside of it, but as we will see, children and adults often bucked familial and social pressures when they testified. They and the court systems treated their depositions as agential.[27] Finally, it bears emphasizing that no torture was authorized in the secular or episcopal courts where this witch hunt was concerned, though it certainly was widespread (and illegal) at the local level.

What Did These Witches Allegedly Do?

In general, suspected witches in Navarre were believed to engage in explicit diabolical pacts: in other words, they intentionally abandoned Christianity in order to venerate the Devil as their god. They could change into animals to carry out harmful magic or avoid discovery. They sought to ruin crops with poison or storms. They could kill livestock as well as people of all ages, but children were their preferred targets. For example, in 1576, a prosecutor for the royal court of Navarre opened a witchcraft case with the following summary:

> The prosecutor accuses criminally Sancho de Irayoz . . . and María de Lizaso . . . and Graciana de Ezcurra . . . prisoners in the royal jails . . . that with little fear of God and the royal justice of Your Majesty, they have been for a long time, even years, witches and sorcerers, and as such they have committed much sorcery and witchcraft with poisonous herbs and powders . . . and they have thrown poison and toxic powders on fields that have been sown . . . and on mountains where there is pasture, and with these substances they have killed and injured many persons, especially children, and the fruits of the earth have been lost.[28]

Witches in Navarre smothered children in their beds, fed them toxic apples, or used their corpses to make poison. They also carried children through the air to their diabolical gatherings: there, they presented their prey to the Devil, who, depending upon his mood and the children's ages, might order the youngsters to renounce Christianity.

These sorts of witch activities were mentioned throughout sixteenth-century Navarre, but they were assembled into a particularly fearsome paradigm in the witch hunt of 1608–14.[29] That archetype was publicized during the auto de fe of November 1610, when the deeds and sentences of twenty-nine witches were read aloud to an audience of thirty thousand in Pamplona.[30] The recitation took hours to complete. According to the inquisition's summary, no one knew who the very first witch in Navarrese territory was, but, presumably, the Devil's vassals (*vasallos*) had been there for years. The Devil had an ugly face and three horns; one was in the front of his head and sent forth flames in order to illuminate his assemblies. Ominously, his witches snatched children from their beds and took them to the Devil's gatherings as new diabolical recruits; up to the age of four, children could be taken against their will, though after that age, they had to agree to be carried away, and the witches could not force them. Though reported as such in the auto de fe, Navarrese villagers never absorbed the idea that young children gave permission to be flown to the Devil's meetings, which may be another reason why parents and communities never treated those children as guilty of witchcraft.

According to the Spanish Inquisition, once the master witches, whether male or female, arrived at the Devil's meetings, they presented their young charges to the Devil as an offering, saying, "here is your new friend, named so-and-so." If the children were at least ten years of age—for the Devil wanted them to understand exactly what they were doing—they repeated what the Devil said to them, and thereby renounced Jesus, the Blessed Virgin Mary, all the saints, baptism, parents, and godparents. They received the Devil instead as their lord and god. Sometimes, they retracted their Christianity under threat of being whipped and burned by the witch who had brought them there. After these revocations, the children kissed the Devil's left hand, face, and chest, and finally kissed him under the tail, which he raised for this purpose. Once these kisses had occurred, the Devil marked the children with his claws if he decided they were of age.[31] If the children were too young, he refrained from marking them and sent them off instead to guard a herd of toads: he warned the boys and girls not to harm the toads and not to say a word about what they had seen at the akelarres. If they talked to any outsiders, the Devil would whip them so hard with barbed branches that the thorns would remain in their skin, though he subsequently removed the signs of the whipping with a certain ointment. But if they guarded well the toads and remained silent, when they reached the age of fourteen or fifteen—or earlier, if they were talented—they would stop guarding toads and begin to do what the adult witches did.[32]

As soon as these young witches renounced Christianity, the Devil handed them individual toads that wore clothing (sapos vestidos), which would act like diabolical guardian angels: these toads woke the witches for the Devil's gatherings and vomited the ointment that allowed them to fly there.[33] The witches' reunions with the Devil had a fixed sequence of activities. First, the witches danced, holding hands, to the sound of unpleasantly harsh drums and flutes. As they proceeded, they passed through flames that appeared to be real, without incurring any harm; the Devil announced that these were the fires of hell, which in fact could not hurt anyone, no matter what Christian preachers said.[34] Next, the master witches presented their child recruits to him. Then, the witches feasted on the flesh of dead adults and children whom they had disinterred. They ate the corpses raw, roasted, or boiled; even if the bodies had been dead for days and reeked, they said this food was tastier than partridges and capons. They also ate tasteless black bread while sitting at "dirty and disgusting tables" (sucias y asquerosas mesas), and presiding over it all was the Devil with the "queen" of the witches. After eating, the Devil had sex with the queen and then with all the adult witches, both male and female, either "naturally" or "like a sodomite." Afterwards, the witches had intercourse with each other without regard for biological sex.[35]

These details undoubtedly shocked the audience at the auto de fe. More surprises followed. For example, the inquisitors reported that after the witches had sex with one another, the Devil performed an upside-down Mass. Given that Catholic Christians were adjured to abstain from sex on feast days and before receiving the Eucharist, that detail is telling. As for the Devil leading his congregation in worship,

> Six lesser demons help the Devil say Mass, and ordinarily stay close to him; and the Devil sings some mixed up words, and the lesser demons respond in a muddled way, with low, roaring voices. At the time of the offertory, the witch community returns [el pueblo brujo se vuelve], and the Devil pronounces a benediction upon them with his left hand, though not with crosses, but with circles or scribblings. Then, the Devil delivers a sermon, to the effect that he is the one true god, and they should adore only him and only hope for their salvation from him. Ultimately, the witches ask forgiveness for the evil they have failed to do, and then the Devil offers them a black wafer.[36]

Once they became part of the Devil's flock, the witches could not see the Eucharist, even at Easter: it always appeared to them as a small black cloud.[37]

The guiding principle behind this long and appalling portrait was known to every social and intellectual class in early modern Europe: the Devil and witches were always conceptualized through inversion, and the same held true for seventeenth-century Navarre.[38] If God created the earth, the Devil and his witches attacked that creation by destroying crops, trees, animals, and even children. If God wanted salvation for men and women, the Devil hoped instead to lead them to hell, and he sent his witches to lure innocents into his diabolical sect. If Catholic Christianity urged believers to abstain from food, sex, and sin, the Devil's flock indulged in all three. Villagers speaking in court as well as learned demonologists in their printed treatises knew that the Devil promoted the opposite of Christian values of faith, hope, and charity. He was the implacable opponent of Jesus Christ, and he behaved like a lion, always seeking people to devour.[39] The Devil's gatherings described in the 1610 auto de fe featured this sort of inversion at every turn: black rather than white, filthy rather than clean, harsh rather than melodious. The witches' consumption of corpses pushed this reversed world to its extreme. While witches across Europe were often imagined as harming and even eating children, the witches' alleged feasting on dead adults in Navarre was unprecedented.

What the Inquisitors Did First

Even if the original witch suspects, arrested in January 1609, voiced only a few details of this paradigm—and we have no way of knowing, since their trials do not survive—it is little wonder that the inquisitors acted quickly.[40] A month later, those inquisitors, Alonso Becerra Holguín and Juan de Valle Alvarado, wrote to the Suprema in Madrid about what they had done so far, and how they intended to proceed.[41] They reassured their superiors that their investigations were appropriate because the witchcraft they were learning about featured overt rejections of the Catholic faith in favor of Devil worship. Their earliest suspects were not talking about simple spells for healing or love magic, which might not indicate heretical intent and might only involve tacit, not explicit, demonic pacts.[42] Becerra and Valle went on to describe how they had searched their tribunal for previous instructions about witches: they had located mandates from the Suprema from 1526 and 1555, which told inquisitors overseeing Navarre to verify the reality of the witches' activities because suspects could have been dreaming. Finally, in February 1609 Becerra and Valle told the Suprema that they had brought four of the most implicated suspects to Logroño for questioning, and those cases were underway. To the inquisitors' surprise, before they had finished interviewing the four original prisoners, six more individuals from Zugarramurdi voluntarily arrived at the tribunal: these adults said they had only confessed to witchcraft under duress, and they wanted officially to revoke their confessions before the inquisition. Becerra and Valle told the Suprema that they did not believe the six had been threatened or coerced and reported that they intended to hold them for interrogation.[43]

Before the first witch suspects ever arrived in Logroño, the two inquisitors there had enough theological education to know that the Devil and his minions embodied the opposite of Catholic Christianity. They understood the concepts of explicit and tacit demonic pacts. They were familiar with the highly authoritative canon law text called the *Canon episcopi*, which stipulated that women in particular could be fooled into thinking they flew through the air, when they were only dreaming.[44] Yet the extent to which the full-blown witch paradigm in this persecution was already in the inquisitors' minds as they began their work is difficult to gauge: throughout 1609, their communications with Madrid seemed to reveal reactions to evidence in real time as well as bias.[45]

Working Toward a Paradigm

When Becerra and Valle told the Suprema in February 1609 that their witch suspects had openly worshipped the Devil, they could have been relaying a crucial element of the first suspects' confessions.[46] Yet even at that early stage, they treated the possibility that the witches were dreaming as moot, as if that prospect applied only to much earlier cases heard by their predecessors in the sixteenth century. The inquisitors again rejected ambiguity when they said they knew the six witch suspects who wanted to revoke their confessions had turned up in Logroño on the Devil's advice. They obviously endorsed John 8:44's portrayal of the Devil as the father of lies.

Two months later, in May 1609, the inquisitors told the Suprema that the Devil had the Navarrese so "drawn in and terrified" that witch suspects would never confess, even if an inquisitor managed to go on visitation. They explained that the four original witches were "adding to their confessions," but declined to say in what regard; they asked the Suprema in particular what they should do about the children and young adults who had been turned into witches. The sect was growing, as was the Devil's command over it. By early September 1609, Inquisitor Valle was on visitation, and inquisitors Becerra and Salazar remained in Logroño. (Salazar had joined the tribunal in late June 1609.) Becerra and Salazar told the Suprema that they looked forward to Valle's arrest of two clerics who had been named by all the witch prisoners in the tribunal. The two inquisitors reasoned that these suspects, "being clerics . . . must speak Spanish, or at least Latin, and thus we will learn from them the foundations, tangles [marañas], and secrets of this diabolical sect"—as if there could be more knowledge for the inquisitors to acquire.[47]

We cannot grasp what the witches told the inquisitors over time, because we lack the trials: it is impossible to know how they might have broadened or revised their narratives in relation to what they were asked. Yet it is clear that the inquisitors were writing to Madrid as if their understanding was shifting according to what they heard. For example, the first witch suspects from Zugarramurdi said that they and the Devil went in search of María de Suretegui after María left their sect. María barricaded herself in her house with supporters; when the Devil and his witches could not recapture her, they destroyed her orchard, then picked up a mill on her property and put it somewhere else. In late September 1609, Becerra and Salazar told the Suprema that they were investigating the truth of these matters: they thought they had enough witnesses to prove that the witches who did *not* besiege María's house had changed into the shapes of pigs and mares and remained in the orchard, waiting to see what would happen. In the same correspondence, the inquisitors said they had been supremely bothered by a contradiction: some of the Zugarramurdi suspects had been seen in the akelarres many times but also had been seen simultaneously in bed, apparently asleep. Becerra and Salazar said they were still pondering the problem, but they "suspected that the Devil is leaving another phantasmal body in the house." Given that so many of these elements—shapeshifting, the destruction of fruit trees and crops, flight through the air, and children as victims—recurred in Navarrese witchcraft throughout the early modern period, it seems obvious that the inquisitors' description of Navarrese witchcraft in 1609 shared popular as well as elite emphases.[48]

Children as Victims and Accusers

Out of the first ten witch suspects interrogated from January to February 1609, three were men and seven were women, and they were all adults. Yet children quickly came to play a significant part in the persecution. When Becerra and Valle wrote to the Suprema on May 22, 1609, they wondered what they should do with "children under the age of twelve who were *brujos renegados*, as well as the *brujos renegados* who were under age twenty-five."[49] The adjective *renegado* comes from the Spanish verb *renegar*, to disown or renounce: here, it indicated that these individuals had renounced their Christian faith. With the phrase "children under the age of twelve," Becerra and Valle were merging girls and boys into the same legal category for an age of discretion. Their reference to brujos renegados under age twenty-five reflected the fact that such was the legal age of majority in Roman and Navarrese law. For our purposes, the larger point is that between January and May 1609, Becerra and Valle were hearing about children as victims of the Devil, not just through harmful magic but via conversion to the Devil's sect.

Earlier researchers thought children only played a substantial role in the witch hunt after the auto de fe of November 1610. Yet the inquisition's own documentation, as well as new materials from the secular legal jurisdiction, illustrates that harm to children and their transformation into the Devil's followers were almost instantly leitmotifs in the persecution. The inquisitors heard testimony about witches and children in their tribunal in the first half of 1609; Valle personally encountered child-witches when he was on visitation in the last half of 1609.[50] Moreover, children were imagined as witch victims far beyond Zugarramurdi and Las Cinco Villas, far earlier than previous scholars realized. (Las Cinco Villas encompasses the villages of Arantza, Igantzi, Lesaka, Etxalar, and Bera.) As early as spring 1609, Becerra and Valle told the Suprema that suspects were telling them about other assemblies of witches in other parts of Navarre.[51] And records from the secular court of Navarre indicate that children were imagined as victims of harmful magic or diabolical conversion before November 1610 in areas south, east, and west of Zugarramurdi and Las Cinco Villas.[52]

The almost instantaneous presence of children in this witch hunt should not be surprising. Navarrese historians have pointed out the pivotal role of children in witch-hunting there; children were central to witchcraft accusations in Germany as well.[53] Where this specific persecution is concerned, scholars always believed that the lack of inquisition trials meant that we would never thoroughly understand the roles that boys and girls played in the catastrophe. Their position turns out to be incorrect. They failed to notice that forty-three witchcraft confessions made by children and teenagers, along with revocations of those confessions, are actually contained at the very end of the crucial inquisition dossier, Legajo 1679, in Madrid.

Even more dramatically, legal materials from Navarre's royal court preserve abundant evidence about youngsters in this witch hunt, including their own testimony. Grasping children's special legal status, what they said they had suffered, and what their parents and neighbors believed they had suffered clarifies the accusatory process and the violence that accompanied it.

In the witch hunt that snowballed after December 1608, children were not only victims but relentless accusers and eyewitnesses. Though they typically participated in only a limited way in diabolical activities at the Devil's assemblies—by watching sex, cannibalism, poison-making, weather magic, and toads—they knew firsthand what the witches had done as well as what they were planning to do. Children who said they attended the akelarres reported that older witches continuously browbeat them to keep silent and threatened them with murder if they should talk. Yet despite such warnings, children transported to the akelarres *always* told their parents what was happening to them. They inevitably announced who had taken them to visit the Devil as well as whom they had seen there. The children noted that their parents might not have known they were being whisked away because the witches could administer a powder that caused mothers and fathers to fall into a deep sleep while their offspring were gone. The children also offered the possibility that parents who remained awake might have been fooled by look-alike phantasms that the Devil put into bed in the children's place.

Concerned Relatives

As parents of child-witches talked to legal authorities about what they knew, they noted that they had repeatedly examined their children to determine if they were telling the truth about diabolical abductions. One mother said she "interrogated her six-year-old daughter, conducting many proofs on different days and in different weeks, sometimes with love [*amor*], sometimes with sternness [*rigor*], so that she would speak the truth." A sixty-five-year-old named Martín Serart had a nephew who said he was taken to the witches' gatherings. Serart told the boy it was a lie, and threatened him to tell the truth, "and the child was strong, to the point that even if they whipped him, he said he was taken while he was sleeping." Juan de Inda had two daughters who volunteered that they were carried by witches to the Devil; when he told them they must have dreamed it, they insisted they went in person. A twenty-five-year-old named María de Mendiburu maintained that she had questioned a child servant for a full year and a half, but the girl's story about the witches' congregations never varied.[54] The fact that young children repeated exactly their accounts, without wavering over dates, experiences, or actors, seemed nearly miraculous to their families and employers and helped persuade them that the children were telling the truth. Two-, four-, and eight-year-olds were not supposed to be able to retain memories in such detail for such a long time. When youngsters demonstrated such narrative fidelity over time, they became a source of wonder. Some parents insisted that their children's ability to recall what had happened to them was a sign of divine grace.

When concerned mothers and fathers told secular legal authorities about their investigations, they proved they weren't gullible or overly rapid in their conclusions and diminished the possibility that their children were merely fantasizing. They also had a keen sense of how to build their narratives for the court in terms of reasoned, logical steps. Once convinced this nightmare was truly happening, parents then tried physical measures to keep their children safe. In Olague, for example, the Echaide family made their offspring stay awake all night. Parents in other villages tied themselves to their children, tied their children into their beds, and then packed those beds with additional siblings and relatives in the hope that their precautions would prevent abductions. Their strategies rarely worked: the children reported that they continued to be snatched and taken to revere the Devil. If the children appeared to be sleeping peacefully, that was because the Devil had left doppelgängers in their place to deceive onlookers. The children insisted that they had truly left.

Parents in Navarrese villages were terrified about the harm being done to their offspring. Their fears were not unusual per se, for Navarrese adults cared when children in their communities were in danger. If toddlers and youngsters went missing, fell under horse-driven carts, or drowned, parents and neighbors helped to search for them, noticed forensic evidence, and gave testimony. In 1559, a two-year-old boy disappeared from the village of Obanos after he had been seen playing with a nine-year-old male companion. All of Obanos's adults turned out to look for the toddler and persisted in their quest through the night; they understood the potential risks of the water in their environment and used tools such as iron hooks and wooden sticks as they searched through rivers, creeks, and pits. Unfortunately, about 9:00 a.m. the next day, the boy was found at the bottom of a well. At that point, shrieks about the discovery pierced the air, and adults gathered to look at the child's body. When interviewed by the local court of first instance, one woman recalled that she had seen the dead child's companion running into his own house on the afternoon the toddler went missing. That circumstance prompted suspicions and interrogations. Fears were confirmed when another child turned out to be an eyewitness to the crime and reported that the older boy threw the toddler into the well after the two-year-old called him crazy.[55]

On March 29, 1596, Fernández de Iruñela and María de Urdiain told a court of first instance that their daughter was found drowned the day before in a pool of water. They had sent their daughter to the mill with wheat to be ground; she was accompanied by a slightly older female friend. The older girl had injured the younger one and caused her death in order to steal the wheat, which she then hid under her own bed. When strangers found the dead girl's body, they immediately walked from one village to another to find out to whom she belonged. Fernández and María instantly went to them and identified their daughter; local law enforcement searched the home of the offender and found the wheat.[56]

Cases of infanticide demonstrate the same sort of forensic attention and community concern. In 1606, in Zabaldika, the village constable was watching a village dance when two men approached him and told him that María de Baztan had killed her two-year-old. The constable, "accompanied by many residents [vezinos]," went to look for María. The search took some time; the crowd finally turned to some decrepit houses that were in the vicinity, where they found her behind a closed door, holding a dead child. They took the body from her and found signs of violence around her throat; María tried to claim that a snake must have bitten her when she was out. The constable took her into custody and placed her under arrest. He also took the corpse home with him to preserve evidence. A crucial witness, a widow named Gracia de Zozaya, told the prosecutor in Pamplona that María originally had come to her to beg for a burial spot for the toddler because she said she would soon be dead. Shocked, Gracia asked María how she could know such a thing when the child was perfectly healthy. María left, but returned within the hour, sobbing and holding the now-dead child in her arms. Gracia, who by then was sitting with two other women, immediately accused María of having killed her child. The three women ran to the resident priest to ask what should be done; the priest found a student who knew where to find the constable, and soon thereafter, the search began.[57]

Accidental or purposeful deaths of children were tragic and keenly felt, but witches and the harm they could do to offspring were even more traumatic to Navarrese communities. Witches looked like neighbors. Witches had no sense of moderation when it came to recruiting followers of the Devil; they had no quota of diabolical converts. To make matters worse, witches stayed put in their villages, unlike other heretics who usually were imagined as moving through or touching down in Navarre, such as moriscos (converts from Islam to Christianity, or their descendants) and conversos (converts from Judaism to Christianity, or their descendants). Without permission, witches in Navarre invaded private household spaces through unexpected routes, such as cracks, windows, and chimneys. Finally, witches harmed their victims physically as well as spiritually: beyond persuading them to reject Christianity, children told their families that the witches whipped and beat them and threatened them with poisoning. Fathers, mothers, and other relatives were stunned and outraged by the injuries their families were suffering; neighbors currently unaffected were terrified that their children would be next. Thus when children told their families that they were taken to revere the Devil, named their witch kidnappers, persevered in their stories, and continued to be abducted, their parents did more than interrogate them and tie them to their beds: they started verbal confrontations with alleged suspects.

In 1610, a mother in the village of Arraioz, in the Valle de Baztan, "pressed Catalina de Barrenechea many times to confess that she took this witness's daughter to the Devil's gatherings, and she always said no, that she was not a witch." In the same village, Pedro de Indart's wife publicly confronted María de Aldico at least three times over the abduction of a toddler. A relative of María de Aldico pleaded with her "to give up the office of witch." María de Mendiburu adjured her elderly neighbor, Graciana de Barrenechea, to stop practicing witchcraft.[58] Because child accusers could rotate through a sequence of witch suspects, it seems likely that the accused were subjected to multiple confrontations of this sort, which occurred in the street, at front doors, and in church. The repetition of the confrontations could have had effects on the witch suspects' self-identities. Moreover, because the children taken to the Devil's juntas always named people they had seen there, including other boys and girls, the circle of victims and witches inevitably grew larger.

Thus throughout this witch persecution, children identified adults and teenagers who took them to revere the Devil and declared whom they had seen in the Devil's gatherings. Even if the children originally spoke only to their parents, their statements never remained confidential; instead, public knowledge of suspects grew as children talked and their parents verbally accosted the accused. Sometimes, child-witches took it upon themselves to deliberately intensify the alarm. In Olague, boys and girls explicitly referred to themselves as the child-witches of that village (*somos los niños embrujados de Olague*) and ran as a pack; as a group, they publicly shouted witchcraft accusations against adults, which astonished bystanders.[59] The same band reported that Olague's witches had disinterred and eaten a former priest. That possibility so terrified the dead priest's sisters that they had him exhumed, whereupon multiple adults confirmed that they had examined his body—wiggling his feet, touching his ears, and so on—and had found that he was really intact. The fact that the dead priest had not been eaten by witches was enough to convince some of Olague's adults that this particular story was false, but no one in the trial record explicitly moved from that realization to doubt about witchcraft accusations as a whole. The cycle of child allegations continued unabated.[60] Meanwhile, in Erratzu, child-witches announced to their parish priest that his portrait was burned in the Devil's gatherings; they told him the adult witches intended to kill him but had not yet managed to do so because of the crucifixes he had all over his house.[61]

Children's accounts of being taken by adult witches to the Devil's meetings had dramatic emotional and social effects, some of which seem to have been intentional on the part of the youngsters involved.[62] Parents took action to protect their offspring; they chased down suspects and verbally confronted the accused. At this point in the process, the fate of the witch suspects took one of two turns: either they were sent to the inquisition tribunal in Logroño, or they remained at home. The outcome for both groups was surprisingly similar in terms of dishonor, suffering, and death.

Witches Sent to Logroño

When the first witch suspects from Zugarramurdi started on the 105-mile trek to Logroño, they had to hire escorts to guide them. They carried their beds, along with enough currency to cover their expenses, for in both the inquisitorial and secular legal jurisdictions, prisoners' families were responsible for their provisions.[63] In late summer 1609, the inquisitors debated intensely whether they should add to the defendants in custody by seizing French suspects: such individuals had crossed the border in order to flee witchcraft prosecutions occurring simultaneously in the Pays de Labourd.[64] The inquisitors ultimately decided to turn those refugees over to French officials, because they had no evidence the French had been practicing witchcraft in Spanish territory.[65]

In the same time period, Inquisitor Valle left on visitation, arrived in Zugarramurdi, and interrogated alleged accomplices of the ten witches imprisoned in the tribunal. He and his colleagues rapidly agreed to send five more suspects to Logroño for trial, two of whom were the clerics Pedro de Arburu, a Premonstratensian friar at the monastery of Urdax, in Zugarramurdi, and Juan de la Borda, a presbyter there. These men were first cousins, and their mothers were among the ten witch prisoners in the tribunal, all of whom had apparently named the men as fellow witches. Arburu and Borda were not told where they were going; they thought they were traveling on ecclesiastical business for the monastery. The other newly seized prisoners were so poor that the inquisitors ordered them to sell whatever they could in order to have money for their food while in jail.[66] The very fact of being taken to Logroño by the Spanish Inquisition would have been enough to wreck the prisoners' reputations in their native villages. Everyone would have known where they had gone, but due to the inquisition's policy of secrecy, family members and friends could not have visited the prisoners, nor would they have received updates on the prisoners' conditions or the progress of their trials.

The surviving evidence does not relay when the prisoners arrived or the frequency of their interrogations. Standard inquisitorial procedure dictated that the inquisitors should have admonished the prisoners three times to reveal or guess why they were in the tribunal to begin with. If a confession was not forthcoming, the inquisitors should have called in theological consultants to assess the potential heresy of the evidence against the defendants: once those consultants had rendered an opinion, the prosecutor attached to the tribunal, in collaboration with the inquisitors, should have prepared formal charges. We know from inquisitorial correspondence that indictments against the first ten witch suspects were formulated by September 4, 1609.[67]

Those first prisoners had started to fall gravely ill as the summer progressed. By August 1609, Estevania de Tellechea had died: she was over ninety years old and so deaf that the inquisitors had found it impossible to reconcile her to the church, though they absolved her judicially before she passed away. By September 1609, there were more fatalities: Graciana de Barrenechea and Estevania de Iriarte, mother and daughter, died, while María de Iriarte, María Pérez, and two of the men were "on the point of death." María de Suretegui also was reported as terminally ill.[68] The health of the ten original prisoners had worsened as new prisoners were arriving; the inquisitors were convinced these illnesses were the Devil's work because he wanted to prevent defendants from ratifying their statements. The Devil would do anything to obstruct the inquisition: without ratification, the witches' depositions could not be used in court. As an example, the inquisitors described to the Suprema what had happened with Estevania de Iriarte:

> [When] our colleague, Dr. Alonso Becerra, went to the house of
> penitence to reconcile Estevania de Iriarte, and began to discuss the

necessary details of her case, she was almost without fever, though very weak, and she was very composed in what she did, up until she was absolved from excommunication. And then Becerra asked her if she recalled having testified against certain persons in the inquisition, and she made an effort to get out of the chair she was in, and Becerra asked her why she was getting up, and she said, "to show him some beautiful trees out that window," and from that point on, nothing could be done with her, and she died without ratifying her deposition [against the others].[69]

Iriarte's strategy here is obvious to us, if not to Becerra. She offered a distraction in order not to further harm anyone else.

By November 1609, six of the twenty-six suspects from Zugarramurdi had died.[70] By the time of the auto de fe, a year later, the death toll had risen to thirteen.[71] The inquisitors told the Suprema that their prisoners' illnesses and deaths were machinations of the Devil, but they also had to have known how profoundly unhealthy their prison was, due to its placement directly above the river Ebro. Raw sewage in the water, the possibility of flooding, and the damp all took their toll. By the start of this witch hunt, inquisitors in Logroño had been complaining about their prison for almost two decades. Original renovations in 1592 had stopped because of the architect's death; a year later, inquisitors put the project out to bid, but the Suprema found the winning proposal too expensive. Nothing more happened until 1601, when the Suprema agreed to reinstate the project, but by that date, the cost of renovation had climbed from 6,400 to more than 10,400 ducats. The tribunal's physical environment also endangered the inquisition's rule of secrecy. In 1601 the inquisitors complained that "many prosecutions have been lost [perdidas] because the prisoners can so easily communicate, due to the weakness of the prison. The highest cells have walls of board; the floors fall down; every day we find holes in the walls."[72] In April 1607, the inquisitors told the Suprema that the location of their prison was so unhealthy that they always had to move sick prisoners to individual houses in the city, which caused many problems in terms of confidentiality. In the same letter, the inquisitors said that Logroño was so inhospitable, and so lacking in properly educated potential employees, that they did not think it was advisable to stay there.[73]

Nevertheless, throughout the persecution the inquisitors and the accused witches remained in place, and the tribunal's employees continued their work. The witch prisoners were interrogated, charges levelled, and trials held. Witches who confessed were reconciled to the Catholic Church and given penances. Witches who refused to confess could be tortured if the Suprema allowed it, which occurred in the case of clerics Pedro de Arburu and Juan de la Borda in autumn 1610. Both men were put onto the rack (*potro*), whereby they were tied down with cords that could be tightened around their arms and legs.[74] The cord broke on the second pull for Arburu; the professional torturer replaced it, and the inquisitors ordered a second turn on the right arm. Arburu said "get off me, I will speak the truth, I am a witch, let me go." He then immediately returned to denying the charges, whereupon they gave the cord a second turn on the left wrist: at that point, Arburu lost consciousness, and the inquisitors halted the torture. Borda was given eight full turns, "and due to certain ailments," they stopped there. Both men persisted in their denials of witchcraft.[75]

As inquisitors Becerra and Salazar worked in the tribunal throughout 1609, their colleague, Valle, spent the last months of that year on visitation. He began in Zugarramurdi and Las Cinco Villas, but then went much farther afield, and he sent long letters to his colleagues about his discoveries. More than seventy people in Tolosa had been accused of witchcraft; in Errenteria, a woman had turned fifteen children into witches in only eight days. Valle interviewed dozens of girls and boys who had been converted into witches by adult neighbors. He also reported that he had seen the Devil's mark: he had experimented on accused witches in Lesaka (*ya lo tengo experimentado en estos de Lesaka*), finding "the mark is small, and in some it is easy to see . . . and touching it with something pointed, or a pin, they don't feel it, even if pressed hard; nor will the pin go in even if you try to sink it. I was amazed to see it."[76]

Valle returned to Logroño in December 1609. Over the next three months, he and his colleagues received letters and personal visits from mayors and parish priests in villages besieged by witches. The pleas from Navarre were always the same: parents and officials were desperate; only the inquisitors could provide a remedy. For instance, in February 1610, the inquisitors told the Suprema, "in this office, Errenteria's mayor and priest relayed, with tears and great pain, the massive need of their republic. They want above all to be free from the extortions of the Devil. They are asking with great urgency for one of us to go and fix the problem, and they are offering to pay our costs."[77] The inquisitors then hypothesized to their superiors that they thought they might be able to take sixteen more suspects into their tribunal for trial. They would focus on the area of Las Cinco Villas and would target the witches who were most energetic in converting children. Their aim was to restrain the Devil's audacity and give some courage to the villagers awaiting help.

The inquisitors also told the Suprema that they had twenty-eight witch cases pending: fourteen people had confessed and were waiting to be sentenced; fourteen others continued with denials, and their cases had reached the stage where the evidence against them would be transcribed and given to them for review. As for the sixteen new prisoners whom they wished to bring to Logroño for trial, the inquisitors reasoned that a stay in jail would make them inclined to confess, but problems included a lack of space and the poor quality of the cells. The inquisitors thought they might enlarge their housing capacity by taking on more rooms in their house of penitence, where they could accommodate twelve female prisoners; then, they might ask the Dominican monastery of Valquerna for four more spots for male suspects.[78] Their forecast about the sex ratio of their intended prisoners may reflect village communications about witches, or the inquisitors' own presumptions as to how the ratio of female and male witches would break down. I have not found documentation that clarifies their reasoning.

To sum up, then, by May 1609 the Logroño tribunal held ten people suspected of witchcraft. During Inquisitor Valle's visitation in the second half of 1609, he sent five more witch suspects to Logroño, and was authorized by the tribunal to gather twelve more.[79] By February 1610, the inquisitors had a total of twenty-eight witchcraft cases pending (rather than twenty-seven) and were aiming to add an additional sixteen.[80] Yet they were severely hampered in their efforts because they had to find space to hold the suspects once they arrested them. Even worse, the tribunal had almost no funds to support so many prisoners. If the tribunal brought sixteen more to Logroño,

> the spending by this tribunal is going to be extraordinary, because the prisoners are so extremely poor. Everyone we have to imprison gets by in that miserable land on what they can receive from their crops and harvests of very few flocks, and things that fetch very little. And because this inquisition is so poor and needy, we cannot pay the salaries and ordinary expenses [of our employees] without a good bit of help. It will be necessary for your Lordship to send aid for the great needs and expenses that we require, because all the time that the twenty-eight prisoners have been here, their expenses have been at the cost of this inquisition.[81]

The prisoners' families apparently had fallen short in practical support, so the tribunal had stepped in to feed and clothe the defendants.

The tribunal ultimately did imprison sixteen more witch suspects, but according to their own correspondence, they could have prosecuted so many more. In July 1610, they noted that they had finally finished reviewing and voting on the case summaries that Valle had brought back from his visitation the year before. While on the road, Valle had collected evidence against some three hundred people of legal age who had abandoned Christianity, not to mention another, larger number of bewitched children who had not formally renounced the faith. Inquisitorial commissioners in the field were continuing to collect depositions about witches; the number of diabolical assemblies had grown to twenty.[82] The three inquisitors told the Suprema that the villages were crying out for some sort of remedy, and they were trying to give them courage; they greatly desired "to chop down so many evils." They were well aware of how much money they needed. They were about to do a rough estimate of their tribunal's income and debts, and they continued to worry about prison space.

What, then, was life like for witch suspects in the inquisition tribunal of Logroño? They spoke Basque, but the inquisitors spoke only Spanish: as defendants endured multiple interrogations, everything had to be translated by interpreters hired by the tribunal. The prisoners conferred with each other through unsecured cells. A number fell ill and died before their cases were concluded. The survivors confessed to witchcraft and were penanced or refused to confess and were condemned to death. A few were tortured in the hopes of securing a confession. Finally, one of the women put on trial, María de Endara, a young widow from Etxalar, arrived in Logroño supposedly pregnant by her parish priest. The inquisitors' solution for this particular problem was to instruct the priest to take the child after it was delivered, so they would not have to cope with it.[83]

By October 1610, the tribunal had received the Suprema's permission to hold an auto de fe. The inquisitors instantly began to research how to run it, including worrying about who should sit where.[84] They publicly announced the impending spectacle on October 19, "to the great applause of this entire land . . . and the concourse of people will be enormous because everyone is moved to attend it."[85] On Saturday, November 6, 1610, the auto de fe began in the afternoon with an enormous procession of inquisition personnel, members of religious orders, and secular clergy: this group walked to Logroño's main square and watched as the inquisition's giant green cross was raised to the highest place in the spectators' stands. The following day, Sunday, November 7, another procession began, this time with the tribunal's fifty-three prisoners in tow, thirty-one of whom were accused of witchcraft. Once the prisoners arrived at the square, they took up positions on a stage across from the inquisitors and spectators. A sermon was preached; the witches sentenced to death heard their lengthy sentences read aloud to the crowd. At the end of the day, six live witches, along with the effigies of five dead ones, were handed over to the secular authorities to be burned at the stake. The executions occurred outside of town. The whole spectacle was designed to educate, entertain, and terrify.[86]

On Monday, November 8, the forty-two remaining prisoners again walked to the stage and heard their sentences. Eleven live witches repented their heresy and were reconciled to the church. Seven effigies of dead witches were also reconciled: they had expressed remorse for their heresy before dying. The penances for the reconciled, live witches were severe: six months, a year, or perpetual reclusion in monasteries or convents and various periods of banishment ranging from six months to perpetual exile.

Meanwhile, the two clerics accused of witchcraft, Pedro Arburu and Juan de la Borda, were reconciled to the church in private in the inquisition tribunal after renouncing a light (de levi) suspicion of heresy. Such private reconciliations were common where clerics were concerned; the inquisition was not eager to sentence religious figures in public. Arburu was stripped of his religious order and ordered to serve five years in the galleys: once that sentence was completed, he was to go into perpetual reclusion in a monastery outside the kingdom of Navarre. Borda was suspended from his clerical office for ten years, ordered into a church or monastery outside Navarre and Gipuzkoa for three years, and then exiled perpetually.[87]

With the spectacle of the auto de fe and their harsh punishments, the inquisitors in Logroño may well have thought that the witch sect would go into decline.[88] Things did not work out as planned. Though the printed pamphlet about the auto de fe trumpeted its spiritual benefits (see chapter 2), the number of accused witches continued to climb, and pleas and complaints from the villages persisted. As Becerra, Valle, and Salazar remained in their tribunal, ordinary people began to seek stronger solutions to their witch problems than conversations and exhortations. Villagers and their local officials could not send accused witches to Logroño without the inquisitors' permission, which was not forthcoming. The alternatives they landed on were often brutal.

Witches Who Stayed Home

Every suspect in this witch hunt was first accused in a village setting, and by far the majority of the accused remained there, rather than being tried by inquisitors. If suspects apologized in public to the families of their alleged victims, they could still be named later the same day, week, or month by other children, teenagers, or adults who insisted they were taking them to the Devil's gatherings. Persistent accusations nullified the effects of public apologies. Verbal exchanges turned physical. For example, in December 1609, Brianda de Mayora and María Castellano engaged in a shouting match from their windows as to which of them, or their family members, had taken each other's child to the Devil's junta. When María's adult son arrived home and saw the ongoing argument, he cried to Brianda, "oh you evil mouth, I will gorge myself on your blood"; he then threw a rock at her and missed, whereupon Brianda howled, "oh you traitor, you want to kill me by stoning."[89] Brianda and her husband filed charges of defamation and assault in secular court and won. On July 17, 1610, in the village of Etxalar, Catalina de Vergara left her house and stopped María de Ansorena as the latter was walking down the public street. Catalina bitterly asked what she had done to make María take her child to revere the Devil; María, who was nine months pregnant, denied she was responsible. Catalina immediately hit her in the head with a rock, whereupon María broke a clay jug she was carrying over Catalina's skull. The two women ended up on the ground, tearing at each other, until other women arrived and broke up the fight. Catalina ultimately was charged with "half homicide" (medio homicidio), which was intent to murder.[90]

Male observers said they had not intervened with Catalina and María because the quarrel was "a woman's affair," but recent studies of European witchcraft have confirmed that witchcraft accusations and prosecutions depended upon taking seriously women's suspicions and complaints. For this particular witch hunt in Navarre, not only did men sometimes step aside and allow their wives to take the lead in confrontations, but the urgency behind suspicions could also prompt women to step over gender lines. Homicide and attempted homicide were profoundly masculine crimes in early modern Navarre, yet in Etxalar, Catalina decided the attack on María was worth it, and she was not alone.[91] Notably, at least two other mothers of bewitched children told the secular court under oath that they had considered murdering the suspected witches who were abducting their children. One testified that despite being female, she would have destroyed her daughter's diabolical kidnapper. Another said she "had often wondered whether [I] could kill the person who was taking [my] son, even though [I am] a woman."[92] As we will see in chapter 3, women tortured other women to death in the village of Sunbilla, and their actions horrified the male clergy who learned about it.[93]

Vigilante Justice

The sort of violence these women contemplated and carried out was called *via de hecho* in Spanish: that phrase can be translated as "the way of the deed," and it meant vigilante justice conducted outside the law. Witnesses reported that the threat of vigilante justice from both men and women against other adults was virtually omnipresent in this witch hunt: they testified as if they were terrified of it and as if the prospect of it enhanced the gravity of both their statements and their situations in the villages.[94] In Bera, in December 1609, the parish priest reported that if he had not intervened, villagers would have slit the throats (*hubieron degollada*) of four witch suspects.[95] Over 1610–11 in Arraioz, Pedro de Caracoechea threatened multiple times to kill a young woman named Marimartín, who allegedly took his daughter to the Devil's gatherings. Pedro swore he would gorge himself on Marimartín's blood if she were not punished, and she took him seriously enough to run away.[96] In one of Las Cinco Villas, a forty-year-old man was lowered from a rope tied to a bridge and threatened with drowning. He subsequently confessed.[97] In February 1611, inquisition commissioner Leon de Araníbar told Logroño's inquisitors that he was sending three prisoners to them despite the fact that he had not received permission to do so. Araníbar explained that in Zubieta, a village of some fifty houses, 103 children had been bewitched over the last five months. The three suspects he had seized, two women and one man, were the ringleaders of the sect, "and it has been extremely difficult to prevent their throats from being cut." Araníbar feared that if the inquisitors did not accept them as prisoners, their neighbors would burn them alive.[98] In another letter from February 1611, Araníbar told the tribunal that vigilante justice had just occurred in Legassa: three or four men had been stabbed and left gravely hurt.

In the village of Olague, the young son and daughter of nobles Don Pedro de Echaide and Doña Graciana de Ursúa testified in June 1611 that two women—a mother and daughter named Margarita and María Martín—took them to the Devil's gatherings, where they forced them to eat black things out of black cups by opening their mouths with their fingers. The two children danced with the witches, and when the dance was over, "the Devil took the women who were of age"; the younger witch told the children that if they breathed a word of what they had seen, their estate would be turned into dust. Their parents, Don Pedro and Doña Graciana, subsequently walked from their manor into the village and attacked Margarita and María Martín in their own homes: they broke down doors and beat the two women with clubs until they were bloodied. Everyone confirmed that the injuries would have been far worse if a male relative of the women had not arrived on the scene and drawn a knife.[99] Meanwhile, a different witch suspect in Olague, Miguel de Imbuluzqueta, had his house burned down, which was the ultimate act of vigilante justice, as there was no village or state charity, or communal responsibility, to rebuild the loss of such a property.[100]

In a fascinating coincidence, the lexicon of violence in these village scenarios matches depictions of anger in Golden Age Spanish drama. Theatrical discourse about rage "is filled with words for burning." Writers of plays call anger "a knife." The thirst caused by anger can only be assuaged through drinking the blood of one's enemies. Angry people in the *comedias* cannot be patient; they trample over everything. Wrath could be prompted by insults, "[b]ut the most extreme provocation to Anger . . . was usually the desire for revenge." Finally, the ultimate outcome of anger in the comedias was death.[101] These attributes and possibilities would have made perfect sense to Navarrese villagers whose children were corrupted by witches.

Village Constables and Inquisition Employees

There was, however, a safer and seemingly lawful way to solve the witch problem in Navarrese communities than vigilante justice, or so parents and neighbors of both sexes believed. Male members of villages could come together under the leadership of their constables (*jurados*), who were elected annually from the pool of legal male residents. As a body, the men could talk about their witch problem; presumably, they had input from the women in their family circles. They then could deputize their constables to seek advice from the closest employees of the Spanish Inquisition, who would have been commissioners (*comisarios*) and familiars (*familiares*). Inquisition commissioners were hired by inquisition tribunals to take down witness testimony and forward it to the inquisitors themselves: they usually were local clerics. Familiars were unpaid lay servants of inquisition tribunals: they were supposed to be prompt and obedient in carrying out whatever the inquisition needed.[102] Inquisition commissioners and familiars enjoyed legal immunity from the episcopal and secular legal jurisdictions.

After residents of the Valle de Baztan—especially villagers in Elgorriaga, Erratzu, and Arraioz—held such councils in 1610 and 1611, they sent their constables to confer with a commissioner and a familiar in the area: Leon de Araníbar and Miguel de Narbarte. This strategy appeared sound on multiple levels. Everyone in Navarre knew that the Spanish Inquisition was officially in charge of this witch hunt; inquisition employees presumably knew the protocols of inquisitorial procedure. If inquisition employees told villagers what to do about their witches, then villagers could not be accused of practicing vigilante justice, or so residents of the Baztan affirmed, according to their later courtroom testimony. After all, the inquisitors themselves were miles away in their tribunal, only the inquisition was presumed to have a remedy for the witches, the villages needed immediate help, and the inquisition employees were right there.

Accordingly, over the autumn of 1610 and the winter of 1611, three constables from Elgorriaga, Erratzu, and Arraioz—Juan de Legasa, Juan Iturralde, and Juan de Perochena, respectively—traveled short distances to find commissioner Leon de Araníbar and familiar Miguel de Narbarte.[103] They told Araníbar and Narbarte that parents were beside themselves: nothing they had tried so far could make the witches stop abducting children. Araníbar and Narbarte consequently instructed the three constables to imprison witch suspects and frighten them into confessions.

It is crucial to note that Araníbar, like all inquisition commissioners, was only authorized to take down sworn testimony and forward it to the tribunal: he could conduct interviews with suspects and witnesses, but he had no official power to imprison, torture, or sentence. As for Narbarte, like all inquisition familiars, he was supposed to help the inquisition in any way possible, but he lacked even the authority to transcribe evidence, much less grill or torture suspects. Both men spoke Basque as well as Spanish. Both were thoroughly ensconced in their Navarrese communities. Later, in extraordinary testimony in secular court—from which they should have been immune, given their status as inquisition employees—they would say they had found it impossible to resist village pressure to fix the witch problem.[104]

Over 1610–11, Araníbar and Narbarte crossed the legal lines of their inquisitorial employment, and they clearly knew they were doing so, given that they refused to put their instructions in writing.[105] Their oral instructions to the village constables essentially gave villagers permission to mimic inquisition procedure, though with significant omissions. No charges were formally made or written down, no witness statements were taken, the suspects had no defense, and any confessions that occurred were not given under oath. Nevertheless, the presumption of guilt, prospect of imprisonment, and elevation of confession were central to the practices of the Spanish Inquisition, and victims of the constables and their neighbors repeatedly made such connections. The accused and abused witches would eventually

charge their torturers with acting like inquisitors but without the inquisition's legal authority.

Local Torture

As soon as Legasa, Iturralde, and Perochena returned to their respective villages, they started seizing suspects, and they had help from their communities. Men took the lead, but women participated as well. In Elgorriaga,
constable Legasa and other residents put women and men into private prisons for eight days, after which some confessed. For those who recanted their
admissions or refused to confess in the first place, Legasa and his companions stepped up their measures: they placed the heads of the accused between the rungs of a ladder and marched them from one village to another in
processions that lasted for hours. Juan de Cosiñorena, a forty-year-old cloth
worker, was put into a ladder with another man, Pedro de Landa, and pa-
raded for a night and a day. When Juan and Pedro appealed to God to save
them, their torturers hit them with clubs and rocks, saying, "you belong to
the Devil, confess that you're witches."[106] When Juan and Pedro refused, their
captors held lighted torches over them, so that embers fell and burned their
heads and clothes. Later, Pedro testified in court that the stoning he suffered
in the ladder took off a piece of a toe, whereby he was unable to wear a shoe
on his foot for two months.[107] After the ladder experience, Juan was tortured
again: this time, his hands were tied, and he was hung from a timber by
a rope tied around his waist. He was left there for a long time; he fainted
from the pain, and to avoid more agony, he finally falsely confessed.[108] The
same sort of treatment also was meted out to young married women, whose
reputations and marriages were ruined not just from the public slurs that
accompanied the ladder torture but from being out all night in the captivity
of men who were not their husbands.[109]

People accused of witchcraft in Erratzu suffered analogous imprisonments, carried out by Erratzu's constable but organized by the village priest.[110]
One eighty-year-old woman was jailed for five months: the priest, Miguel de
Aguirre, called her a "wicked woman, an evil witch," and told her, "say and
confess that you're a witch."[111] A male resident testified that Aguirre had ten
or twelve honorable people imprisoned who never before had a reputation
for witchcraft. The same witness said he personally was put into the stocks
for a day and a night; he sent for Aguirre twice, but he never came, and
when he did arrive, he said that this witness had been accused by many. The

witness was terrified: he had five small children and "a little wife" (*pequeña muger*), and they had no means of support except what he earned. He consequently falsely confessed.[112] He had to weigh the social shame of a confession against his need to feed his family.

In Arraioz, groups of men with clubs, rocks, and guns took witch suspects from their houses and put them into private prisons. Some of the accused ended up in the basement of the noble manor of Jauregizar, where they were left for days without food and water, over the objections of the manor's female owner, who intervened quickly and secretly.[113] Other women in Arraioz, of all ages, were confined in water-filled mangers, where they were made to stand overnight as the water froze. Others had their arms pinned behind their backs and were hoisted into the air by their wrists, dislocating their shoulders: that procedure mimicked one of the inquisition's methods of torture, called the *garrucha*. Some were tormented with cords tied so tightly around their waists that the victims believed they were dying and begged for a priest to administer the last rites: binding, too, was an inquisitorial method of torment. Other residents of Arraioz were tied to trees and left there for days.[114] All the witch suspects were told repeatedly that they would be burned if they did not confess, another obvious reference to the Spanish Inquisition and the burnings carried out in its auto de fe. The secular jurisdiction in Navarre only hanged convicted witches.

The fact that village constables had sought advice from inquisition employees clearly persuaded many residents that this violence was authorized. Significantly, the surviving documentation suggests that no other witch hunt in Navarre in the early modern period featured this kind of widespread, village-based torture. It thus looks as if villagers in Navarre improvised: after November 1610, they knew witches had been burned at the stake; they may have guessed at the inquisition's methods of torture. They applied what they thought they knew to their neighbors, on the advice of inquisition employees.[115]

Remarkably, those employees, Araníbar and Narbarte, never consulted their bosses in Logroño before counseling the constables of the Valle de Baztan; Araníbar kept his own pivotal role hidden until October 1611.[116] When the torturers and their friends defended themselves in secular or episcopal court, they insisted they had been sanctioned by their communities to consult with inquisition employees and were simply trying to avoid vigilante justice. Their reasoning did not work; the prosecutors refused to believe them. The accused witches who sued their torturers steadfastly reported that their abusers never said they were sanctioned by the inquisition or any other justice system, even though they "behaved like inquisitors."[117] In turn, the secular court was adamant that Araníbar and Narbarte did not have the authority to order what would turn into private imprisonment and torture, despite being inquisition employees. The same court also stipulated that the constables had no right to act in such ways against their fellow citizens.[118]

From 1608 to 1612, every affected community in Navarre wanted suspected witches to confess and seek pardon from the families they had injured. If suspects were lucky, they could confess, apologize, and not be accused again.[119] They also could flee, although we don't know whether they continued to be identified as witches as they moved around; perhaps they hoped that the infamy of being named as a witch would not follow them.[120] In any case, if suspects were less lucky, they would confess, apologize, be named again, and admit they could not stop being a witch and injuring children. In terms of vigilante justice, men and woman who said they could not stop being witches, and men and women who refused to admit they were witches, ended up in the same place: both groups faced private imprisonment and torture, as did suspects of both sexes who confessed and then revoked their statements.

Social and Spiritual Loss

Under any of these circumstances, the accused witches' lives changed fundamentally if they were adults and teenagers whom their communities believed to be guilty.[121] Being denounced as a witch brought social ruin. In Erratzu, one man said, "his honor was on the ground, and he would prefer to go on pilgrimage than continue to live in that place." In Elgorriaga, one of the married women put into the ladders testified that afterwards she could not leave her house: she and her husband were living "such a cruel life that she was on the verge of going crazy."[122] What we don't know—because we haven't yet found the right kind of evidence—is whether the dishonor from being publicly labeled a witch dissipated with time, especially if the accused had no familial reputation as such. Only very occasionally did a witness for the witch torturers try to excuse the violence with the claim that a particular victim's ancestry was tainted with witchcraft.[123]

Being accused of witchcraft also turned people into religious pariahs in a way that could have endured for months if not years. This particular heresy was an "exceptional" one and hence reserved, meaning it required the attention of higher ecclesiastics for absolution. As a result, people who confessed to being witches could not receive the ecclesiastical sacraments until a representative of the bishop of Pamplona or an inquisitor appeared in person to absolve them. Thus unless or until such figures reached their particular village, the confessed witches there could not receive the Eucharist or Extreme Unction, or engage in the sacrament of penance.[124]

For older people, these restrictions were extremely worrisome. In Erratzu, parish priest Miguel de Aguirre declared publicly that one of his flock, an elderly shepherd named Juan Miguel Chiperena, was actually a witch. When Chiperena fell sick and died, Aguirre refused to administer Extreme Unction to him, which appalled Erratzu's residents.[125] In Elgorriaga, Pedro de Landa, age sixty-three, who had survived the ladder torture, commented in secular court on his profound disquiet over not receiving the sacraments: "[I am] fearful of dying without them."[126] At the same time, accused witches who *declined* to confess could continue to receive the sacraments, which stoked community tensions in all sorts of directions, from the shock of village priests and neighbors that the Eucharist was being given to potential heretics to the dejection of confessed witches at their exclusion from crucial religious rites.

While Logroño's three inquisitors busied themselves with witches in their tribunal, they created a vacuum in the countryside: eventually, actors there decided to fill it. In the absence of inquisitorial solutions, villagers pressured, coerced, and assaulted the supposed assailants of children on the advice of inquisition employees. They created in turn a substantial group of outcasts who had lost their former social and religious status. A number of those outcasts eventually would seek vengeance against their tormenters before the secular and episcopal legal jurisdictions; in the meantime, however, local life was torn apart.[127] The next question is how religious values and social conflicts galvanized this persecution.

2

SPIRITUAL AND SOCIAL COMBAT

There is no doubt that this witch persecution was suffused with theological anxieties about the Devil. Parents, priests, relatives, and neighbors were aghast to see children converted into the Devil's followers. Many said they would rather see their offspring dead; some asked witch suspects to go ahead and kill their children, rather than continue to torment them in this way.[1] But it also is true that more worldly motives entered into this witch hunt, and the challenge for modern historians and modern readers is to keep both possibilities in play at the same time. Easy as it would be to view religious fears as mere "cover" for earthly motives, sources from Navarrese communities do not allow a one-sided explanation for what happened, because they contain too much evidence to the contrary. Moreover, if we want to capture realities from so long ago, it seems especially risky to elevate causes that we intuitively think are more likely because of our later vantage point. As historians, the responsible way forward is to view all the possibilities as plausible when it comes to why people were suspected and accused of witchcraft. Witch-hunting on a large scale in early modern Navarre, or Europe, for that matter, never came down to single causes or explanations.

The Religious Environment

The Catholic world that inquisitors and Navarrese villagers inhabited in the early seventeenth century was replete with religious warfare, and it's worth stressing that the threats were close by. Navarre's geographical boundaries touched France and the sea: Protestants could enter the region by land or water, or in print, in the form of banned books that the inquisition never successfully suppressed.[2] Navarre's proximity to borders made it a threshold in terms of religious space, at least as far as inquisitors were concerned. The ones in Logroño worried intensely about religious dissidents from other nations. Once Portugal was annexed by Spain in 1580, Logroño's inquisitors fixated as well on the possibility that Portuguese conversos, who descended from Jews, could be traveling through Navarre to get to St. Jean de Luz, on the French side, in order to practice Mosaic Law there. The inquisitors worried too about the less frequent presence of moriscos, for fear they were crossing Navarre in order to reach the Ottoman Empire.

Meanwhile, in the late sixteenth and early seventeenth centuries, the bishops of Pamplona were engrossed with the theological, ceremonial, and moral errors of Navarre's parish priests.[3] They were convinced that bad examples led to religious discord. Often, the Navarrese clergy could fail to deliver the ecclesiastical sacraments in the right way, or even disrespect the saints. For example, in 1604, the mayor, constables, and council of Carcastillo initiated a hearing about their vicar, Don Juan Garcia de Eulate. Don Juan was very old, and stuttered; he could not preach the Gospel, and his parish could not understand him even if he tried.[4] Residents of Pitillas, thirty-seven miles south of Pamplona, went to the bishop to announce that their vicar, Don Pedro de Abaurrea, was not saying Mass on all the days he should. He also was refusing to execute the necessary processions and prayers to banish clouds during storms, "as always has been done, forever, by taking the statue of Our Lady to the door of the church." (It was routine in early modern Spain to carry crosses and statues around churches during hail or thunderstorms, as part of a petitionary procession.[5]) The episcopal court ordered Don Pedro to say Mass daily for the village and to "conjure clouds day and night, as might be needed."[6]

Meanwhile, Don Bernardo de Jauregui, a stand-in priest for the village of Luzaide-Valcarlos, became convinced that the statue of Saint Martin in his parish church was spying on him: Don Bernardo consequently buried the statue, explaining to his parishioners that the image was talking to him. The community consequently dug up Saint Martin and locked him away for safekeeping. Residents were convinced that the "harsh whirlwinds and storms" that they had suffered was due to the priest's having buried the statue, which amounted to neglecting the proper reverence due to Saint Martin.[7]

Moreover, clerics in Navarre could be violent toward each other as well as toward the laity they were supposed to serve.[8] Presbyters could kill one another with guns or swords. Two clerics in Azpeitia bloodied each other's noses in church during the Feast of Corpus Christi while the Eucharist was on display, a circumstance that compounded their offense; two months later, they took up their argument again, and one attacked the other with a switch. In Sesma, a parish priest was brought to episcopal court after shooting someone else's dog while out hunting and then threatening to kill the dog's owner. In Azpeitia in 1601, parish priest Fermín de Loyola was prosecuted by the bishop "for being disorderly, going out at night with a sword and a shield, playing excessively at cards, and fomenting quarrels, in one of which he charged at Francisco de Aria with a candlestick."[9] Another beneficed cleric in Azpeitia interfered with local government officials as they attempted to seize the equipment of fishermen who were casting with prohibited nets: the priest said the nets were his, tried to take them back, and called the officials "greedy."

At the same time, parish priests very often scandalized their congregations because they refused to give up women. The bishop of Pamplona could order a priest to throw a female servant out of the house, but the priest might merely place her in a home across the street. One priest in Azpeitia had multiple offspring by multiple mothers in his home; he recently had taken up with a woman from Azkoitia, with whom he'd had yet one more child.[10] In Ziritza, the priest had carried on so long and so publicly with a married woman that his parishioners were convinced their relationship had called down the wrath of God, since for the last five years hailstorms had razed their harvests.[11]

Priests stationed in remote Navarrese villages often became bored and looked for entertainment: gambling, drinking, concubines, running with bulls, dancing, and hunting helped pass the time.[12] Gambling and hunting were not entirely recreational; the clergy could pursue both to supplement their usually tiny annual incomes. Navarre's poverty was well known; bishops and inquisitors always commented on it. A subsistence economy in the mountains meant that tithes from villagers were necessarily restricted. Impoverished priests consequently tended to seek income elsewhere, which put them on the same economic plane as the laypeople they were supposed to be guiding and correcting.

For example, in the first decades of the seventeenth century, Pamplona's bishops prosecuted dozens of clerics for hunting for profit. Priests borrowed ferrets to hunt rabbits and then declined to return them. Two clerics and a student formed a rabbit-killing trio that allegedly seized more than two thousand hares through prohibited means, namely, ferrets, dogs, and nets. One priest was so dedicated to hunting with a gun that he often stayed overnight in the forest. Another took his hunting dogs to church, where they peed on the altar and barked during Mass.[13] The larger point is that Navarrese priests were usually thoroughly integrated into their native environments, just like inquisition employees. This fact helps to explain why those priests often became active witch-hunters between 1608 and 1614: they too felt religious and social pressures, participated in village enmities, and perhaps didn't care one iota about being role models.

Efforts at Religious Reform

Nevertheless, Pamplona's bishops had a guide to remedy priestly misbehavior in the form of the decrees from the Council of Trent.[14] The Council of Trent was an ecumenical gathering of Catholic clerics, originally called by Holy Roman Emperor Charles V to define Catholic doctrine and rituals in the wake of the Protestant Reformation. The council met from 1545–47, 1551–52, and 1562–63; it was suspended in 1547 and 1552 because of European wars. In Spain, Philip II promulgated Trent's extensive mandates on July 10, 1564.

The Tridentine decrees elevated tremendously the pastoral responsibilities of bishops. After 1564, bishops were supposed to reside in their dioceses and monitor their clergy for scandal and ignorance. Trent's mandates also laid out for Catholics the duties that they should expect from local priests. Residence in parishes was now obligatory.[15] Priests had to administer the sacraments to the laity or explain why not to their bishops; if they were absent from their parishes, they could be required to hire a vicar to provide the sacraments to their flocks.

Still, because Pamplona's bishops had no luck whatsoever in formally calling or concluding diocesan synods until 1590, there was no operational link between Trent's decrees and episcopal recommendations in Navarre for decades. What finally made Trent enforceable in Navarre was a synod called by Bishop Bernardino de Sandoval y Rojas (r. 1588–95), which occurred in 1590 and formally ended, whereby its mandates could be put into effect.[16] (Bishop Sandoval eventually became the inquisitor-general; he was officially in charge of the entire Spanish Inquisition during the 1608–14 witch hunt.) Not only did Sandoval's synod in 1590 explicitly and repeatedly refer to the content of the Tridentine decrees, but its outcome was printed in 1591, which meant it was theoretically available to anyone literate in Spanish.[17] The synod's directives were called "constitutions," and they followed standard topics: explanations of mortal versus venial sins; details on the sacraments; reiterations of the most important Catholic prayers, such as the Our Father (*Pater Noster*) and the Hail Mary (*Ave María*); descriptions of the various church offices; and specifics on how the episcopal court and its officers should function.

The 1590 synod also tackled, at length, requirements for clerical behavior. In a section titled, "on the life and virtue of the clergy," Sandoval adjured his clerics not to play games or eat in church; not to dance, sing profane songs, or attend the running of bulls; not to drink in taverns unless they were traveling; and not to walk with women on public streets. The clergy were not to carry arms. Perhaps not surprisingly, the synod's constitution lay particular stress on the clergy and sex. They could not have lovers or suspicious women in their houses. If their superiors reprimanded them for connections to women—and the women were not put aside "actually, and with results"—the bishop could categorize those clerics as guilty of "public concubinage."[18]

The synodal constitutions also commented at length on the obligation for clergy to reside in their parishes. That residence was absolutely crucial if those clerics had the care of souls (*cura animarum*), which meant they administered the sacraments. For decades before 1590, theologians throughout Spain had argued that clerical residence was a divine mandate, ordered by Jesus in John 10:1–16 and John 21:15–17, and Bishop Sandoval agreed.[19] His 1590 synod quoted John 10 to the effect that Jesus had told his disciples to "know" their sheep: that verb was expressed in Latin as *cognoscere* and in Spanish as *conocer*, which meant to know a person rather than knowing a fact. Residence was a divine command; Sandoval bluntly stated that Navarrese clerics couldn't know their sheep if they didn't live with them. Significantly, in this respect, Sandoval and his Spanish peers went further than the Tridentine decrees, which said residence was obligatory but declined to say where or how the obligation originated. In 1590, Sandoval pledged to deprive priests of their benefices—their church offices, or sources of income— if they were not physically there to administer the sacraments. He wrote that as their bishop, he would first publicly issue a summons to them in their churches, on a Sunday, to stop their fraud. Once that summons was given, he would proceed to remove them if they persevered in their absence, even if they had been away when the citation was read.[20]

Yet despite a completed synod and explicit, printed constitutions, bishops in seventeenth-century Navarre had trouble monitoring the clergy due to topography, climate, and the expanse of their diocese. They never perfected their priests—but then, neither did any other Catholic bishop in early modern Europe.[21] Still, they had a great deal of success in catechetical instruction in Christian doctrine. Navarre's clergy were ordered to teach the basic elements of Christian salvation every Sunday and feast day, "after eating, at a convenient time": the church bell should ring as a sign for the children to gather. Every feast day, the entire *pueblo* should be instructed in the Gospel reading for that occasion.[22] Clerics who failed to complete these two tasks were supposed to pay fines. After Trent, Pamplona's bishops also adjured village priests and rectors to start schools for their communities' children, to teach them to read and write. What went along with these pedagogical efforts was the publication of catechisms, including bilingual ones in Basque, though the extent to which such texts reached readers is anyone's guess.[23]

The Witches' Inversions of Catholic Theology

Navarrese people clearly absorbed the religious lessons sponsored by Pamplona's bishops. They knew how to identify misbehaving priests and complained energetically to the episcopal court about them. They knew the sacraments as well as their prayers. Significantly, Tridentine theology was directly relevant to the ways in which they talked about and reacted to the witch hunt that began in 1608. Trent's decrees explained in detail how Catholic Christians received salvation from God, which was a gift that no one could ever merit by faith or works, due to original sin. God called people to Him, and people could decide whether or not to cooperate because they possessed free will. If people heeded God's call, they were "aroused and aided by divine grace, receiving faith by hearing . . . they [were] moved freely toward [Him], believing to be true what has been divinely revealed and promised." At that point, understanding themselves to be sinners, they turned from "the fear of divine justice . . . to consider the mercy of God"; they began to hope and then to love God as the fountain of all justice. They started to hate sin and desire the sacrament of baptism. Once justified, people received not only the remission of sins, thanks to the merits of Jesus's Passion on the Cross, but the infusion of faith, hope, and charity.[24]

Crucially, justification always began as a free and unmerited gift, but Catholics could increase their hopes of salvation through "the observance of the commandments of God and of the Church, [as] faith cooperat[ed] with good works." Trent's decrees told Catholic Christians, "with fear and trembling work out [your] salvation, in labors, in watchings, in almsdeeds, in prayer, in fastings, and chastity. For knowing that [you] are born again unto the hope of glory, and not as yet unto glory, [you] ought to fear for the combat that yet remains with the flesh, with the world, and with the devil."[25]

One of the most important ways in which Catholic Christians could increase their justification was by receiving the Eucharist. The churchmen at Trent took great care to explain that the bread and wine in the Mass were literally transformed into the body and blood of Jesus Christ, though their external appearances ("accidents" in the Aristotelian sense) remained unchanged. Transubstantiation was one of the great mysteries of Catholicism, and though parish priests were forbidden to celebrate the Mass in the vernacular, Trent told them, "during the celebration of the mass, explain some of the things read during the mass, and explain some myster[ies] of this most holy sacrifice, especially on Sundays and festival days."[26] At the Fourth Lateran Council of 1215, Christians throughout Europe had been directed to receive the Eucharist at least once a year, at Easter, after completing the sacrament of penance, but by the second half of the sixteenth century, Catholic writers often urged more frequent reception of both penance and the Eucharist. Penance involved the oral confession of sins to a priest or friar, who then prescribed a means of atonement, which the confessant accepted. The formal structure of penance required a prayer of contrition by the penitent that expressed sorrow for sinful thoughts, words, and deeds. Afterwards, the confessant was absolved of sin by the priest or friar and reconciled to the body of the Catholic Church.

When suspected witches in Navarre described their participation in dancing, feasts, and sex, they were overturning Trent's command that Christians engage in prayer, fasting, and chastity. When those witches expressed sorrow to the Devil for the good works *they had done* and the evil works *they had failed to do*, they were inverting the actions that Catholics were expected to perform to increase their justification. The witches' lack of regret for evil works overturned the moral basis of the sacrament of penance, which required contrition for sins committed. Witches in this persecution allegedly could not even see Catholicism's fundamental sacrament, the Eucharist: instead of a white wafer, they saw a black cloud. Their separation from the Eucharist was furthered in a practical way because, again, their heresy was exceptional: ordinary priests or friars could not reconcile them to the church, which would have allowed them to regain access to the sacraments. Instead, they required the intervention of an inquisitor or a representative of the bishop.

The witches' entanglement with Jesus, Mary, and the saints was just as deep. The Tridentine decrees made it exceedingly clear that Jesus should be worshipped and Mary and the saints venerated. Spanish Catholic culture in general thrived on Christocentrism, but Marian devotions, pilgrimages to saints' shrines, and the dedication of villages to saintly protectors also were commonplace in the early modern period. Inquisitors and villagers alike attributed special power to pronouncing the name of Jesus: between 1608 and 1614, when witches accidentally said that name, the Devil's akelarres disappeared. Though the Devil in this witch hunt instructed novice witches to abandon their belief in the Virgin Mary, child-witches said they had visions of her while they were in the akelarres, and she always implored them to be strong. The Devil helped his witches attack churches; the witches often met near shrines. These were yet more signs of disrespect for the Catholic heavenly hierarchy.

And yet the line between Catholic orthodoxy and heresy could be porous. Even self-identified Catholics in Navarre, as was the case elsewhere in Europe, thought hard about the parameters of sin, as well as the theology and moral guidance they were hearing from the pulpit and perhaps reading in print. The inquisition tribunal in Logroño sentenced multiple people a year for maintaining that sex between unmarried men and women was not immoral, proposing that Mary was not a virgin when she gave birth to Jesus, or blurting "I renounce God" while losing at cards. Many of these offenders voluntarily appeared before inquisitors Becerra, Valle, and Salazar to confess their errors, while others were denounced by bystanders who were aghast at what they had heard. For example, in 1609, Navarrese men turned in an English sailor for saying publicly that "Catholics were papists, demons, and devils, and they believed in stick figures and rocks, and even if they broke him into pieces by dragging him behind horses, he would not believe in the Catholic faith. When they showed him a statue of Our Lady, he grimaced at it, and gave signs of hating the name of Our Lady." One Navarrese friar was known to be walking around La Rochelle in France, "in layperson's clothes, like a Lutheran": when Navarrese friends recognized him, they "tried to put him back in his habit, and forced him to board a boat, in order to return him to Spain and take him away from the bad state he was in."[27]

In general, early modern people in Navarre thought of themselves as Christians. They comprehended what the Catholic sacraments meant. They knew the saints might work as intercessors on their behalf with God, which is why they called them lawyers (abogados) in their wills. They understood the difference between morally good works and morally deficient ones. They cared about religious error. Between 1608 and 1614, the concepts and language that witch accusers, witch suspects, and village bystanders used in court consistently reflected the Catholic environment shaped by Trent.

The Religious Values of Bishop Venegas

One of the chief arbiters of this witch hunt—Alonso Venegas y Figueroa, who became bishop of Pamplona in 1606—was also an enthusiastic advocate for Tridentine culture. By the time of his appointment to the Pamplona diocese, he had already enjoyed an illustrious career. Born in Madrid, his father was one of Philip II's ambassadors to Germany, while his mother was from a noble Portuguese family. Venegas entered the University of Salamanca in 1577 and ultimately obtained a licentiate in canon law. Thereafter, he became one of the cathedral canons of Toledo, whose archbishop was the primate of Spain; while beneficed there, Venegas also acted as an inquisitor in Granada from 1592 to 1600. He served on the Suprema in Madrid from 1600 to 1606. He acted as Pamplona's bishop from 1606 until 1612; he then was promoted to the episcopal see of Sigüenza, where he died in 1614.[28]

Venegas has been described as bringing the Council of Trent to Pamplona, and it is easy to see why.[29] He followed Bishop Sandoval's example and promoted Tridentine values in the city.[30] He established a teaching position on sacred scripture in the cathedral. He endorsed the printing of pamphlets on Christian doctrine. Though he could not read the language, he licensed the printing of a religious catechism in Basque and ordered that it be used throughout the diocese.[31] In 1608 and 1609, Venegas published two tracts for the education of his diocesan clergy.[32] He also did his utmost to create a seminary for the training of priests: when consulted, his cathedral chapter told him, "[Navarre's clerics] are in the mountains, and cannot reach the universities. They need a seminary desperately, on account of living in such an isolated way and on the French border."[33] In addition, Venegas found that his cathedral had no steady source of income to pay singers; when the cathedral did attract good vocalists, they quickly left for other locations because of the unpredictability of their salaries. Venegas therefore decided to use his own funds to support "twelve boys, the sons of poor parents, who might practice music, and many of them could study grammar, and the whole enterprise would be in service to the Church." Venegas attempted to start beatification proceedings for Ignatius of Loyola as early as 1606–7; when Ignatius's beatification occurred, in July 1609, he invited members of the Society of Jesus to attend vespers and Mass in Pamplona's cathedral in honor of their founder.[34]

Furthermore, Venegas was captivated by the Feast of Corpus Christi, which celebrated the Eucharistic mystery of transubstantiation, and he was determined to promote it.[35] To that end, he supported enormous festivals for that feast day in 1609 and 1610 in Pamplona. Given that the witches on trial during those years claimed not to be able to see the Eucharist, Venegas's efforts in this regard were perhaps especially significant, though we have no idea what he knew about the inquisition's investigations over that two-year period. The commemorations he sponsored began with processions of all the clergy in the city, including Venegas, who carried the Most Holy Sacrament himself. The following morning, the Eucharist was exhibited in the cathedral for all to venerate. Musical performances occurred all day for three days. There were poetry competitions in honor of the sacrament; the head preacher of the college of Jesuits in Pamplona gave sermons.[36] These festivals were so noteworthy that pamphlets about them were printed.[37]

The Devil in Print

Venegas and his contemporaries were well aware that it was a struggle to practice Tridentine Catholicism. Human beings were tempted at every turn to sin. They had a powerful adversary encouraging their pride, avarice, lust, anger, gluttony, envy, and spiritual sloth: namely, the Devil.[38] Vernacular treatises on witchcraft in early modern Spain, which were deliberately aimed at a wide audience, described the Devil as God's foremost enemy.[39] The Devil could attract followers through explicit or implicit pacts; his followers could fly through the air in their dreams or in reality. Disciples of the Devil were traitors to God: they had forsaken their baptismal vows and should be punished as apostates.[40]

If printed advice about witchcraft implied that the laity should be mindful of the Devil's snares, devotional books in general promoted the same awareness. For example, in *Exercicios espirituales*, printed in Pamplona in 1618, author Antonio Molina repeatedly noted the hatred that demons had for Christ. He affirmed that the Devil was full of lies and tricks. He reported, "the Devil's aspiration in his temptations, always, is to make man despair . . . and you should greatly fear such a powerful and astute enemy." Molina tried to encourage his readers with the thought that "the Holy Angels are always watching those who battle against temptations, and they are happy when people vanquish them, and they help them."[41] The child-witches who saw the Virgin Mary begging them to resist would have perfectly understood Molina's point.

In his widely circulated *Parayso virginal de discoursos predicables en las fiestas de la siempre Virgen María, madre de Dios*, the Dominican friar Juan de Mata devoted whole pages to the power of the Virgin Mary vis-à-vis the Devil. The name "María" gave exorcists the power to expel demons from the possessed; her name was feared more than anything in hell.[42] In another tract, *Oraciones cristianas sobre los evangelios de los domingos de advento*, Matías Jiménez confirmed that the Devil was a liar who took from Adam and Eve the fear of death and who now took from human beings the fear of the Last Judgment. Hell was an evil without remedy: sacred scripture called it "the lake of God's anger," and meditation upon it was a remedy for sin. Jiménez wanted his readers to "arm themselves with strong weapons and provide themselves with good ammunition" to fight the enemy of Christ.[43] Finally, and somewhat oddly, given its ostensible subject was marriage, Ignacio de Andueza began his *Manual de casados, con un tratado del Santíssimo Sacramento* with entire paragraphs about hell. "The fires of Hell roast and burn . . . tormenting the condemned without consuming them . . . and Hell doesn't just have fire, but also intolerable cold . . . and then Death enters to snap at [the condemned], and as it snaps at them, it doesn't kill them, nor can it kill them, but rather, it bites them." Later in his treatise, Andueza wrote, "the Devil loathes God, and wants only vengeance; he turned his wrath against the creation of God, which was man, and he conducts war against that creation."[44]

Such messages were not out of reach for Navarrese people who could read Spanish, and the same spiritual content could have been easily transmitted through sermons and conversations in Basque. We know that despite Navarre's reputation for poverty, ignorance, and liminality, books circulated: a recent study of thirty-seven private libraries confirms the interest of Pamplona clerics and lawyers in vernacular works on Catholic devotion and theology.[45] Pamplona's clergy owned confessors' manuals, treatises on how to die well, compilations of sermons, manuals on how to prepare to receive the Eucharist, catechisms for priests and confessors, and collections of spiritual exercises. They also owned the infamous witch-hunting treatise, *Malleus maleficarum*. Navarrese clergy and laity, as well as the inquisitors who supervised that territory, understood enough theology about Christ and the Devil to invoke their enmity as the conceptual foundation of this witch hunt.[46]

Warfare

What has gone unnoticed up to now, however, is the all-encompassing rhetoric of spiritual combat that infiltrated the witch persecution of 1608–14. Expressions of struggle between God and the Devil were employed by literally everyone, including villagers of all ages, local officials and priests, and judicial authorities. For example, when Logroño's inquisitors first wrote to the

Suprema about the witches in February 1609, they noted that the six suspects who turned up of their own accord had explained why they were there with exactly the same words and reasoning, which the inquisitors found highly suspicious. After the inquisitors questioned the guide who had brought the six to Logroño, he maintained that none of the six was being pursued by any justice system; the inquisitors consequently decided that the suspects must have come to their tribunal out of "some consultation and counsel with the Devil."[47] When the Suprema wrote back, its members signed their response, "Dios os guarde," meaning "may God protect you."[48]

In the summer of 1609, when witch-prisoners began to die in the tribunal's jail, the inquisitors wondered whether those deaths might be a diabolical ploy to prevent the ratification of evidence and thereby wreck their cases. The inquisitors' misgivings were heightened because the witches fell so desperately ill without any previous symptoms, as the doctors noted who were brought in for consultation. The inquisitors wanted to investigate whether the Devil was having sex with the ill female witches, or whether he was appearing to them in the house of penitence, "because even the doctors have thought that such is going on, and yesterday they told us that we should make new dresses and beds for the witches, and remove the ones they have, and the jail warden and those of his house have started to express great suspicion and shame about it all." If the inquisitors found proof that the Devil was having sex with the prisoners outside the tribunal's jail, they would have to arrange for all the witches to move back in, "because we are certain that the Devil never would commit such acts in [our] secret cells."[49] These passages from inquisitorial correspondence raise so many questions. Were the witches' original beds diabolical by nature, which meant they could not resist the Devil's sexual advances? Was the witches' original clothing too enticing for the Devil, or did it contain talismans that called him? Were the warden and his family expected to monitor phantasmal sexual activity and fall into dishonor when they knew nothing about it?

As the inquisitors in Logroño listened to witnesses and suspects, they stockpiled anecdotes that they would use in later debates about the reality of the witches' activities. They highlighted the stories of child-witches who saw the Virgin Mary at the Devil's reunions: Mary often had the infant Jesus in her arms and pleaded with the children not to renounce their Christianity. One young woman who could not bring herself to reject the Virgin Mary at an akelarre fell ill and remained that way until she was absolved. Another woman was terribly maltreated by witches: when she told her husband, they thereafter went to bed with a "lit candle, an armed pistol, and a drawn sword." An eleven-year-old boy was given a cross and a slip of paper with holy writing on it by an inquisition commissioner: when the witches came for him once more, they could not lift him out of bed, no matter how hard they tried. One fifteen-year-old male wanted to return to the Christian fold and began to walk to Logroño on his own: later, he reportedly told the inquisitors about his spiritual battles on the way. The Devil had confronted him as he traveled, but "he didn't want to follow [him] anymore, or be swept up in his deceits and trickery, and he wanted to return to Jesus Christ, as he had proposed; and so to be cured, he came to Logroño. When the Devil pointed him toward a different road, [he] rejected it, saying that he would continue his journey and would look for the faith of Jesus Christ in Logroño." Of course, the implication was that only Spanish inquisitors could help him, which in one crucial respect was true: they had the power to absolve him and restore him to the sacraments.[50]

Spiritual zeal also was built into accounts of the auto de fe. In the pamphlet printed on January 6, 1611, Gaspar de Palencia, a Franciscan friar, wrote in his approval for publication, "the content therein was very true, and it was appropriate that it come to the notice of all the faithful, so that their eyes might be opened to the deceits of Satan."[51] The same pamphlet relayed that when Inquisitor Becerra removed the sambenito of María de Suretegui during the auto de fe, he announced he was doing so to exemplify the inquisition's clemency. Becerra told the thirty thousand onlookers that Suretegui deserved this mercy because of her extreme pain over her sin and her struggle to resist diabolical forces. After she left the Devil's flock (gremio) in Zugarramurdi, she had been harassed by her former witch-companions. She fought back energetically and refused to return to their sect. Both printed and manuscript sources contain descriptions like this: "[S]uretegui was in her house, in the company of many people who were guarding her for her own safety. Many witches arrived there, and begged and threatened her to return to them, and with the power of fifty voices, she said she no longer wanted to serve the Devil, that he had tricked her long enough, and she showed them the Cross of the Rosary. Seeing that they could not take her, they went to her orchard and pulled out its vines and trees."[52] During the auto de fe, Becerra's description of Suretegui's return to Christianity "caused such great devotion and piety in everyone in the audience, that they did not stop giving a thousand benedictions and praises to God and the inquisition."[53]

The audience at the November 1610 auto de fe also would have heard about the astonishing events in Bera, one of Las Cinco Villas. There, children who had stopped being witches were placed under the vigilant eye of the rector, Lorenzo Hualde. One night, the witches and the Devil came for them, but Hualde was on the lookout, wearing his clerical garb. Hualde "exhorted them, and then the witches and demon climbed onto the roof and began to break the tiles, with so much noise that the entire pueblo was disturbed." The next day, the witches grabbed (*cogieron*) the children and took them to the akelarre, where, on the Devil's orders, they whipped them with hawthorn branches. A few days later, as the children left school, one of the witches passed through the street; yelling, the children pursued her and stoned her until she could manage to get inside her house, where she spent many days in bed.[54] Similar dramas even allegedly happened with witches in custody. The Devil visited María de Zozaya both in the village jail in Errenteria and in the inquisitors' prison: "he told her to deny the charges, and not to name his witches, because the inquisitors would burn her, and he wanted to smother her one time because she didn't want to promise."

Catholics who heard such accounts might be led to reflect on their own behavior. The witches explained that they and the Devil mocked Christians who did not bless their table before eating or give thanks after eating. The Devil's crew was delighted when people forgot to thank God, who sustained them; witches preferred to invade such houses.[55] The Devil revealed in the akelarre which people were more likely not to pray before eating, "and the Devil opened those persons' doors for the witches, and the witches cast a spell over the persons inside, and danced in their houses, and broke plates, and committed other injuries." Spiritual carelessness created a diabolical opening, literally, as witches crossed, unnoticed, into private household spaces, with destructive consequences. Conversely, shouting the name of Jesus while being pursued by witches could make them powerless, and ships that carried a visible cross could not be assaulted.[56] When such anecdotes were transmitted—whether aloud, in print, or in manuscript—they may well have instructed, terrified, or even entertained listeners and readers, who could then go on to circulate what they had learned.

Ardent rhetoric appeared as well in the language of the inquisitors' employees. When commissioner Leon de Araníbar wrote to Logroño from Elizondo in February 1611, he commented that the three prisoners he had in hand from Zubieta were the most "obstinate, bold, and pernicious" he had ever encountered. Araníbar remarked that he had never seen such zeal as in Zubieta's rector, who had discovered the entire witches' sect through his industry and solicitude, and who was refusing to spare even his own relatives from investigation.[57] Spiritual combat was also taking place as relatives, neighbors, and priests tried to correct the witches in their midst.[58] In Erratzu, the vicar Miguel de Aguirre "was very much troubled by the thought that anyone in the village could be part of this sect, and he had a great desire and zeal to cure them, thinking about the salvation of their souls. And thus he exhorted many people."[59] When Aguirre visited Teresa de Iturburu, he told her to make a complete confession of it all, "and if she did so, the inquisition would be merciful, and without a doubt would pardon her . . . and he gave her other good and beneficial advice, pointing out the pains and torments of hell, and the [heavenly] reward of the blessed."[60] In Arraioz, Graciana de Perochena, age forty-six, had a substantial fight with her relative, accused witch María de Aldico:

> [Graciana] spoke to her and exhorted her with all possible force to leave the office of witch, and María responded that she could remember being a witch her entire life, and her relatives had abandoned her; she wanted to stop being a witch, but the Goat [i.e., the Devil] had her so blinded that it wasn't in her power. She often wanted to go and confess her sins . . . but the Goat made her turn back, and [she always did] what he wanted. And this witness then took her to confess, and when they reached the church, the priest read the holy Gospels. And despite all this, it was not possible to make her confess.[61]

This account of their conversation appears to demonstrate that the label of "witch" had become a part of María's identity—though it could reveal as well the way her relative imagined María's spiritual and emotional state.[62] We lack sufficient evidence to discern how María's self-identification as a witch developed, but the sense of spiritual combat is palpable.

In another deposition before the secular court, a man in Arraioz relayed his efforts to rescue his niece, who was a servant of Sabadina de Zozaya, one of the witches who was extensively tortured by her neighbors. This man brought his niece covertly to Elizondo, where he questioned her in secret; he demanded she confess if she was a witch, "and even though he spent a long time exhorting her, he could not make her say. At the end, she said it was true she was a witch, and her mistress Sabadina had bewitched her about a year ago." The uncle then took his niece before commissioner Leon de Araníbar, whereupon she confessed. A few days later, she told the same uncle that Sabadina, in the presence of other relatives, wanted to hit her with a burning stick: they terrified her and whipped her to say what she had deposed before Araníbar.[63] The niece's description called up a number of different scenarios, both real and imaginary: the fact that witch torturers in Arraioz had threatened male witch suspects with burning torches; the inquisition's burning of witches in November 1610; the witches' supposed habit of whipping their young converts at the akelarres.

Accusations: Debt, Sex, and Mental Illness

The surviving documents about this witch hunt reveal that religious understanding and religious fears played critical roles in the way people envisioned witches, accused them, and confessed to witchcraft. Between 1608 and 1614, people in Navarre were terrified of losing their families to the Devil in both a spiritual and a physical sense. Yet sometimes, the documents also open windows onto more mercenary and personal motives for allegations, which allow us to see conflicts that the historical record often conceals. One such motive in early modern Navarre was loaned and borrowed money. On July 4, 1608, Guillén Elizamendi, from Elizondo, confirmed in a notarial document that he owed six ducats to the vicar of Zugarramurdi and six more to Juana de Miñir, also a resident of Zugarramurdi, on account of a cart horse he had bought from her. In 1610, in the village of Narbarte, Pierre de Sanchigorena admitted he owed money to at least sixteen people: he said he didn't remember any other debts, but if some appeared, and they were true, they should be paid.[64] In Arraioz in 1613, the widow Catalina de Arrechea made her last will before Miguel de Narbarte. She owed one ducat and four reales to one neighbor; she also had borrowed a ducat from Adam Monena of Lekaroz for her daughter's wedding. In turn, five neighbors owed her money, including the owner of the manor of Jauregizar, Catalina de Iturbide.[65]

In one instance, we can see debts behind a witchcraft accusation in this persecution.[66] When Miguel Zuito called Sabadina de Zozaya a witch in spring 1611, she immediately called him a thief. A later witness clarified their conflict: Zuito had "stolen" from Sabadina's family by borrowing money and declining to repay it. The witness, García Michelaberra, learned from Zuito himself that the latter had borrowed money from one of Sabadina's sons-in-law; the son-in-law asked for the money to be paid back in order to travel to Logroño. Zuito told Michelaberra that he could not restore the money without selling cattle, and commented, "those wicked women [of the Zozaya family] will never be satisfied." Zuito then said, "if justice were not done about those wicked women, he would take the matter into his own hands, and when they passed by his door, he would kill them with a gun." And [Michelaberra] understood Zuito to mean that those women were witches, and if they weren't punished, he would kill them. And he remembers well that in his presence, Zuito said to a two-year-old child of his, "Look, son, tell me how Tristant de Ursúa, the husband of Sabadina de Zozaya, dances in the devil's akelarre." Michelaberra immediately objected to what Zuito was doing, and then Zuito shut up and went into his house, without saying another word. And all of this seemed very wrong to [Michelabarra], because such statements from children were enough to defame neighbors.[67]

Michelaberra was fifty-eight years old. His statement is direct evidence of the power of children's insults. Equally importantly, because Arraioz was in the Valle de Baztan, legal residents were on the same economic plane, given that they were explicitly stipulated as equals in terms of ancestry, and held pasturelands in common. Yet conflicts there over borrowed money were still entirely possible.[68]

Sex out of wedlock and illegitimate children could also fuel personal conflicts and witchcraft accusations. In August 1611, in Elizondo, a woman revoked her original confession to witchcraft made five months earlier. She explained that her own daughter had originally named her as a witch, "but that accusation was false on account of the hatred her daughter has for her, and the many troubles they have had between them. Her daughter has given birth twice without being married, like an evil woman, and this witness has rebuked her many times."[69] In Elgorriaga, María de Echeverría had multiple children by different men and remained unmarried: she insisted that the constable who had tortured her over witchcraft accusations, Juan de Legasa, had fathered one of her babies. Under oath, María said she had pleaded with Legasa to have mercy on her as the mother of his child; he then allegedly raped her. Witnesses remarked that when it came to the fathers of María's offspring, she "threw the children at whomever was at hand."[70] They also stated that relations between María and Legasa had been strained for years, and asserted that if María really had been raped, she certainly would have brought charges.[71]

Mental illness, too, could enter into the process of witch-hunting. In June 1610, María Aziariz was hit in the head with a rock by María Argonz.[72] Aziariz's husband retrieved the rock, showed it to his village's mayor, and demanded a legal hearing. (The rock in question weighed about two pounds.) He reported that his wife was gravely hurt. The mayor in turn asked why the one woman had assaulted the other. The husband reported that his wife had been standing at their door with a male grandchild. Argonz approached "and began to say that [Aziariz] was a witch, and a killer of children, and she would kill her son's baby." Aziariz "felt those words deeply" and moved toward Argonz; Argonz then "raised a stone and hit her with the sharp edge." Significantly—perhaps he thought he had discovered a real witch in their midst—the mayor asked why Argonz would have said such a thing. Aziariz's husband replied that Argonz didn't need a reason: "she frequently insults many very honorable women with that sort of language, and because everyone views her as more crazy than sane, they put up with it."

Other witnesses backed up the husband's story. On her way home from Mass, Lucia Landa saw and heard the confrontation. Argonz said to Aziariz "that she was an evil wicked whore, and a child of Aziariz's wasn't by her husband, but by another; and she was a witch and a child killer . . . and soon, she would get rid of her grandchildren."[73] Landa reported that if Aziariz's headdress had not blocked the rock, she would have been dead.[74] Landa described Argonz, the attacker, as "a woman of evil life: she has left her husband and household and goes walking through the whole valley, and even beyond it, doing much harm to people in terms of what she says, as well as taking and stealing things that come to hand." Other villagers agreed that Argonz was both mentally ill and a thief. She was known to have taken wheat and bread from other people's houses; multiple witnesses repeated the phrase, "she stole things that came to hand." Argonz, then, neglected to follow some of the key gender expectations for honorable women. She left her house and her husband. She walked unaccompanied and without apparent purpose. She stole when the opportunity presented itself and entered other people's houses in order to do so.

Argonz's "invasions" of homes were reminiscent of witches' incursions into domestic spaces, and some deponents even moved from Argonz's thievery to the abduction of children. One female witness testified that her four-year-old son once went missing from her house: she looked for him for more than two hours, until finally the entire village was in an uproar. Then, "walking with the mayor and constables in search of the child, with some fear and suspicion, they came to the house where María Argonz lived, where they found the child, who was very frightened. And when they went to the door, María Argonz didn't want to open it, but rather locked it with a key . . . and then they forced her to open the door. And this witness knows for certain that if they had not arrived at that moment at the house, she would have lost her child."[75] The testimony about Argonz reveals multiple village truths: the power of compounded insults, the boundaries of wifely expectations, community concern for missing youngsters, and the way villagers made connections between activities and character.[76]

After this case moved to Pamplona, Argonz's own lawyer insisted, first, that Aziariz had originally hit Argonz with a stick, which is why Argonz lashed out with the rock. Second, "[Argonz] is always in a frenzy, and she's crazy by nature, and as such, she has done many things that a person would only do if he had no judgment or understanding, as the witnesses will attest."[77] Indeed, three defense witnesses for Argonz confirmed this portrait. She was mad and behaved like an insane person; it was said she came by this state naturally because her father and grandfather were also mad. Her grandfather used to eat the worms that he found under rocks. Her neighbors didn't do anything about her because they knew she was crazy. The royal court sentenced Argonz to a year of exile. She had to be out of Navarre within six days, or by June 28, 1610.[78] Her case was not unique, nor was mental instability or bad neighborliness always gendered female. In Doneztebe-Santesteban, in December 1610, Gracián de Irissari was accused of defaming Brianda de Mayora as a witch. The prosecutor's statement said that Irissari, too, had a habit of insulting and defaming people for no reason and had been punished previously for it.[79]

Accusations: Pressure, Hatred, Torture

Money, sex, madness: all three figured at least occasionally as a foundation for accusations in this witch hunt, but they were outweighed by subornment, familial pressure, and private loathing. Children were bribed to accuse particular people through gifts of food and clothing. Two women in Etxalar promised a young shepherd a shirt and four reales if he would denounce particular people. They "catechized him every morning, and he admitted that they had also suborned three other boys."[80] In Sunbilla, a French boy, age fourteen, said he could detect witches through marks in their eyes; he had been bribed with food.

The role of family pressure was more complicated, emotionally and practically. Between 1608 and 1614, Navarrese villagers appear to have been convinced that they would lose their houses, property, and all their movable goods if their sons, daughters, mothers, or fathers were named as witches and ended up before the inquisition in Logroño. One woman explained that her neighbors told her that if she did not confess and was not reconciled and absolved under the inquisition's edict of grace in 1611, her house and property would be razed and lost (*la casa y hacienda quedaría asolada y perdida*). Given that witch suspects who were reconciled or executed in the November 1610 auto de fe did lose their property, these fears were understandable: the villagers perhaps were unaware that the Spanish Inquisition in general tended not to confiscate property where witches were concerned.[81] The worry that anyone might suffer the same loss simply by appearing in the tribunal was persistent, and it could lead to false confessions in an attempt to stop the accusatory process and stay away from the inquisitors.

For example, in December 1611, Inquisitor Salazar challenged María de Indart's efforts to revoke her witchcraft confession. He told her that she had never been imprisoned or mistreated by village justices or neighbors; why, then, would she have falsely admitted to such a crime? Indart replied that her husband and her only daughter were in torment over her being named a witch by others. They were terrified they would lose the house and all their goods if she did not confess. One day, "her husband persuaded her for a long time and begged her to confess, and asked her to do it for him. And he began to cry. And she had never seen him cry, and she softened so much that she confessed."[82]

When family anxieties over property were backed up with physical mistreatment, confessions happened that much more quickly. In Ziga, an older teenage girl was assaulted by the constables of her village because she had been named as a witch, "and she was even more pressed by her parents and other people of the household, who told her that if she confessed, she would be free of trouble." Another sixteen-year-old finally confessed in Elizondo after "being vexed and troubled by certain relatives and members of the household." One young woman was tortured into confessing by two aunts and her mother, while a teenage boy was beleaguered by his mother and other relatives.[83] Family pressure to confess was not gendered in either direction: the demands came from mothers and fathers, aunts and uncles, as well as sisters and brothers, and they were directed toward an equivalent range of individuals.

Male or female employers also could try to coerce their employees, and here the motivation seems to have been anxiety for the reputation of the household, rather than fear over the potential loss of that household. In San Sebastián, a single woman, age thirty-one, confessed at tremendous length to being a witch in November 1609. When she retracted her statement in

August 1611, she said she was terrified of her employer and had been pressured into the confession by him.[84] In February 1611, María de Sansetena, age thirty-six, admitted being a witch in bleak language. She said she had been bewitched years earlier, in 1607; the Devil "told her that she had a vile face but said she would be all right" (*era de ruín gesto, pero que bien estaría*). The Devil had sex with the attractive women who were his disciples but left her alone because she was ugly.[85] In this case, Sansetena seems to have transferred a part of her self-consciousness—her perception that she was unattractive—into her confession to witchcraft. She went on to tell the inquisition commissioner that she had seen poison-making among the witches. Her list of accomplices was more than a full folio in length.

Then, in August 1611, Sansetena recanted. She explained that when she first confessed to witchcraft, she had been sick, with continuous fevers. Some children of the village had named her as the witch who had corrupted them. Her employers began to tell her that she had to confess, and warned that if she refused, they would put her down a well. They showed her the ropes they would use to take her there. Because she was so very sick and weak, she confessed, and then her employers threw her out of the house. There was no one to take her in; she went to a mountain hut, where she stayed for two days without food. Her parents finally came to find her and take her home to the village of Elbete, but her troubles were far from over. Once there, Sansetena told some neighbors that she was not, in fact, a witch. Her fellow villagers reacted by putting her into the stocks with her hands tied behind her back.[86] They left her there for four months, saying that she would not be released unless she confessed. Not having any other way out, she confessed again, and they insisted once more that she name accomplices. She had then identified other witches, but what she had said was all lies.[87]

Finally, hatred could be a potent force for accusations of witchcraft. As we saw in the case of Sabadina de Zozaya and Miguel Zuito in Arraioz, the cause of their dislike arose from a loan that was not repaid. For a widow, Catalina de Alduncin, and her son in Goizueta, their social inferiors wanted to wreck their standing, and those enemies saw a golden opportunity when general rumors of witches began to fly.[88] When it came to parish priest Lorenzo Hualde and the residents of Bera, Hualde and his neighbors had filed multiple legal cases against each other before the witch persecution even started. In 1605, dismayed that Hualde was being installed as their parish priest despite being French, Bera's residents tried twice to stop his investiture.[89] The same year, Hualde responded by filing a suit for defamation against Bera's current mayor "and his friends."[90]

A Family Catastrophe

In one remarkable instance, hatred and familial ties intersected to produce a disaster in the village of Olague. It was a tiny place. In a census taken on June 26, 1606, Olague had twenty-four houses owned by legal residents (*vezinos*); assuming there were five people in each of those households, the number of legal residents, with full legal rights, would have been 120 people, give or take a few servants and apprentices. Net worth in the village varied. Some people had land, animals, and houses worth only 26 ducats, while others had the same in the amount of 150; the standout was Lope de Baquedano, who had a net worth of 562 ducats.[91] As for the village's spiritual environment, it is doubtful that the architects of the Tridentine decrees would have been satisfied with Olague's parish priest, Pedro de Ostiz, since he was prosecuted four times in episcopal court between 1592 and 1612. Ostiz had a habit of not paying for services rendered and hesitated as well to pay back loans.[92]

The surviving evidence does not tell us how witchcraft accusations in Olague began, but in the winter of 1610–11, multiple children in that village announced to their families that they were being taken by neighbors to revere the Devil and renounce Christianity. These youngsters ran together as a gang and shouted witchcraft accusations at adults; they also named other children whom they had seen at the akelarres. One of the adults they accused was a former widow, María de Alzate: she had married for a second time with Olague's blacksmith, Juan de Unciti, who also was marrying again. María had two children from her first marriage, though the sources say nothing about their names or ages; she also had a girl from her union with Unciti named Marimartín, who was twelve or thirteen years old in 1611.[93] In June 1611, in a secular court hearing, Marimartín was called as a prosecution witness in a defamation case over the insult of "witch." In the process of testifying, Marimartín labeled her own mother a witch and said her mother had converted her into one of the Devil's disciples.

While being named as a witch by neighbors and neighborhood children was bad enough, being identified as a witch by your own child was probably the apogee of dishonor and horror for any Navarrese family in the early modern period. Children knew their parents very well; they were assumed to be loyal in the extreme; presumably, a child who accused a parent of witchcraft had little or no motivation to do so, and hence the accusation must be true. When Marimartín first testified about witchcraft in Olague, her deposition was quite muted. It read:

She said she was thirteen, more or less. We declined to receive an oath from her [on account of her age], and [even] without it, she volunteered to speak the truth, and she deposed as follows. That Mariacho [*sic*] de Alzate, her mother, took her to the akelarre where the witches carry out their meetings. After that, María de [___], called Agullano, took her three times to the meetings. And in the meetings, she has seen [the children] Don Pedro and Doña Juana de Echaide . . . and María Martín de Olagüe took them there, and this witness has seen her many times in the junta, and she is well-known for being a witch in this village, and such is public and notorious in the village.[94]

Notaries read the statement back to Marimartín, and she ratified it; because she could not sign her name, the notary signed for her. She had named her own mother as a witch in a single sentence that lacked all detail.

The truth emerged ten days later, on July 4, 1611, when residents of Olague were asked again about witchcraft in a different secular prosecution for defamation. Marimartín testified once more, but very differently:

After Easter Sunday of the present year, a servant of her father, along with Martín de Unciti, her brother, took her to the house of the widow, Graciana de Olagüe. Graciana's son, Sancho, as well as her own brother and her father's servant, began to talk about the witches that they said Olague had. And turning to her, they said she was a witch too, because the children said she was, and the children declared they had seen her and her mother in the akelarres. And so [they said] she had to confess to witchcraft, and say what happened in the akelarre, and who took her there, and which adults in Olague were witches. And she said and assured them many times that she was not a witch, nor did she know who was, and it wasn't true.[95]

Then, they told Marimartín that she had to say that she, her mother, and the other people they named were all witches, whether she wanted to or not. If she didn't, she would be burned as a *negativa*, or someone who refused to confess; the implicit reference to the inquisition was clear. The group threatened and menaced Marimartín so fiercely that her "free will became disturbed, and they forced her away from the truth, and she said she and her mother were witches."[96]

A day after this pressured interrogation, Marimartín's brother caught up with her once more: he told her that if she varied one iota in her story, he and her father's servant would put ropes around her throat and throw her over the dam.[97] In this persecution, villagers consistently imagined and feared that witches would smother or drown their children: the verb for either is the same, *ahogar*. Water is everywhere in the mountains of Navarre; drownings occurred often. Marimartín's brother knew exactly what sort of threat he was making.

Marimartín was not the only child to be coerced in this way. The same figures—her brother, Graciana de Olagüe, and even her father—also intimidated other children in Olague into witchcraft accusations, sometimes against their own parents. In Graciana's house, eight-year-old Pedroco Imbuluzqueta was forced to drink "an enormous quantity of wine, undiluted with water," and was then threatened with maltreatment until he agreed to accuse his own father.[98] Guillendo de Oyeregui, a son of Olague's woodworker, Miguel de Oyeregui, was caught in a field by Marimartín's father, who promised to club him to death if he did not name certain people as witches.[99]

Plenty of other child-witches in Olague insisted they really were being taken to the Devil's gatherings and never gave any sign in their depositions that they had been bullied into their confessions and accusations. Marimartín, Pedroco, and Guillendo also stuck with their forced narrative for some time.[100] Eventually, though, they began to disclose what had happened to them. Pedroco and Guillendo found parish priests from neighboring villages and told them in public that they had been strong-armed into their witchcraft confessions and the naming of accomplices. Before her court appearance in the second defamation case, Marimartín was examined by her mother, María de Alzate, at home, in front of a number of adult witnesses called for that purpose. One of the men there recalled: "Her mother asked Marimartín with much gentleness and softness to say where, when, and how she had seen that her mother was a witch, and not to hesitate to speak the truth before the others who were there. And the girl began to pour tears, and she said she didn't know her mother was a witch, nor had she seen as much, nor could she truthfully have said it. At which point her mother asked her ... how and why had she publicized and said such a thing, that her mother was a witch."[101] Marimartín then told her audience about the intimidation she had suffered and noted that her brother had threatened her with death.

In June 1611, Marimartín named her mother as a witch in the tersest possible way. In July 1611, she became braver: when she testified again, in a different slander case, she deposed for folios, and her revelations were dreadful. It turns out that the brother who had intimidated her was her

VILLAGE INFERNOS AND WITCHES' ADVOCATES

stepbrother, a child from her father's first marriage. That stepbrother was acting in partnership with his and Marimartín's father, Juan de Unciti, to destroy Unciti's current wife and Marimartín's mother, María de Alzate. Unciti apparently thought that the dishonor that would accrue to his household from being married to a witch and having a witch for a daughter was worth the destruction he hoped would befall his spouse.

To make matters worse, the spendthrift priest of Olague, Pedro de Ostiz, was Juan de Unciti's first cousin, and he, too, was in on the scheme to ruin Marimartín's mother. In July 1611, Marimartín told the secular court that she previously had told the whole truth to inquisition commissioners who recently had visited Olague. After she had left the session with the commissioners, the priest Ostiz called her into his presence: he was accompanied by her father and stepbrother. Ostiz was angry. He asked her why she had changed her story when she appeared before inquisition employees—he must have learned something about her interview, even though that interrogation should have involved the strictest secrecy since it was conducted by inquisition personnel.[102] Marimartín looked Ostiz in the face and responded, "[I changed my story] because everything I had said and publicized was false and full of lies, against all truth, on account of the violence, and I know how to retract." Hearing this, the priest raised his hand and slapped her to the ground, saying "you wicked pig, if you don't go back to your original story, I will have to rip your guts out with a dagger." Her father and brother simultaneously told her that unless she returned to her original story, they would soon be embracing her in her death shroud. Shaking and dazed, in order to placate them and get away, Marimartín promised she would go back and say whatever they wanted before the commissioners. But the next day, she told those inquisition employees about the latest violence that had been inflicted upon her.[103]

At the end of her second deposition in July 1611, Marimartín told the secular court that other child-witches had told her they would persevere in their witchcraft denunciations and confessions before the inquisition commissioners, because the priest, Ostiz, had promised to give them the houses of those they identified. Ostiz had no recognized authority or ability to deliver private property into the hands of children or teenagers. Perhaps the village's child-witches did not realize that, or perhaps just the faintest chance of such possessions was enough to keep them steadfast. This was a world of deprivation, not abundance.

Child-witches in Olague not only believed they could effect change but also were capable of acting as a group for collective purposes. Their self-identification as child-witches (*niños embrujados*) and their public naming of witches stunned the adults around them. At least a few of the ones who persevered in their accusations in 1611 hoped to gain their neighbors' property: even if that goal was originally offered as an inducement to denounce, some of them appear to have taken up that goal explicitly—or other children felt comfortable describing them in that way. At the same time, child-witches in Olague who revoked their confessions and accusations admitted to adult coercion but then created or seized opportunities to oppose it.

As we saw in chapter 1 and will see again in chapter 3, children's accusations of witchcraft had just as much weight as adults' and equally dire consequences. Yet the predicament of Olague's child-witches who reported violent threats behind their witchcraft confessions did not mean that the wider community stepped in to help as the coercion was underway. Children were immensely valued in Navarrese society, and not just by their immediate families: as we have seen, entire communities would look for missing children and seek to have murderers prosecuted. Yet such concern did not mean that what we would think of as child abuse found its way into the secular legal jurisdiction. While infanticide and homicide resulted in court cases against parents, as did the deaths of children at the hands of neighbors or strangers, I have never seen a secular prosecution against parents for starving, beating, or physically abusing their children in this epoch. Village communities disapproved of the mistreatment of children when they knew it was happening, but neighbors did not step over household lines to protect children who were not their own, unless death had occurred.[104] No matter how much onlookers pitied her father and stepbrother's treatment of her, Marimartín had no protectors to turn to besides her mother.

Her mother did not let her down. She defended Marimartín's side of the story. She told the secular court that her stepson was deliberately manipulating Olague's children into false accusations of witchcraft. She asserted that he and Graciana de Olagüe had been drilling the children in what to say and were achieving their goals with gifts and intimidation. She understood their motives: they were "hoping to defame and insult many well-born, honorable people of Olague, to turn their lives upside down with grief and troubles."[105] She affirmed that their parish priest, Pedro de Ostiz, was one of the miscreants. She also knew her second husband was a key malefactor in the village's tumult.

Accordingly, to protect her daughter, at some point after July 1611 Alzate took Marimartín to Pamplona and installed her in the household of a widow named María de Iribas. When the secular court went looking for Marimartín in September 1611, to see if she would ratify her original June 1611 confession to being a witch—in which she had also named her mother—she could not be found. The investigator stated, "I have looked carefully for Marimartín de Unciti . . . both in Olague and in the city of Pamplona, in the house of María de Iribas . . . and I could not find her in either that village or this city. And having asked María de Iribas about her, she told me that persons had taken Marimartín away two weeks ago, and she did not know where she was."[106]

A Ruinous Marriage and a Separation

Though Marimartín could have ended up dead at the hands of her stepbrother, possibly with her father's endorsement, her mother was not about to let that happen, as another archival find makes clear. In fact, Alzate herself moved Marimartín around and put her into hiding for four months, while Alzate filed for separation of marriage with the episcopal court in December 1611.[107] Alzate told the bishop's judges that her married life with Juan de Unciti had been ruinous. He had thrown her son and daughter from her first marriage out of the house. He had thrown her out of the house. He had knocked off her headdress. He had broken her left arm with a fire shovel and hit her in the face with a closed fist (*puño cerrado*).[108] (A blow with a closed fist was much more serious, legally, than a slap with an open palm.) Furthermore, Unciti refused to allow Alzate to eat with the family, to the point that his apprentices gave her food; some of his servants intervened when he abused her. Their neighbors often heard screams and punches in their house. Sometimes, they saw Alzate running down the street, trying to escape.

Alzate's marriage to Unciti was so miserable that she violated gender norms in pursuit of peace and safety. Multiple witnesses, both female and male, attested, as a critique, that Alzate had left Unciti's house: "All the time they've been married, without cause, this witness has seen María leave the house some five times on her own authority, and she has walked wherever she wished."[109] A female walking around on her own caused scandal and dishonor to her husband. One witness reported that Unciti told Alzate, "what kind of craziness possesses you to walk around in such a way? Have you not done enough harm already? You should remain in the house without giving anyone the opportunity to see your whims and madness."[110]

As we have seen, women who left their houses and spouses, proceeded beyond their village's perimeters, or even walked from one village to another greatly endangered their reputations.[111] At some point before 1611, Alzate even tried living on her own in Lantz, a village almost three miles from Olague.[112] Unfortunately for her, the Tridentine ambitions of Bishop Venegas affected her for the worse, because when Venegas's inspector discovered that she was living apart from Unciti, he ordered them to reunite. Alzate was the one who had left; she faced excommunication if she did not obey. This is how María de Alzate and her daughter came to be living once more with Unciti and his son when witchcraft rumors in Olague began to circulate. His hatred for her explains why he decided to try to ruin her life with accusations.[113] Still, he may not have succeeded. Alzate was never prosecuted as a witch by the secular or inquisitorial legal jurisdiction nor did she ever confess to witchcraft in her community. She even won her case in episcopal court and was granted a separation. That court ordered Unciti not to worry or disturb her under any circumstances. He had to pay her court costs; she was no longer prevented from attending divine offices, no matter what the episcopal inspector had previously said.[114] Not only could Alzate speak publicly about the testimony she had given in secular court, but she could also publicize the episcopal ruling against her husband as well as its financial burden upon him. In terms of honor, she took at least a degree of vengeance, though she might well have suffered economically after her legal success. Before she was ever swept up in witchcraft accusations, Alzate had told witnesses she would rather die in poverty than go on living with her second husband.[115]

Retractions and Remorse

Clearly, being the object of a false witchcraft accusation produced social and spiritual anguish. Yet individuals who were the agents of false accusations often found themselves in a similarly miserable state. From December 1608 to mid-1611, everyone who confessed to witchcraft in this persecution was pressured to name accomplices. Adults and children who knew they had deceitfully labeled themselves and others as witches could be in agony over their sin against themselves and their neighbors. They had violated both charity and the eighth commandment not to bear false witness.

Some of their remorse may have been in response to inquisitorial expectations. When individuals appeared before Inquisitor Salazar in 1611 to revoke earlier confessions to witchcraft, they had to convince him they were sincere and were not acting out of any sort of worldly interest. Thus a woman from Ziga told Salazar through a Basque interpreter that she had come to "remedy her conscience from the great charge and qualm she had, from having said she was a witch in a certain confession she had made." Similar phrases about "remedying one's soul" were routine for witch suspects of all ages who spoke with Salazar while he was on visitation.

Nevertheless, the inquisition did not require people to cry as a sign of sincerity, and yet witches revoking their confessions frequently did, often copiously. The woman from Ziga rejected her original witchcraft confession "with great weeping and grief" (con grandes llantos y lastimas), saying, "everything in it she had said falsely, against reason and truth." Another woman from the same village said she was tortured into confessing in February 1611 by the actions of the constables and her parents. Later, in July, she said "the certain and exact truth is that she is not and never was a witch, and she made that confession falsely, against all reason and truth, bearing false witness against herself and all the accomplices named therein." A seventeen-year-old told Salazar she wanted to discharge her conscience and save her soul.[116] In Lesaka, Marimartín de Legarra said she had confessed to witchcraft in 1609 under pressure from her master, who was both Lesaka's priest and an inquisition commissioner. Two years later, in 1611, she appeared voluntarily before Salazar to discharge her conscience and remedy her soul. She had suffered greatly in the interim from spiritual qualms and grief, to the point that she could not bring herself to receive the Eucharist. She had wanted to go to Logroño to retract her first confession in front of the inquisitors, but she had delayed because she wanted to travel there with someone safe, and without her journey coming to the attention of her employer, who was the same man who had pressured her to confess. She only dared come to Salazar on August 11, 1611, because her master was out of town.[117]

Individuals displayed the same kind of distress even when they were not speaking to inquisitors. In 1610, Bishop Venegas of Pamplona sent members of the Society of Jesus into witch territory, to investigate and offer whatever spiritual solace they could.[118] One of those individuals, Hernando de Solarte, told Venegas that he was hearing children take back their confessions in order to clear their consciences. The children asked Solarte "if Heaven would open for them if they told the truth." He described adults who were weeping all night over the sins they had committed against themselves and others; he told Venegas that they had lost hope.[119] Whether uttered for sincere or deceitful reasons, accusations of and confessions to witchcraft could create spiritual torment. Navarrese villagers could hate each other enough to accuse falsely, with the intent to ruin. But they also could ache for the damage they had done to themselves and their neighbors when their confessions and accusations were forced.

The Strange Case of María de Ulibarri

One especially intricate example captures the themes of this chapter. María de Ulibarri, married, age thirty-six, came before an inquisition commissioner in September 1611. Her goal was to discharge her conscience and remedy her soul.[120] Ulibarri told the commissioner that three years earlier, she had been lured into witchcraft by a single woman who also lived in Corres, where Ulibarri was residing. This individual came to Ulibarri's house in the late afternoon and wheedled and pleaded with her to attend a gathering that promised to be highly entertaining. Ulibarri replied that she was wasting her time. In no way would she leave her house; she would not violate that cultural standard. Still, the persuasions of the other, older woman had an effect, and Ulibarri eventually agreed to meet her at her home that evening. Once there, Ulibarri's new friend took out a pumpkin, from which she removed some powder: with that substance, she anointed Ulibarri's breasts, belly, and shoulders and told her not to speak Jesus's name or commend herself to God and His saints.

At that moment, the two women rose off the ground, flew through the doors of the house, and "without touching the earth, went to Islarra, which was about a half a league away." There, Ulibarri saw a great light from fires, as well as many people. The Devil was present too, in the form of a man: he was brownish-gray in color, seated on a throne, with two enormous horns on his head. He greeted Ulibarri by bowing, "as if to say, 'welcome,'" and he told her to kiss him "in the lower part," which she did. He instructed Ulibarri to sit with the others, and she obeyed. Then, everyone got up to dance, and "we all were disheveled, with great joy"; afterwards, they kissed the Devil under the tail, dined on bread and wine, and returned home.

The commissioner was anxious to discover accomplices: he pressed Ulibarri for names not just from Corres but from surrounding villages. He also asked her how often she went to the Devil's gatherings. She corrected his impression that these reunions were held three times a week; instead, she asserted that they were held three times a year, and hence she had attended only six sessions over twenty-four months. In the second session, the Devil had marked her with his claw, on her shoulder: the pain had been immense and had taken more than three months to heal. It was at that gathering that Ulibarri denied her Christian faith. The commissioner asked for more details. Who had provided the bread and wine, and who had paid for it? Who performed the music for the dancing? What else did the witches do besides kiss the Devil under the tail?

Ulibarri's responses were the very incarnation of legal prudence. She explained that two fellow-witches, both male, provided the food: the Devil paid for it, but she could not say for certain with what sort of coin. The Devil had sex with both women and men, but he only had sex with her once. Intercourse with him was "so horrible, and so unbearably hot, that she could not endure it, as she told him." When asked whether she owned any poisonous powders or had taken dead bodies out of churches, first, Ulibarri noted that her master witch, who had converted her to the Devil's sect, had asked her to take the powders, but she had refused; second, she had never touched corpses. She was extremely repentant for having belonged to the Devil's congregation and begged for mercy and help for her soul.

There was nothing accidental about Ulibarri's guardedness in her testimony: she knew how much to say to limit the damage to herself and others. She offered minimal details in her confession and curbed her participation in witch activities. She never declined to answer the questions but restrained her responses. She identified accomplices in the single digits, and only put forward names from surrounding villages when she was specifically directed to do so. Her version of the akelarre mostly featured dancing. Her account of the poisonous powders was limited to the Devil's distribution of them; she never touched them, and her fellow witches never actually put them to use.[121]

Meaningfully, Ulibarri also injected spiritual combat into her witchcraft confession in September 1611: taken in conjunction with her refusal to handle poisons or corpses, this was another sign that she was drawing a boundary as to how much of a witch she had been. She reported that when her master witch pressured her to take the poisonous powders, she told that woman, "she didn't want to take them; rather, she told her that she should go to hell with them, for she no longer wanted her company, and with that, they said goodbye." Here, we see the same tone, adamancy, and decisiveness offered by other witch suspects as they narrated their resistance to their former diabolical colleagues. Moreover, though Ulibarri managed to extricate herself from her master witch after that woman left Corres, and no one else tried to take her to the akelarres, she was persecuted anew by Juan Ibáñes, a male follower of the Devil. He told her, "if she confessed he was a witch, he would have to kill her; and he wanted to guarantee it by cutting her tongue with some scissors, so that she would not confess the truth." She also said that Ibáñes had "persuaded her a thousand times to commit indecent acts, and she never wanted to consent, telling him that he could go to the Devil . . . and one day, [she] was very big with pregnancy, and she had just come from confession in Bujanda, and Ibañes went into the street [to confront her], and he mistreated her to the point that he made the baby stir."[122] The drama of her statement was palpable. Ulibarri was threatened by the Devil's servant immediately after she had taken the sacrament of penance; she was making paradigmatic connections between witches and illicit sex, and witches and harm to children. Ibáñes not only tried to sway her into sexual misconduct but also mistreated the baby in her womb. Her statement in September 1611 highlighted temptation, struggle, and consequences to a child, this time in utero.

Ulibarri was not reconciled after her September confession; we do not know why.[123] Instead, her statement was sent to Salazar while he was on visitation, and he ordered her to appear before him in Vitoria on November 29, 1611, for reconciliation.[124] His Basque interpreters read Ulibarri her original statement. She ratified it but corrected herself on the number of her accomplices: "while she was certain she had seen some of them, she was very doubtful about others, because she suspected she had only seen their phantasms [in the akelarres], and not the persons themselves." She also noted that her husband never knew she had gone to join the witches, because a doppelgänger stayed in bed with him.

Salazar reconciled Ulibarri that morning, but in the afternoon of the same day, he called her back. The manuscript evidence suggests that he had noticed a contradiction between Ulibarri's first confession and her current one: in the former, she said she always went to her master witch's house before flying to the akelarre; in the latter, she said she went to sleep in her own house before attending the akelarre.[125] When she reappeared, Salazar took a harsh tone with her.[126] He adjured her to tell the entire truth, under obligation of the oath she had sworn; he told her not to give false testimony about herself, or anyone else, and not to cover up the truth. He then asked Ulibarri for another oath and demanded that she tell him whether she had said or done anything against the Catholic faith. Ulibarri replied that she recalled being a witch and keeping the rites and ceremonies of the false sect of witches.[127] Salazar became less stern: he asked her if she was sure she didn't want to remove, change, or add anything to her confession. The confession was read back to her. She said that every word she had spoken was true; she had nothing to remove, change, or add.

Then, abruptly, Ulibarri spoke up: "Besides what I have said, for the sake of my conscience I declare that Mariquita de Ataude, my mother, wife of Juan de Ulibarri, my father . . . died in a state of despair [desesperada] more than twenty days ago, in a pool of water."[128] Ulibarri explained that her mother had been in the Logroño tribunal for more than a month on suspicion of witchcraft; Ulibarri knew her mother had confessed to that heresy and believed the tribunal had penanced her for it. When her mother was released, Ulibarri "wanted to console her as a daughter, [and told her] she should be happy for having gotten out of the bad state she was in from going to Logroño. Her mother replied, with great pain and sadness, that her effort had brought no relief, because her soul was condemned as infamous on account of the evil and damage she had done in her confessions in Logroño, from having named and declared many persons as accomplices who were not such, and who had no guilt at all."[129] Mariquita de Ataude told her daughter that two friars had pressured her constantly inside the tribunal "to say that certain clerics were guilty of belonging to the witches' sect, even though it had not occurred to her to do so, nor did she want to." Those friars could have been acting as confessors to the witch suspects; they also could have been Basque translators employed by the tribunal. Once again, the evidence reveals that Basque-speaking employees of the Logroño tribunal could manipulate or hide testimony in ways that the inquisitors either could not see or refused to see.[130]

Ulibarri encouraged her mother to find an inquisition employee and tell him the truth. Ataude consequently went to Philipe Diez, an inquisition commissioner in Maestu: when she said she wanted to retract the accomplices she had named, he called her a wicked, evil woman for trying to back out of what she had said under oath. Diez informed her that she was likely to be burned at some future date and refused to reconcile her to the church. The daughter then pressured the mother to find a confessor who could lift her burden in some way, but it was useless. Her mother could not find any relief from an anguish that grew larger every day.

Ulibarri and Ataude last saw each other on a Sunday; Ataude's body was discovered the following Thursday. Her daughter said that her mother had been found in the river with her feet on the ground and her head uncovered, looking toward the sky: she interpreted her mother's physical position in the water as a sign that she had committed suicide by drowning. Ulibarri told Inquisitor Salazar that "she had great pain in seeing her mother like this: she was afflicted to be her daughter, and to remember these events."[131]

Suicide was both a secular crime and a mortal sin, and shame undoubtedly came with being related to anyone who carried out their own death. More enigmatic and revealing, though, were Ulibarri's opening words to Salazar, when she said that she was going to reveal what happened to her mother "for the sake of my conscience." Matters of conscience implied recognizing the difference between right and wrong. One wrong turned out to be Ulibarri's advice, since her mother was received so cruelly by inquisition employees. Another was the fact that Ulibarri's mother had been persuaded or coerced by friars into making false statements to inquisitors. Yet a third was Ulibarri's awareness that her mother had falsely named thirty-three accomplices while she was in the Logroño tribunal, whom the daughter went on to list for Inquisitor Salazar. All these "mistakes" could be seen as ultimately indicting the Spanish Inquisition for spiritual and legal wrongdoing. Ulibarri's matter of conscience amounted to telling Salazar about the legal misconduct that was the context for her mother's confession and death.

According to the surviving transcript, Salazar did not react upon hearing Ulibarri's details of malfeasance. Instead, he asked her to renounce her own heresy of witchcraft, reconciled her to the church, and issued penances for her to carry out. He commanded her to say ten Our Fathers and ten Hail Marys every day for the next two months, whether in church or at home, and to beg "Our Lord most sincerely to forgive your sins." He told her to fast every Friday during those two months and to engage in the sacrament of penance. She promised to fulfill his orders.

Ulibarri clearly was uncomfortable with her mother's confession, and there are signs she was also disquieted over her own. When she attempted to retract some of the identifications of accomplices she herself had made—saying instead that they could have been figures, rather than real—she may have been gesturing toward lies. Moreover, at the very end of her last statement, in November 1611, Ulibarri told Salazar that her mother, while in Logroño, had named her as a witch, "though her mother indeed never saw her or recognized her in the gatherings of witches, nor did she remember having seen her mother among the witches."[132] Logically, Ulibarri should have been able to assert that she as well as her mother had only appeared in the akelarre as phantasms. Instead, Ulibarri continued to maintain that her admission to witchcraft was most sincere: she heard her confession read back twice and ratified it twice.

The fissure between the mother's consciousness of deception and the daughter's simultaneous recognition of that deception but doggedness about her own status as a witch is baffling. Perhaps Ulibarri, like so many others, was terrified of losing her property if she too denied her original confession and simply tried to remedy what she could in terms of her mother's false testimony.[133] Yet her psychological state remains provocative. Despite the fact that she described her integration into the Devil's congregation as full of resistance and combat, and put limits on her witch activities, she later insisted on her witch identity despite exonerating evidence. Whereas we modern readers tend to think of early modern witchcraft as swerving between two bookends of duplicity and derangement, Ulibarri's testimony illustrates the endless combinations of treachery, coercion, self-deception, sincerity, and quests for exoneration that could go into witchcraft accusations and confessions. No matter where accusers and defendants fell on that continuum, it is overwhelmingly clear that as the persecution arose in the villages and was presented in the courts, spiritual, social, and familial conflicts were fundamental to the dynamic of this witch hunt. A sense of struggle was also a backdrop to the legal choices and legal blunders that occurred as the hunt progressed. Those tangles are the subject of chapter 3.

3

LEGAL DECISIONS, LEGAL ERRORS

This chapter investigates the circumstances and values that led Logroño's inquisitors and certain Navarrese villagers into disastrous legal choices in this witch hunt. The men in the tribunal that oversaw Navarre, like inquisitors everywhere, were bound by directions from the Suprema in Madrid—unless their priorities led them to neglect or reject those mandates. They could only prosecute as many cases as their budget would allow—unless the Suprema was willing to give them more money. Their sense of honor and privilege made them stubborn and competitive with other legal jurisdictions. Ironically, their choices aggravated the witch hunt rather than remedy it.

A parallel dynamic affected some men and women in the village of Olague. These individuals had enjoyed stable, moral reputations in their community until the witch hunt spread. When they were accused by children, and then defamed and assaulted by adults, they fought back with public slander of their own. Like the inquisitors, these villagers were obstinate due to their sense of honor and failed to look after their best interests; for them, the results were devastating. As was the case for the inquisition tribunal, villagers in Olague found that their financial circumstances critically affected their legal options, and they too should have known that they were headed into dire situations. Examining the how and why of these two groups' legal decisions further clarifies the processes and consequences of this witch hunt when it was in full force.

Micromanagement by Madrid

Earlier scholars asserted that Logroño's inquisitors were basically unsupervised in the witch hunt, but in fact, the situation was much more complicated.[1] In many respects, the Suprema called the shots on what the tribunal was supposed to do throughout the early modern period. In 1595, for example, the Suprema wrote that they had received the results from a visitation recently performed by Inquisitor Salcedo. Henceforth, they wanted the tribunal to meet to look over all the cases that Salcedo had collected and to vote on the same; then, the inquisitors should write their opinions in the margin before sending the document on to Madrid.[2] In January 1606, the Suprema reminded the tribunal that it was time to send someone on visitation: whoever went "should take particular care to restore the sambenitos [in the churches] that have been battered with age and can no longer be read."[3] In May 1608, the Suprema warned the tribunal about moriscos who might be moving through Navarre: commissioners and familiars should be on the lookout for morisco families, and if found, they should be seized and prohibited from traveling.[4] The tribunal was also instructed to notify the viceroy and secular justice system to take the same precautions.

The Suprema was capable of sustained attention to Logroño's problems and did not hesitate to press inquisitors there into further investigations. In the summer of 1608, for example, the church of Nuestra Señora de la Redonda, seeking to display its sambenitos in another part of the building while the church was being repaired, presented a petition to the inquisitors. The inquisitors asked the Suprema for its opinion; the council wrote back to say that the inquisitors should determine whether the sambenitos were truly in the way of the reconstruction. When the inquisitors determined that the sambenitos were indeed an inconvenience, the Suprema told them to place the garments in a "clear and public place."[5]

Though the Suprema did not seem to grasp the terrain and weather of Navarre, its members did realize that the territory was full of borders.[6] The council repeatedly cautioned the inquisitors to respect those borders and to notice where heresy had actually been committed. If the inquisitors collected testimony about French heretics, they could not be punished in Spanish territory unless the inquisitors discovered that they had apostatized after moving there. The tribunal was not to prosecute "the English who have sinned against our holy Catholic faith in their own land or on the sea, if they haven't committed such sins in these kingdoms."[7] The Suprema also coached the Logroño tribunal, often in contradictory directions, in the minutiae of what sort of penalties it could hand out to convicted heretics. In 1568, the Suprema told inquisitors that suspects who were reconciled should not be sent to the galleys. In 1570, it told inquisitors that people reconciled for judaizing or for practicing Islam or Lutheranism could be sentenced to the galleys if they were physically fit. In 1590, the Suprema opined that when people were condemned to the galleys but also were given a sentence of perpetual reclusion, "tell the criminals that once their time in the galleys was up, they shall return to the tribunal, so that the inquisitors may order what is appropriate for them so that they shall be instructed in matters of our Holy Catholic faith."[8]

The Suprema was also absorbed with the tribunal's witchcraft cases. In 1526, when Navarre had been rocked with witchcraft accusations for a year, the Suprema wrote multiple letters to the inquisitors about their responsibilities. The council affirmed that the inquisition had legal jurisdiction over the cases if the witchcraft in question involved apostasy.[9] In February 1526, the Suprema told the inquisitors that it had seen the four prosecutions they had forwarded a month earlier. Though the inquisitors believed the witches really flew to the Devil's gatherings, the council wanted "greater verification of the truth of the crimes . . . and more investigations about them."[10] In the same letter, the council asked Logroño's inquisitors to verify that people really had died from witchcraft: they should "specify how they died, and whether they were found dead outside their homes and beds. If [they died] inside, whether they had fevers, and when were they last healthy."[11] When the individuals perished, were the doors to their houses open or closed, and how big were the doors and windows? If the witches claimed that they had caused hailstorms and lightening, the inquisitors should find out when and where these storms had occurred, to confirm that they actually had happened, and to rule out mistaken attribution. For example, did the storms allegedly caused by witches occur in the stormy season?[12]

Later in 1526, Inquisitor-General Alonso Manrique took a further step with the witch problem in Navarre by calling a conference of ten theologians to confer over these puzzling heretics.[13] Those theologians debated six propositions, which covered

- whether the witches who truly commit murders should be exiled or relaxed to the secular authorities after their reconciliation to the church for heresy;
- whether the witches "really and truly commit[ted] the crimes they have confessed," or are in fact fooled;

- whether the witches should be punished in the same way if they were fooled and did not really commit their deeds;
- whether knowledge of the witches' harmful magic and their punishment by secular authorities should concern inquisitors, or whether inquisitors should even know about those deeds;
- whether the witches can be sentenced to the greatest ordinary penalties solely through their own confessions, without other proof or support; and
- what "remedy will destroy the plague of those witches."[14]

In 1526, the theologians' decisions were mixed. They all agreed that the Spanish Inquisition should handle witch suspects first, and that inquisitors should inquire into the evil magic they might have practiced. After they turned the first proposition—on the reality of the witches' evil doings—into a question about whether witches really flew, six out of the ten decided that they did. They disagreed as well on whether witches who were fooled should be subjected to the same penalties as ones who truly committed crimes and whether a witch's confession should be enough to convict. They then turned their creativity loose as they pondered what pastoral and legal measures could end the witch sect. Good preaching and new monasteries would be a start. Frequent reception of the Eucharist, holy water in homes, and the distribution of crosses were also needed. The current bishop of Pamplona should be told to reside; new shrines should be erected in places where the Devil held his assemblies. All agreed that the witches should be punished in an exemplary way, as a warning to others.

Significantly, two of the ten theologians at the conference then took up the task of counseling Navarre's inquisitors. In their new document, titled "Instructions for the Inquisitors of Navarre about Witches," also dated 1526, they emphasized pastoral efforts and a cautious approach.[15] Navarre's inquisitors had to be kind. If witch suspects who were of legal age appeared spontaneously, they should be treated "with love or words of charity"; if they showed signs of repentance and confessed their errors, then they had to be reconciled to the church without confiscation of goods and given some helpful penance. Inquisitors should notice if the suspects had done anything against the ecclesiastical sacraments; if so, they should be punished more severely. Yet inquisitors also had to inquire into whether the suspects had previously been tortured by secular justices, and they should not seize or condemn people on the basis of others' testimony without first investigating themselves. The memo ended with a list of activities—daily Mass, sermons

VILLAGE INFERNOS AND WITCHES' ADVOCATES

in Basque, carrying crucifixes, and so on—that could ward off the Devil's influence and should be encouraged in Navarre's villages.[16]

The steps and approach taken in the correspondence from 1526 exemplify the Suprema's line on Navarrese witchcraft throughout the sixteenth century. It usually voiced wariness, along with admonitions to investigate.[17] For example, in 1538 the Suprema told Navarre's inquisitors, "it is a huge problem that people think only witches can do [harm], and they should be warned not to believe everything the *Malleus maleficarum* says, because the *Malleus* talks about witchcraft as if it were actually seen and discovered, [when] the material is of such a quality that one can be deceived."[18] Furthermore, a lone witch's word or confession was not enough proof because the witch could be deceived, too.

In a remarkable message from September 12, 1555, the Suprema told the inquisitors that on the previous July 24, it had received a petition and report from towns in Gipuzkoa about witches. The council thought the matter had little substance and consequently did not write to the inquisitors about it. Then, on September 9, the council received yet another report about the same witches, "and the council has been greatly pained to realize that [the secular authorities] have imprisoned so many, because based on what we know from their report, and our experience with other witchcraft cases, we think there is little foundation in it, and many innocent persons will receive offense from it." The council ordered the inquisitors to go into Gipuzkoa's secular jails and question the witch suspects separately and secretly, "with all care and diligence, asking them questions and cross-examining them to discover the truth. If you find that [the charges and confessions] are spurious, send the suspects home without penalty, and punish the [false] witnesses as they deserve." If the inquisitors did not find that the cases were false, they should go ahead and take charge of them and proceed in their usual way. Once they had consulted with the bishop's representative and the tribunal's theological and legal advisors, and formed a judgment as to the suspects' guilt and sentencing, they should send a report to the Suprema, so that it could give its opinion.[19] Under no circumstances were they to carry out any sentencing or punishment without the Suprema's permission nor were they allowed to imprison more suspects.[20] In 1575–76, when Navarre once more suffered multiple accusations of witchcraft, the Suprema again authorized the Logroño tribunal to take over the cases and then approved letting the suspects go, without penalty, when they revoked their confessions.[21]

In April 1595, when witchcraft denunciations overwhelmed the tiny village of Intza, the Suprema was not quite so generous: it recognized that multiple suspects had revoked their confessions before an inquisition commissioner but nonetheless commanded the inquisitors to return those people and their cases to the secular jurisdiction. In this witch incident, child suspects died of illnesses and starvation.[22] As a precaution, the Suprema did advise the tribunal to absolve Miguel de Baiena as a precaution, because he was a minor whose witchcraft confession seemed like fantasy.[23]

The Suprema and This Witch Hunt

In the correspondence that survives, the Logroño tribunal and the Suprema did not mention witches from 1596 to 1608. From 1609 to 1611, the Suprema was both assertive and silent where the witches were concerned: the inquisitors alternately followed instructions, froze when no instructions were forthcoming, or postponed instructions they did not like. For an example of the Suprema's forcefulness, on March 11, 1609, that council sent the tribunal a list of questions to put to the witch suspects from Zugarramurdi.[24] Its mandates were specific: any cross-examination inside or outside the tribunal should conform to its memo, and the same held true for any other accused witches the inquisitors might seize. In order, the Suprema wanted the inquisitors to discover:

- On what days did the witches gather with the Devil, and how much time did they spend there, and what time did they come and go[?] While they were there, did they hear clocks, bells, dogs, or chickens from the nearest place, and how far were they from the nearest place[?]
- Did the witches know in advance the time and days of their meetings, or did someone else know and then tell them, and who might that person be[?]
- Did they have husbands, wives, fathers, mothers, relatives, or servants, and did they all sleep in the same room, and were they ever missed by anyone, and if not, why not[?] Did anyone ever quarrel with them about this[?]
- Were they breast-feeding, and did they take the infant with them, or entrust it with someone, and if not, what did they do with it[?]
- Did they go clothed or naked, and where did they leave their clothes, and did they later find their clothes in the same place[?]
- How long did it take them to get from their house to the Devil's gathering, and what distance lay between the two[?] Did they ever

run into anyone on their way[?] Did they go quickly or slowly, on their own two feet or by someone else's, and did they go alone or in company[?] As they were in route, did they run into shepherds or other persons[?]

- If in coming from or going to the gatherings, or being there, did saying the name of Jesus Christ end the gathering[?] Did any other action have the same effect[?] Did they find themselves on the road, without the Devil being able to help them[?]
- Did they anoint themselves to go to the gatherings, and where[?] Did they say certain words, and what were they[?] What was the ointment [for the anointing] made of, and who made it[?] If they admitted they had the ointment, the inquisitors should look for it, and once found, it should be shown to doctors and apothecaries, who could determine what it was made of and say what its natural effects might be.
- Was it better to anoint oneself to go, or could one go without the ointment[?]
- In between the gatherings, did they talk to each other about what had happened in the last gathering, and when another one would occur, or other things[?]
- Have they confessed [to a priest] during the time they have been a witch, and have they confessed these things[?] How many times have they confessed, and have they received the Most Holy Sacrament, and how many times[?] Do they say Christian prayers, and which ones[?]
- Are they certain that they go bodily to the gatherings, or do they go to sleep with ointment on, whereby these things are imprinted in their imagination or fantasy[?]
- Have the deaths of children or other persons come about[?] Have the hearts of children been removed from their bodies[?] The inquisitors should try to verify these crimes, and with witnesses. (*Crossed out:* if it is true, do [the inquisitors] find many hearts removed from children, and in what form[?] In each case it should be said.)
- When the inquisitors examine a witness or defendant, they should ask about accomplices, and they should ask each accomplice the same questions, to see if they answer the same about acts, crimes, and complicity, in order to better find out and clarify the truth.

It is important to note what the inquisitors themselves had proposed to do before receiving this list from their superiors. In February 1609, they told the Suprema that they had found (and read) its correspondence about witches from 1526 and 1555. They understood that there could be a problem of suspects merely dreaming their witch activities, though they doubted that such was the case with their suspects. They envisioned finding eyewitnesses. They waffled on sequestration of goods: they intended to vote for it in their judgments, but they would also suspend carrying it out until they had the Suprema's opinion. They planned to use interrogatory questions that "would be most appropriate to verify intent."[25] Significantly, none of the Suprema's fourteen queries in March 1609 addressed intent. Questions of purpose typically were key features of inquisitorial investigations. Heresy was supposed to be self-conscious, not accidental.

If we put the Suprema's earlier and later correspondence together, the inquisitors had an abundance of advice from which to choose. The Suprema's letter from 1526 ordered Navarre's inquisitors to seek greater verification of the witches' crimes; it asked about the reality of homicides and storms. It inquired into whether suspects could have conferred about confessions before they made them. It implicitly warned that suspects could have been tortured by secular justices and forbade any arrests made on the basis of another person's uncorroborated testimony. It prohibited the confiscation of goods that belonged to individuals who freely confessed and repented the heresy of witchcraft. Meanwhile, the Suprema's letter from 1555 explicitly raised the possibility that witnesses were lying and that witches under investigation could be falsely accused.

What is telling, then, about the Suprema's missive of March 11, 1609, is what it did not say. There, the Suprema did not remind inquisitors about the links between witches' deeds and dreams. It did not refer to torture or collusion. It did not warn about over-eager indictments grounded in too little evidence. It did not tell Navarre's inquisitors to keep in mind the possibility of false witnesses and false confessions. Instead, the council demanded that the inquisitors acquire the names of accomplices from everyone they interviewed and treat their statements as truthful by default. It then ordered them to put the same specific questions to all suspects and accomplices to see if their testimonies matched. Thus the inquisitors in March 1609 could choose between newer and older guidelines. The directives from the Suprema from 1526 and 1555 contained far more cautions than the instruction issued in March 1609. Perhaps the Suprema's members thought in 1609 that the inquisitors would blend what they were reading from the past with what they were reading from the present, but they did not specifically instruct them to do so, nor did they explain how that amalgamation could be achieved.

The Drive to Verify

In March and July 1609, the Suprema hammered the tribunal to send an inquisitor on visitation to Zugarramurdi.[26] Inquisitors everywhere hated going on visitation and resisted departing for as long as possible. When Inquisitor Valle finally appeared to be setting out in July 1609, the Suprema sent a letter with exhaustive advice as to what he should do in the field. There should be no sequestration of goods for the time being; anyone Valle sent to Logroño should be required to come up with enough money to pay for their food and upkeep while in jail.[27] Valle should look for accomplices of people already under arrest. Once found, he should pursue lines of questioning to establish "the deeds that are coming out of these trials, such as possessing toads, making ointments and powders, killing children, and digging up and eating the unbaptized dead, as well as witches." Valle should "always try" (*procurando siempre*) to investigate whether the "injuries that [the witches] say they have done are certain or not, with the people to whom the injuries were done, or with others who came to know about them." Valle also should seek out the means that the witches used for their flight and harmful magic, such as powders, ointments, or toads: once located, these objects should be examined by doctors and apothecaries, who could declare how they were made and what their natural effects might be. The Suprema reminded the tribunal that "the chief matter of this witch business consists of proving and verifying that the witches' acts and materials were visible and lasting."[28]

Checking and verifying, proving and verifying: it was rhetorically common for Spanish inquisitors to double their verbs in their writings, but the Suprema's preferences in 1609 could not have been clearer. In mid-1609, Becerra, Valle, and Salazar were devoted to carrying out their superiors' directives; they were driven to find out what the Suprema wanted to know.[29] They consequently became overwhelmingly engrossed with *comprobación*, that is, scrutinizing whether the witches really accomplished what they said they did with the materials they said they used. Older warnings about dreams, torture, and false witnesses went out the window.

Valle did his best to substantiate matters while he was in the field. On August 19, 1609, he wrote, "with holy zeal, and the great desire I have to administer justice, over the last few days I have seized Mariana de Iriarte and other companions, all of them French, through signs that I had that some of them are witches . . . and I have performed feasible investigations to ascertain their crimes, as you will see from the original acts that accompany this letter."[30] In late October or early November, Valle wrote to his colleagues in the tribunal about the new complicities he was discovering: "Fortunately, I have discovered an akelarre in some places close to the village of Doneztebe-Santesteban; I have two accomplice witnesses—one is nineteen years old, the other fifteen—and the persons doing the accusing have testified . . . the complicity of witches in Lesaka is proven with seven accomplice witnesses, all between the ages of twelve and fifteen." A week later, he updated his colleagues about Lesaka, noting, "the complicity of witches in the village of Lesaka has been sufficiently witnessed [now] with ten accomplices; two are older, fifty-five and thirty years in age, and the rest are older than ten, and going up to sixteen years of age."[31] Valle did not comment on the fact that so many of his witnesses were young.

Back in Logroño, Becerra and Salazar were checking and verifying as well. For example, at the end of September 1609, they wrote to the Suprema about authenticating deaths by witchcraft. In the tribunal, witnesses said their family members had been murdered through poison or vampirism, just as the witches on trial had confessed. Still, because the witnesses were asleep when the deaths occurred, they could not explain for certain how the poison had been administered; they thought it might have been delivered through milk or some other food.[32] The two inquisitors labeled these deaths by witchcraft as "proven acts" (actos comprobados). Becerra and Salazar also told the Suprema that they were continuing to interrogate all their witch prisoners to learn if the Devil had replaced them with phantasmal bodies when they attended the akelarres. One suspect had told them that it would be fatal for the Devil if the inquisitors found that such was true, because then the inquisitors would know beyond doubt that the witches went in person to Devil's reunions.[33]

Crucially, in March 1609, the Suprema had presented Logroño's inquisitors with a standard script of questions to put to every suspect, witness, and accomplice. We know the inquisitors took that questionnaire very seriously and even communicated its contents to their employees in the field. At the same time, throughout 1609 and 1610, the Suprema never stated that the inquisitors should prefer eyewitnesses to the witches' acts nor did they encourage them to seek witnesses "outside complicity," meaning people who had seen, heard, or learned what the witches did but who were not witches themselves. The Suprema also never told the inquisitors to distrust children. Instead, the council enjoined the inquisitors in 1609 to take testimony about accomplices and to confirm that the accomplices matched each other when asked the same queries. Thus, the Suprema's instructions encouraged depositions that addressed exactly the same processes and circumstances, and the inquisitors only had to select the replies with details in common to have basically homogeneous testimony.

The distinctions, then, that should have been in play in inquisition cases—between seeing something firsthand and hearsay, co-conspirators and outsiders, people of legal and nonlegal age—became confused in this witchcraft persecution from the start of 1609 to the end of 1611. Spanish inquisitors were supposed to observe hierarchies of proof in their cases: conviction only should have been secured via a confession or two eyewitnesses to the same event. Multiple eyewitnesses to different events should only have been treated as a sequence of partial proofs, and partial proofs should not have been enough to convict.

Furthermore, the best witnesses in inquisition trials were always imagined as adults who were not implicated in heresy, who could state what they had seen and heard firsthand through their own sense perception. That standard crumbled here. From 1609 to 1611, Becerra, Valle, and Salazar reacted to child-witches and child witnesses as if they were believable by default.[34] They did not distinguish legally between witnesses outside and inside complicity: thus in August 1610, they told the Suprema that they had twenty-three witnesses against the witch clerics Arburu and Borda, "fifteen of whom are eyewitnesses," and yet they did not note whether any of their twenty-three deponents were also accused of witchcraft.[35] The inquisitors heard innumerable confessions to witchcraft, and confession was, indeed, the queen of proofs. But the inquisitors treated the uniformity of those confessions as legally telling, without grasping that their own relentlessly consistent interrogations were behind the depositions' homogeneity. Such uniformity was only encouraged by conversations inside the holding cells, among the prisoners and Basque translators, about what the inquisitors wanted to hear.[36] In February 1526, the Suprema had warned the tribunal about collusion; in 1601, the tribunal told the Suprema its prosecutions were disintegrating because of prisoners' secret communications. It is remarkable that none of the inquisitors from 1609 through 1611 took steps to limit possible complicity inside the tribunal's jail or its house of penitence.

The Suprema Approves

From 1609 through 1611, the Suprema never told Becerra, Valle, and Salazar that it was displeased with their priorities and methods. On the contrary, in July 1609, the council wrote, "all appears to be going well in the way the [witch] cases are proceeding."[37] In October 1609, the council sent word that it had received the inquisitors' report on the "proven acts" (*actos comprobados*) of the witches and thereby appeared to accept the tribunal's standards of proof. In February 1610, two surviving letters were sent from the Suprema to the tribunal about the witches. The inquisitor-general had seen the most recent documentation from the inquisitors themselves as well as from the village of Bera: "since you are getting to the bottom of the matter, proceed as you think most appropriate, and do look about to see what kind of solution might be had for those children who have been turned into witches." In addition, the Suprema told the inquisitors to write to the villages of Bera, Lesaka, Arantza, and Etxalar: the inquisitors should console them and tell them that an inquisitor would soon depart to remedy the matter, even though Valle had only just returned from visitation two months earlier.[38]

Finally, in August 1610, the Suprema's members wrote up their thoughts on the witches and directed their report to King Philip III. They had given the inquisitors an order to take up another visitation and to go once more to Zugarramurdi and the surrounding villages; despite Valle's discovery of almost three hundred witches on his visitation the previous year, they now understood that the witch sect was surging anew.[39] The residents of Navarre were greatly lacking in Christian doctrine. The Suprema hoped the king would order various archbishops and bishops to send learned clerics into Navarre's mountains to preach and to teach Christian doctrine there; it would be a great service to God and to "that poor people and miserable land." The council assured the king that "the inquisitors [in Logroño] are not lacking in conscientiousness and diligence, nor do they run from the labor they are undertaking, which is greater than could be believed."[40]

Money

Far from being uninvolved in the witch hunt, the Suprema in Madrid corresponded often with Logroño and praised the tribunal's work for years. Still, as the quantity of witch suspects continued to climb, and the November 1610 auto de fe had no effect on the number of denunciations, the inquisitors pleaded for practical, financial help from their superiors. The Suprema declined to respond. The tribunal had highlighted its poverty since the witch hunt began. After Valle returned from visitation in December 1609, the inquisitors told their superiors that his expenses had been extraordinary because he had felt pressured to feed everyone who appeared before him.

In December 1609 and July 1610, the inquisitors wrote explicitly that they needed relief (*socorro*) for the expenses they had incurred. In December 1610, the inquisitors told the Suprema about the horrors happening in Doneztebe-Santesteban: they wanted to imprison about eight more people from that village, "but we have nevertheless suspended that action until we could tell your lordships about it, whom we humbly beseech to provide in this matter."[41] Throughout 1610, the Suprema refused to address money, or so it appears from the surviving evidence. The council in Madrid continued to receive witches' trials, reports on torture, and accounts of what was supposed to happen with the auto de fe. But it declined to comment about financial exigencies and remedies.

The extant sources imply that the inquisitors in Logroño felt trapped over the late summer of 1610 through February 1611. Their commissioners were adamant that witch conflicts in the villages were out of control. As early as September 4, 1610, two months before the auto de fe, commissioner Araníbar wrote:

> this evil grows so much every day in this territory that I am compelled to bother you and beg for a solution to so many evils. I know how much your lordships feel it, and the desire you have for a solution, with hearts full of pity. . . . There are so many infected children that it is worth crying tears of blood to see their parents shriek to heaven, begging for a remedy. . . . They are desperate because we have prohibited them from vigilante justice [*via de hecho*], and if not for that order, there would have been deaths.[42]

Araníbar went on to report that it was heart-wrenching to see what was happening around his own monastery of Urdax, where even little girls were carrying children to the akelarres. "María de Burga, or Barrenechea, and her four [child] companions have all confessed and relapsed, and they made spontaneous confessions about their recidivism that I am sending with this letter. And then, the very next night [after their second confessions], they all returned to the akelarre."[43] Araníbar lamented that these events were being treated with so much publicity that it wasn't possible for him "to maintain exactly the procedural style of the inquisition." He wasn't allowed to send suspects to the tribunal without the inquisitors' permission; he was under siege. As we saw in chapter 1, he eventually authorized the private imprisonment and torture of witch suspects in order to quiet those desperate, shrieking parents.

In 1610, the number of accused witches exploded, and the inquisitors begged the Suprema for monetary assistance that never came. Inquisition employees in the field, and the villagers who knew those employees, wrote to the tribunal and appeared there in person, desperate for a remedy. Logroño's inquisitors had no room to house more witch suspects, and no means or time to prosecute them. Eventually, the quantity of accused heretics that they were supposed to handle exceeded every other prosecution in Spanish Inquisition history by the thousands. The inquisitors consequently began to look for ways to decrease their workloads. As early as February 1610, Becerra, Valle, and Salazar told the Suprema that the defense lawyer assigned to the tribunal had agreed not to put forward defenses for the witch suspects.[44] In July 1610, the three men asked permission to bring witch suspects face-to-face with each other.[45] Both were violations of legal protocol. The inquisitors excused these innovations with the remark that witch suspects were so convinced they would die if they confessed that bringing a confessed (and living) witch before them had an immediate effect on their willingness to talk.[46] The more confessions they could obtain, the fewer trials they had to conduct.

Legal Competition

As if the predicament with their superiors was not enough, Becerra, Valle, and Salazar had a keen sense of indignation when their witch cases were touched by the other legal jurisdictions. Throughout the early modern period, Spanish inquisitors were convinced that they had better procedures and better jails for the investigation of suspected witches and other heretics than either the secular or episcopal justice systems. When Valle went on visitation in the second half of 1609, he learned that the royal secular court in Pamplona was hearing complaints about slander over witchcraft accusations. He wrote to the tribunal, "Three or four persons reputed as witches—and others in the name of certain dead persons, who also were reputed as such—have complained before the royal secular court of Navarre about two honorable girls who traveled to Lesaka to tell me what they had heard about witchcraft. The offended persons are saying the girls defamed them and raised false testimony."[47] The word Valle used for "girls" was *mozas*: that term signified women who were past puberty but under the age of twenty. Though I have never seen a teenager sued for slander in early modern Navarre, apparently the secular jurisdiction was at least entertaining such a possibility in 1609.

VILLAGE INFERNOS AND WITCHES' ADVOCATES

Valle told his colleagues that the royal court had even sent out a commissioner to collect evidence. He noted that these new secular cases were causing great scandal and fear among those who had come to speak with him, given that it appeared the secular jurisdiction might go after them for telling him what they knew. He consequently wrote a letter to Dr. Jiménez de Oco, a member of the viceroy's council. There, he pointed out that the royal court had very little reason to admit such complaints and told that court not to impede the inquisition's work. After all, no one would dare come to discharge their consciences and make a sworn declaration before an inquisitor or an inquisitorial commissioner if they thought they could be punished for it. If the royal court heard such cases, people who chose to testify before an inquisitor would be terrified, as would those called to depose. Valle consequently asked Dr. Oco to tell the viceroy and his council how harmful this legal overreach was and to fix it.

When Dr. Oco replied, Valle sent that letter, along with his own, to the tribunal. Dr. Oco reassured Valle that he had communicated with the royal council: that council had agreed that they should not be impeding the inquisition's work, given how serious this witchcraft business was. In the end, the royal council ordered its commissioner to come back immediately, without collecting evidence or imprisoning anyone. Dr. Oco reported that from this moment forward—as of November 1, 1609—and as long as Valle was investigating witchcraft, the court would not receive any slander complaints over witchcraft accusations. When they forwarded this correspondence to the Suprema, inquisitors Becerra and Salazar told the Suprema that they were still disturbed by the royal court's initiative. Dr. Oco had merely said the court would not receive slander complaints so long as Valle was in the field: his concession left the door open (*puerta abierta*) that the court might act otherwise, later on.[48] The inquisitors thought it appropriate to request and take any papers that had been generated by the secular commissioner on his travels. There is no evidence that the tribunal was able to seize any papers that the secular court collected about slander complaints in 1609; contrary to their demand, that court also did not cancel all its slander cases that year, either. One, filed by Catalina de Alduncin and her son, was prosecuted to the end and in February 1610, resulted in guilty verdicts and exile for the slanderers, who were adults.[49]

The inquisitors in Logroño faced interference as well from Pamplona's bishop Venegas, though they did not seem to recognize him as their tormentor at the time. Venegas went on visitation at some point in late 1609, when Inquisitor Valle was in the field as well. Venegas began his journey in Gipuzkoa, but then circled through some of the same villages as Valle before returning to

Pamplona in March 1610. In late November 1610, after the auto de fe, Venegas sent Basque-speaking members of the Society of Jesus into Navarre's mountains for pastoral purposes, without telling the inquisitors. The Jesuits were directed to console, teach, and preach in the villages afflicted with witchcraft accusations. In January 1611, one of them, Hernando de Solarte, sent two letters to Venegas about his experiences in the field. His missives first went to his provincial in Pamplona, who was supposed to pass them on to the bishop. Instead, the provincial sent the letters to Inquisitor Becerra in Logroño, who promptly reviewed them with his colleagues in February 1611.[50]

The Solarte Letters

Solarte never named Venegas in his letters; instead, he framed his messages as reports to an anonymous supervisor. Writing from Bilbao on January 17, 1611, he explained that the week before Advent the previous year, he had started out by going to Lesaka. There, out of three hundred inhabitants, some two hundred had been denounced as witches. Solarte noted that witch suspects in Lesaka confessed and then revoked. Their absolution was reserved; it gave Solarte great pain to not be able to hear their confessions, and it seemed like an unfortunate innovation to not allow them even to hear Mass. In Bera, things were worse. None of the witches' statements accorded with one another. Bera's priest, Lorenzo Hualde, had beaten his nephew so badly in pursuit of a confession that the boy lost consciousness and they had to wrap him in sheets.

Slowly, however, children and teenagers began to tell Solarte in private that they had been coerced into witchcraft confessions by their relatives. In Bera, an older girl told him that her parents had forced her into lies, saying that if she confessed, she would not be sent to Logroño. And then there was food. In Bera, Hualde's beaten nephew told Solarte that the child accusers were now very well fed, though previously they didn't even have the wherewithal to stuff themselves with millet, which was fodder for farm animals. In Etxalar, when Solarte challenged the truthfulness of a boy's statement, the boy admitted that three women offered him coins and a shirt to make accusations. Solarte concluded that parents "were so jealous of their honor, and so concerned that their children not be condemned, there was nothing they would not do, just or unjust" in the face of a witchcraft allegation. Once an accused child confessed, "the parents are content . . . because in confessing, it seems to them that the matter is fixed."[51] Solarte's remarks confirm the trajectory of honor we have seen before. Witchcraft accusations against children affected their families' prestige in the villages; witchcraft confessions by children may have carried some temporary shame. Still, appearing before inquisitors overwhelmed local disgrace, especially when villagers believed the inquisition would seize their family property.

Solarte understood the role of the honor code in confessions, but he was desperate over the pastoral effects that the witch hunt and the Spanish Inquisition were generating. He wrote, "the land is lost, people are defamed, evils are caused that not even current prisoners of the inquisition can explain or tally. The confessed witches tell us they are ready to take back what they had said if it would save their souls, and despite being so eager to do this, they nevertheless remain without confession [and absolution], with extreme danger to their well-being, given the seriousness of their sins." The inquisition had absolutely forbidden ordinary clergy from administering the sacrament of penance to confessed witches, even if they wanted to revoke; Solarte and his peers dared not cross that line. As a result, they could only "[console] them as best we could, and [offer] to return to hear them in time."[52]

Solarte also described the outrages committed by village constables and mayors, who had allowed the houses of witch suspects to be stoned by neighbors.[53] Solarte had no idea who would pay for the damage, especially since local officials were covering it up. Finally, in a remarkable sequence of paragraphs, he explained that he knew these witch suspects were lying because they contradicted the witches who had been sentenced in the November 1610 auto de fe. Now, just a month later, the details were all wrong. The witches he was hearing didn't anoint themselves to go the Devil's gatherings. Holy water, rosaries, and the name of Jesus had no effect on their situation. They were taken to the akelarres absolutely against their will, to their great distress. Solarte admitted to Venegas that he might be deceived because anything involving the Devil was awash in lies and snares. He understood that it might look as if he and his companions were disputing what the inquisitors had decided in terms of guilt, but the fact was, the inquisitors had not yet conducted trials against any witches from the five sites that made up Las Cinco Villas. It was true that the inquisition currently had imprisoned some people from that area, but it wasn't because the inquisitors knew they were guilty: if they had not taken the suspects into custody, their neighbors would have killed them.[54] In this way, Solarte informed Bishop Venegas about coercion, lies, vigilante justice, and significant inconsistencies in the witches' narratives.

When Solarte wrote a second report to Bishop Venegas on January 27, 1611, his stated aim was to transmit information from the parish priest of

Igantzi, Martín de Irissari. Solarte called Irissari "the most learned man in that territory, and his words are venerated almost like the Gospel . . . and he was the furthest from anyone in thinking that this witchcraft business was a fraud." Solarte thus presented a case for Irissari's intellectual and religious credentials. Now, Irissari had written that an old woman from Sunbilla, over age seventy, had been tortured for more than an hour by three other women in the village. When she would not confess, her torturers took her to the parish church and cross-examined her. When they threatened to torture her once more, she said she would confess to being a witch but insisted she never had committed any act of witchcraft. Irissari told Solarte

> they then pressed her to name her accomplices, and she would not . . . and the same women returned her to her house and tortured her again, whereby she died, without the sacraments, a will, nothing. I tell you, she died in the middle of the torture, without them lowering her body. It's true, because at night they came to me to see if they had to bury her in sacred ground, and I told them to carry out every funerary honor for her, as if she had never confessed, because that confession [she made] was null and void, and did not harm her honor and conscience.[55]

Irissari and Solarte were aghast at the gender inversion of women carrying out torture and murder. Undoubtedly, they expected Bishop Venegas to be stunned, as well.

Irissari went on to tell Solarte about other torments with freezing water in Lesaka. Some women there were tied into stocks and their feet were put into some troughs, filled with cold water up to their knees. They were ordered to confess, or else face transport to Logroño. When they "remained strong in their denials," their tormenters left them there. The victims began to scream for a priest to come and hear their confessions to witchcraft, "and they confessed, and then they were let go."[56] These abuses were identical to ones carried out over the winter of 1610–11 with witch suspects in Elgorriaga and Arraioz, on the advice of inquisition commissioners.

The Inquisitors' Reaction

The inquisitors found Solarte's letters highly upsetting. Though Solarte had been fairly circumspect in his comments about the inquisition—noting, for instance, that he was not saying that verdicts had been incorrect in the auto de fe—he counter-balanced that restraint with critiques. He was amazed to see that witch suspects who had confessed were not allowed in church at all and called that decision "an innovation." Given that inquisitors imagined heresies themselves to be innovations, Solarte's vocabulary here was barbed. Moreover, for years the Logroño inquisitors had championed their suspects' uniformity as a pivotal sign of their guilt, but Solarte pointed out that he was hearing contradictions.

Solarte also highlighted a cause behind the witches' confessions that the inquisitors had apparently never considered: fear over the dishonor and the potential loss of property for appearing in the inquisition tribunal. And whereas the inquisitors had been trusting the statements of children since the start of 1609, Solarte cast doubt on the youngsters' trustworthiness. He wrote that information networks across the villages could easily explain why children told similar stories and offered similar descriptions: "there was not a child in the region who did not know what happened in the ake-larres, as the information moves from one pueblo to another. So, in a few short steps, children in each pueblo gain the knowledge [ciencia] of what witches do."[57] Significantly, those communication webs were horizontal as well as vertical, and children could have informed each other of the witches' characteristics. Finally, the inquisitors were positively steeped in the con-cept of the Devil as a liar and were convinced their suspects were lying in only one direction—to cover up their deeds and escape punishment. In contrast, Solarte did not hesitate to point out that he had discovered fraud that went in the other direction: to convince authorities of diabolical in-volvement. One boy told Solarte that he used a scar from an abscess as the Devil's mark.

What must have made the inquisitors that much more infuriated was Solarte's tacit contrast between his methods and theirs, as well as his descrip-tions of his effectiveness. He emphasized that he had nothing but love in his approach. He explained how he persuaded a teenager to tell the truth about being bribed: "once they see the love I have for them and their well-being, they become anxious to talk to me."[58] To make matters more maddening for the tribunal, Solarte was on the ground, in the villages, where he was personally watching the violence and talking to witch suspects. He was a real eyewitness, not an eyewitness by proxy, as the inquisitors were so long as they stayed in Logroño. Solarte was also observing firsthand many more people than the inquisitors could because the latter limited themselves to prisoners in their tribunal.

In their cover memo about Solarte's epistles, inquisitors Becerra, Valle, and Salazar gradually built their case for the Suprema. They began by commenting on how shocking Solarte's correspondence had been to read. They then noted that a small band of clerics in Etxalar had experimented on witch suspects. Those clergy had kept the accused under observation overnight because they wanted to see whether they remained in place and whether children nevertheless would say that the accused had appeared in the akelarre. When the children contended they had seen the women in the Devil's assembly, the clerics deduced that the accusations of witchcraft were false. Yet, the inquisitors pointed out that these clerics were deficient in morals: after all, one of them, a licentiate Labayen, had allegedly impregnated one of the witch suspects, the widow María de Endara, when she was confined as part of the experiment.[59] Logroño's inquisitors consequently maintained that Labayen's motive for denying the truth of witchcraft was his carnal passion for the widow.

The inquisitors then asserted that Solarte had formed a conspiracy with Labayen and the latter's friends and asserted that this band had been encouraged in their behavior by the attitude of Bishop Venegas's personnel.[60] A Dr. Zalba, one of Venegas's visitors, apparently engaged in debates with Labayen and the other clerics in public and even in front of the bishop himself, during which they all disputed the reality of witchcraft. The inquisitors insisted that Dr. Zalba was related to the pregnant widow Endara; hence, he too had a pernicious motive. If the inquisitors saw conspiracies everywhere, they also appreciated hierarchy. They thought Dr. Zalba's official authority made it impossible for Solarte, Labayen, and the other clerics to resist his opinions.[61]

The inquisitors moved rhetorically from ulterior motives and guilt by association to a caustic appraisal of Solarte. Under "pretext of preaching," he and his Jesuit companions really had gone into the mountains to cause a racket. They intended to upend matters of the inquisition; they were leading simple villagers to believe that the inquisition would not go forward with what it had started. Given that the Devil hoped to upset the inquisition's cases, Solarte was doing the Devil's work, and the pride of the two was identical. Solarte thought he was the only person to really understand these matters; he did not realize how much divine assistance the inquisitors had received over the previous two years, which allowed them to have a far deeper grasp of what was truly happening. Everything Solarte had reported was false, and he was only hearing what he wanted to hear. For example, he wrote as if the stonings in Bera had no valid basis, whereas the inquisitors' investigations had proven that the so-called victims of those attacks were indeed witches.[62] As for the village torture and death of witch suspects, Solarte and Irissari were utterly wrong. Leon de Araníbar had already written to the tribunal about it. Those tortured females had been interviewed later by the inquisitors in the tribunal, and everything Solarte and Irissari had written was an exaggeration.[63] One of the women was put into the stocks in her village, "and she has a dislocated arm"; another was imprisoned in her house with a pair of chains. There never was any water torture, though, and people's legs were never put into troughs.[64]

As for the idea that parental pressure was making children confess falsely to witchcraft, the inquisitors found that unimaginable. The children actually had denied being witches and their parents couldn't bear it: that's why they encouraged their children to confess. As if to distance themselves even further from the chance that children had lied to them, Becerra, Valle, and Salazar flatly denied that they had ever relied on the testimony of children—which, of course, was false. The inquisitors opined that if Solarte had ever heard revocations of confessions, it was the Devil's work to encourage the *negativos*. Finally, the inquisitors insisted there were no meaningful discrepancies between the confessions made by the first witches from Zugarramurdi and the ones heard later from other villages. Solarte talked like a young man with little experience in these matters. He undoubtedly was trying to please whoever had deputized him. The inquisitors closed their memo by telling the Suprema that they wanted to call in Solarte and Irissari for interrogation. As far as we know, such interviews never occurred, though the inquisitors pursued them.[65]

It is remarkable to consider what Logroño's inquisitors were willing to risk—or did not realize they were risking—by sending Solarte's letters to the inquisitor-general and the Suprema. Solarte's communications were well-organized and intensely pastoral. They were filled with details and eyewitness specifics. By combining his experiences with those of Martín de Irissari, a highly reputable priest known throughout the district of Las Cinco Villas, Solarte increased the weight of his findings. He explained how accusations were occurring on the village level, as familial pressure, fear, and intimidation combined with honor to produce a positively toxic environment. Yet the inquisitors apparently believed they had nothing to fear from Solarte's correspondence. Their position only makes sense in the context of an inquisitorial culture of legal and even theological superiority. The inquisitors had experience, status, and privileges. They knew they possessed authority. Competition and discordant opinions from others simply provoked their disdain.

A Remedy Rejected

In February 1611, at the end of their diatribe against Solarte, the inquisitors repeated their usual refrain: the inquisition alone could solve the witch problem, but only the Suprema could tell the tribunal what it needed to do. They wrote, "we are obliged to prostrate ourselves at your feet, and tearfully cry out for the remedy."[66] The fact is, they had been given the remedy many months earlier, when the Suprema told them in December 1609 to promulgate an edict of grace for the confessed and suspected witches. At that time, Valle was returning from visitation, but the Suprema thought he was still in the field, and hence could administer the new order. In December 1609, the Suprema told the tribunal that the new edict of grace had been approved by the inquisitor-general. It affirmed that an edict of grace was warranted, based on the number of male and female witches being discovered in Navarre, along with the fact that the witches were most often underage, female, poor, or of little mental capacity.[67]

It is worth noting the difference between an edict of faith, which Valle had carried into the field, and the edict of grace that the Suprema wanted to issue thereafter. Edicts of faith demanded that the people suspected of heresy appear before inquisitors to confess their own guilt and name accomplices; it did not promise penances. Edicts of grace, by contrast, invited suspects to appear and promised reconciliation if appropriately regretful confessions were made. What the Suprema intended to offer as of December 1609 was forgiveness and reconciliation to the church for witch suspects who were willing to admit their guilt, but the inquisitors in Logroño would have none of it. When they replied in January 1610, they *rejected outright* an edict of grace. They wanted to wait until after their auto de fe, though as yet no date had been set for one. They did not think an edict of grace would have any effect on the master witches and rebel witches; they dismissed the idea that everyone should be admitted equally to reconciliation.[68] In January 1610, they used their proximity to the situation, their greater familiarity with witch suspects, and their conviction that some if not most of the witches were already lost souls to nix a solution handed down by their superiors.

The Suprema agreed to delay the edict. In the surviving correspondence from January 1610 to March 1611, the inquisitors never mentioned the edict of grace, and the Suprema didn't remind them of it.[69] The inquisitors nevertheless remarked in virtually every message that they were not being given any direction by Madrid. By March 1611, Becerra, Valle, and Salazar explicitly told the inquisitor-general that they were stalled. They were successfully reconciling witches who came to the tribunal but had no ability to stop the witches ravaging Navarre.

This state of affairs was the inquisitors' own fault. Their refusal to administer the edict of grace allowed the witch hunt to gain steam. Their lack of action substantially increased the spiritual and physical suffering in Navarre, since not only the accused but also the accused's families were afflicted. The inquisitors could not see what was in their best interest; they seemed unable to respond to the pastoral needs of villagers. Theoretically, the Spanish Inquisition was supposed to combine justice with mercy, but for much of this witch hunt, Logroño's inquisitors were overwhelmingly interested in severity. Their inclinations undermined the purpose of their own legal system, which always aimed, theoretically, at the reincorporation of heretics into the church.

Legal Blunders and Death, Part 1: The Case of Miguel de Imbuluzqueta

Ominously, the inquisitors were not the only people trapped by their legal decisions at this stage of the witch hunt. The widespread practice of suing people for defamation meant that in the village of Olague, three accused witches found themselves the targets of the secular court system when they answered insults with calumny of their own. In these instances, the original slanderers ran to court first and thereby ensnared the accused witches in judicial processes. Significantly, the witch suspects in question were only ever tried for libel in any legal jurisdiction, never for witchcraft.

As we have seen, Olague was the scene of rampant witchcraft accusations in the spring of 1611. Some of that village's adults took vengeance on their enemies by threatening youngsters into accusations. As detailed in chapter 2, one of those individuals, Graciana de Olagüe, allowed her house to be used as a site of intimidation, wherein, for example, the adolescent Marimartín was forced to name her own mother as a witch. From the same location, Graciana and friends also coerced an eight-year-old named Pedroco into naming his father, Miguel de Imbuluzqueta, as a witch on Holy Thursday, 1611.[70] That evening, Pedroco entered Graciana's house to get warm, along with many other village children: they were spending the night in their parish church, across the street, in order to thwart adult witches who said they intended to carry fifty youngsters to the Devil's akelarre.[71] Once he was in that house, Pedroco said that Graciana and a student—Marimartín's stepbrother—began to work on him. They forced him to drink an enormous amount of wine, undiluted with water; next, they tied him up with ropes and

hung him from the chimney, threatening him all the while. When he testified later in court, Pedroco said he had been "like a boy without mental capacity, driven out of his judgment by fears and threats . . . [Graciana and the
student] made him promise to say that he would say, both inside and outside
the house, that his father and mother, and the wife of Juan de Echeverría and
his two daughters . . . were witches, this being false and against all reason."
Pedroco then told the royal court that he was a child who did not know and
understand the offense and injury he had committed; he now realized he
had removed the honor and good reputation of people in Olague.[72] Despite
his claim not to have understood the harm he had caused, before his first
appearance in secular court Pedroco had sought out priests from adjacent
villages to confess that his witch claims were false, even though those clerics
could not absolve him.[73]

Marimartín's mother, María de Alzate, confirmed that Pedroco was telling the truth. She testified that her stepson Martín hated Miguel de Imbuluzqueta and his wife, though she did not explain why. She simply stated
that her stepson, in collaboration with Graciana and Graciana's son, Sancho,
hoped to defame and ruin many honorable people of Olague. The trio threatened, maltreated, and bribed Pedroco and others, including Alzate's daughter: the three adults "taught the children and instilled in them what to say."[74]
At the same time, an unrelated witness, Juan de Azcarraga, a laborer, age
forty-six, told the court "it was common knowledge in Olague that Graciana
de Olagüe, and her son, and Martín Unciti, a student, took into [Graciana's]
house Pedro[co] de Imbuluzqueta and many other underage children, and
forced them to say that their parents, and the wife of Juan de Echeverría and
his two daughters, and other honorable people were witches, and had been
seen in the Devil's gatherings."[75] Azcarraga went on to report that the trio had
suborned and gifted (dadivar) the children with food and drink, and sometimes threatened them with bad treatment.

Pedroco's father, Miguel de Imbuluzqueta, did not handle this situation
calmly. Accounts vary, but it appears that about five weeks after his son first
publicly named him and his wife as witches, Miguel walked up to Graciana de
Olagüe's front door on May 6, 1611. There, he said aloud, to her face, that she
had threatened and persuaded his son to denounce his parents as witches,
when they were not.[76] Graciana replied that he was lying; Miguel responded
that *he* was no witch, but *she* was a proven one, as well as a thief.[77] Miguel had
thus fulfilled the three conditions for defamation: he spoke to Graciana in
public, in front of witnesses, and in a loud voice. He compounded the insult
by calling her a thief; to make matters even worse, he then put his hand on a

dagger in his belt, which onlookers took as a physical threat. Multiple eyewitnesses testified that Miguel was so angry and beside himself that they felt sure he would have stabbed Graciana if they had not intervened.

The problem for Miguel was that according to most witnesses, Graciana never labeled him a witch in public: only children did. He could not pursue a legal case against those children because they were too young to be prosecuted for slander. On the other hand, multiple witnesses attested that he had called Graciana a witch in public. He was an adult; Graciana was an adult. She consequently could file charges of defamation against him, which she promptly did. By the end of May 1611, Miguel was in jail in Pamplona, and his lawyer was pleading with the court that his client's children were dying of hunger.

Miguel begged for bail for months.[78] He finally was released on bond around September 1611. In the interim, however, he filed his own case against Graciana on June 3, 1611, and the court agreed to collect information for that case on July 1.[79] Miguel's witnesses deposed from July 4 to July 10, 1611; Graciana's witnesses testified from July 13 to July 19, 1611.[80]

Miguel had a lawyer, Juan de Urrizola, who was capable of finding good witnesses and writing feisty legal petitions.[81] Urrizola presented multiple deponents to confirm that Graciana had indeed been a thief twenty-two years earlier, in 1589, which meant that Miguel could not have defamed her in that regard. Slander wasn't slander if the insult was true. In regard to Graciana's theft, one fifty-year-old woman told the court that when the burglary was noticed in 1589, "the whole neighborhood began to cry out about the theft, and this witness, with others, went to the house where the robbery had occurred, where they found that the chest had been [tampered with]." The group then went to Graciana's house: by a process of elimination, they realized that she was only person at home at the time of the theft because everyone else was at work in the fields. When they confronted Graciana about the robbery, "she confessed that she had tampered with the chest, and had taken a packet with paper and some coins, and the Devil must have made her commit such a low act [bajessa], and she would return it."[82]

Witnesses for Imbuluzqueta also affirmed that Graciana had coerced children into false denunciations of witchcraft in Olague and had slandered the defendant. One stated that when Miguel confronted Graciana at her front door, Graciana "said the following words: 'come here, Miguel. People say that you have said that I made your child say that you and your wife were witches.'" Miguel replied it was true he had said it, because his son had told him so; Graciana replied, "you are lying, you dirty proven witch."[83]

Meanwhile, María de Alzate, Marimartín's mother, could confirm all three of these points. Her father, now dead, had been the victim of Graciana's theft.[84] She saw Miguel's son say, "in public, in front of her and other neighbors, in Olague's public street," that Graciana forced him to say that his father and mother were witches. Finally, Alzate had heard about the public quarrel between Graciana and Miguel.[85]

Miguel's lawyer, Urrizola, struck hard when he summarized the defense. Graciana had severely insulted Miguel with ugly, confrontational, and prejudicial words, calling him a "despicable, dirty, vile, low man and witch": her invective more than warranted vigilante justice on Miguel's part. Graciana had given Miguel the reputation of a witch thanks to her manipulation of children, none of whom should be believed. It was well-known that she induced those children to say those lies; she thus deserved to be punished with enormous, rigorous criminal penalties. Graciana had been the aggressor in this case. It was Urrizola who called Marimartín to testify and heard her statement about her father's and stepbrother's intimidation. Later, Urrizola referred at length to Marimartín's deposition, hoping her dramatic testimony about lies and threats would make Miguel's case against Graciana even stronger.[86]

Gaspar de Eslava, Graciana's lawyer, based his case on the testimony of youngsters and their alleged persistence in their statements. Like parents throughout Navarre, Eslava thought duration and consistency were telling. He argued that Pedroco had said for weeks that his father, Miguel, was taking him to the witches' gatherings; he alleged that Pedroco had said the same before secular court officials. Other children of Olague confirmed that Miguel led the dances at the akelarres. One of the children from the noble Echaide family, a girl who was too young to swear an oath, testified that Miguel had taken her by the hand at the dances. Pedroco had told the same child that his own father attended the akelarres.[87]

Eslava then moved to doubts about whether Pedroco was coerced in Graciana's house. An eleven-year-old boy attested that he was there, too, on that fateful Holy Thursday: as an eyewitness, he knew for certain that Graciana never said a word to Pedroco about his father, gave him food and drink, or mistreated him in any way. Rather, "this witness saw that freely, without being pressured by anyone, Pedro[co] said and confessed that night that Miguel his father . . . with his mother, took him to the witches' gathering." The witness knew this to be true because he "was one of the bewitched children of Olague . . . and many times all the children, with one voice, had publicly called Miguel a witch to his face." Graciana had no blame in the matter whatsoever. Additionally, a fifteen-year-old male, who had been a witch for a year, said that he had seen with his own eyes that Graciana never laid a hand on Pedroco: she didn't need to, as he told everyone on Holy Thursday that his parents were witches. Another girl reported that all was quiet in Graciana's house that night; she was very certain that Graciana did nothing to Pedroco, as she was an eyewitness. When she was taken to the akelarres, she had seen Miguel, his wife and their two children, and "ordinarily Miguel occupies himself in dancing with the other witches, and in performing vile and low exercises, offering himself to the Goat as his own, and saying he would not leave the Devil's flock even if they burned him. And Miguel praises the Devil to the point of saying that even his own breath was his."[88] Olague's children had absorbed the idea that the Devil was amassing his own troops.

For the sake of Miguel's case, the child-witches of Olague must have been acted upon; for the sake of Graciana's, they had to be acting freely. From our standpoint, Miguel's arguments seem persuasive, and modern readers could be forgiven for thinking that Miguel would win. In the next stage of the trial, his defense lawyer Urrizola called adults who confirmed that they either heard Pedroco and his friends take back and explain their false witchcraft accusations or witnessed Marimartín do the same. Adults had also noticed that Marimartín's stepbrother, a key player in the coercion, constantly tracked the child-witches' movements, which was a significant forensic detail.[89] Some of the adults who deposed for Miguel were priests; two were a laborer and miller; many were men in their forties who had known Miguel for upwards of twelve years.[90] They were perfect witnesses in terms of sex, age, and status, and they recognized how serious the trial was: one of the priests who testified for Miguel stated at the end, "he wishes that his deposition not be used for the effusion of blood or the mutilation of limbs." In other words, he did not want his sworn statement to lead to violence, either through a legal verdict or through vigilante justice.[91]

The difficulty for Miguel was not only that Graciana filed charges first but also that he was poor, and she was not. Though the royal court was willing to collect evidence for his defense as long as he could pay for its acquisition, his countersuit, which he was right to file quickly, was doomed to fail because he ultimately could not underwrite it.[92]

Although Miguel did finally manage to post bail, he then sabotaged his community's goodwill. The evidence is confusing, but it appears that in September 1611, Miguel acquired a bondsman—Miguel de Echeverría, from Olague—as well as a further guarantor of the bail, Sancho Garchotena de Lanz, who was the mayor of Lantz. Garchotena's responsibility was to pay the difference if the court ended up demanding more money than either Miguel or Echeverría could lay their hands on. The problem was that upon Miguel's release, he and Echeverría vanished. They allegedly ran to the Basque province of Gipuzkoa.

When Graciana and her lawyer learned of their disappearance, they demanded in turn that Garchotena, the arch bondsman, capture and turn over Miguel and Echeverría. Understandably, Garchotena protested: he thought his only responsibility was to come up with cash if Miguel and Echeverría fell short. He also opined that Miguel and Echeverría's departure had only been witnessed by a single person, so who could tell if they were really gone? By October 1611, Echeverría had returned to Olague, and was under judicial threat because he had not been around to represent Miguel when the court needed to see the latter. He was given fifteen days to find Miguel and bring him to Pamplona; he obviously failed, because he went back to jail and was not released until December 10, 1611. Miguel must have returned or have been found by that date, or else Echeverría would not have been freed. The royal court referred to Miguel as a prisoner in February 1612.[93]

By the time he was re-imprisoned in Pamplona, Miguel had no money at all. Given his previous actions, it is doubtful the royal court would ever have granted him bail again, or that he could have found anyone to advance it. The legal correspondence that ensued after he was jailed by February 1612 came only from him, not his lawyer, and that detail is telling in terms of his rapidly dwindling support. Beginning that month, he sent one petition after another to the royal court, informing its members that he was deathly ill.[94] In early April, still sick, he relayed that the court reporter had not yet read his case against Graciana to the judges; he asked the judges to make the reporter do his job, which by now was moot, since Miguel, as the plaintiff, couldn't pay for the taking of further testimony. Perhaps a week later, Miguel wrote again to the court: this time, he admitted the court reporter didn't want to move his case forward because he couldn't pay the fees. He noted, "[I] am so poor that I have nowhere to turn to pay them. And, still being sick, [I am] suffering extreme necessity for want of provisions. Concerning which, I beg Your Grace to order me provided for, and the legal case to be determined."[95] The only response Miguel received was the verdict: he was condemned to retract publicly his statements against Graciana before a notary and witnesses and then was exiled for four years. He was ordered to depart within six days. Miguel objected, saying that he possessed the same status as Graciana; he was only being condemned because his extreme poverty did not allow him to pursue his case. His plea was useless; his sentence was reiterated. Meanwhile, Graciana was judged free of all costs from Miguel's case against her.

If Miguel had not called Graciana a witch and a thief in public, before witnesses, the prosecution against him would never have materialized. If he had been faster in getting into court when Graciana called him a witch, he might have had a chance, though he still would have needed enough money to pay for the unfolding of the litigation process.[96] As we will see in chapter 4, occasionally neighbors banded together to finance prosecutions for defamation, but no one in 1611–12 was willing to come to Miguel's aid in that regard. It seems likely that his community viewed him as untrustworthy given his flight to Gipuzkoa and the ensuing legal consequences for his bondsmen. By the time he was sentenced in April 1612, his family's house had been burned down by neighbors. By 1615, he had died, and his wife was facing a long secular trial over being thirty-six ducats in debt to a resident of Olague.[97] We do not know whether Miguel died in exile or died in prison before he could leave: the trial record does not specify.

Legal Blunders and Death, Part 2: The Case of the Two Widows

Other neighbors of Miguel's were caught in identical legal circumstances and experienced similarly awful consequences. In June 1611, two widows—a mother and a daughter, Margarita de Olagüe and María Martín de Olagüe—were victims of vigilante justice carried out by the married noble couple Don Pedro de Echaide and Doña Graciana de Ursúa.[98] Two of the Echaide children were adamant that the widows had been taking them to revere the Devil, where they whipped them and forced them to consume loathsome food and drink. As a result of his children's stories, Don Pedro left his manor and walked into Olague on a Saturday morning, where he attacked María Martín in her house. On Sunday, Doña Graciana and two servants went into Olague and attacked Margarita and María Martín in Margarita's house, where María Martín had gone for shelter. Don Pedro joined Doña Graciana and participated in the beatings.[99] The Echaide servants who were there on Sunday said that Margarita's son had rushed into the room with a knife drawn, whereupon he slashed the hand of one servant and the fingers of Doña Graciana.

Fatefully, as Don Pedro and his wife left after Sunday's attack, the two widows allegedly leaned out a window and told Graciana that "she was a wicked witch, and she herself took her own children to the akelarre. And they called Don Pedro a witch, public heretic, and a traitor. The women said these words publicly and with great anger." Another witness said the widows' insults ran like this:

> She [Graciana] was a wicked evil woman, and Don Pedro was a de-
> ceiver, a cursed traitor, and falsifier, and those who dealt with him
> were heartless and treasonous, and because he and his wife were
> evil, they wanted to make the widows like them, when the wid-
> ows were better than they were. And they made the children say
> what they did, giving them food and drink, telling them to say what
> wasn't true, and he and his entire house and his generation weren't
> worthy to interact with them, and they were just as clean as he was,
> and even more so than he would be in his entire life.[100]

Margarita and María Martín responded to the beating with as much rage as
they could muster; they fought back with statements about lies, honor, and
lineage. Other witnesses looking up from the street as these epithets were
uttered saw that Margarita and María Martín were bloodied in the faces and
shoulders from Don Pedro's battering them with a club.

While some of the witnesses reported that Margarita and María Martín
publicly shouted the insults, others insisted that María Martín was so terrified of encountering Don Pedro a second time that she jumped out a window
and landed in a stream behind her mother's house. It is certainly possible
that the relatively few witnesses who testified to the women's defamatory
actions were encouraged to do so by Don Pedro, who, as we will see below,
inspired some trepidation among Olague's villagers.[101] More to the point, in
terms of honor versus legal intelligence, when Margarita and María Martín
supposedly insulted Don Pedro and Doña Graciana out their window in late
June 1611, Miguel Imbuluzqueta, their neighbor, had already been on trial for
seven weeks for having publicly insulted Graciana de Olagüe. The arrest and
imprisonment of Miguel would have been known in the village. Everyone
in early modern Navarre knew the penalties for defamation were harsh and
usually included significant terms of exile. Why, then, would Margarita and
María Martín have made such a mistake? Perhaps their adherence to community norms gave them no choice. Perhaps their emotions got the better of
their reasoning. Yet contrary to witches elsewhere in early modern Europe,
numerous village sources for this witch hunt demonstrate that it was the accusers, not the witch suspects, who were originally infuriated. Suspects only
became enraged once an accusation was launched in their direction; anger
was not attributed to them as part of their character by any of the witnesses;
testimonies never said that wrath made them convert to the Devil's sect.[102]

Of course, Don Pedro and his wife immediately went to the royal
court in Pamplona and filed charges against the two women for "words of

defamation." The plaintiffs presented multiple youngsters for the prosecution, including their own, who affirmed that they had seen the two widows in the akelarres; it was thus implied that Echaide and his wife had just cause to beat the women.[103] The plaintiffs also summoned two men who could verify the insults that the two widows had hurled out the window.

Margarita and María Martín were represented by Juan de Urrizola, who was simultaneously acting as Miguel de Imbuluzqueta's lawyer. The two cases had almost identical trajectories. These three adults had been accused by many of Olague's children of taking them to the Devil's akelarres; the same three spat venomous public insults against other adults, whereupon they found themselves prosecuted for slander in the secular jurisdiction. Multiple witnesses had heard the three defendants utter the defamatory language. Unless they could prove that they had not spoken such words, they were on the hook for the crime of slander. What Urrizola attempted to do in both trials was to show that the insults uttered by his clients were justified. In Miguel's case, Urrizola argued that Graciana had indeed coerced Miguel's son Pedroco into naming his father and mother as witches and that she truly was a thief.[104] In Margarita and María Martín's case, Don Pedro de Echaide and Doña Graciana de Ursúa had beaten them with a club and scratched their faces in their own home. Much as witches invaded households to do harm, Urrizola argued that those noble plaintiffs had also crossed domestic lines in inappropriate and shocking ways.

In the case he was defending against Margarita and María Martín, Urrizola eventually elicited overt compassion from his witnesses, but not at the start. Most of the deponents Urrizola called early in the process said they knew very little, though one woman volunteered that Don Pedro and Doña Graciana put their hands on the two defendants without reason. That witness relayed that the Echaide couple gouged out Margarita's flesh with their nails and drew blood from her face and also knocked out a tooth from María Martín, Margarita's daughter.[105] The same witness noted that if Miguel de Olagüe had run in with a knife, it was to defend his mother and sister; she also said that Doña Graciana had told the two women they would be burned at the stake. Another female witness said that María Martín was a poor widow: she never had possessed the reputation of being a witch, and she lived in a contemplative (*recogida*) way, with four young children, in a little house that she had in the village. This deponent saw María Martín in the street after the attack, "screaming [*daba vozes*] 'oh my God, oh my God, without fault people wish me ill for having been born.'" The deponent talked to her and asked her who had done this injury, and she named Don Pedro.[106]

After the Echaide couple filed their slander case in Pamplona, Margarita and María Martín were jailed there. Margarita remained a prisoner for about twenty days, after which she was freed on bond.[107] For whatever reason (the evidence is not clear), María Martín remained in prison for months, despite her lawyer filing multiple petitions that she should be released while the women's counter-complaint was being prepared.[108] The court voted sometime in September 1611 on a verdict: it sentenced Margarita de Olagüe to two years of exile, and demanded that María Martín take back the insults she had uttered against Don Pedro de Echaide and Doña Graciana de Ursúa.[109]

I have not found evidence to explain why the September verdict was not immediately carried out. Instead, sometime between September and December 1611, María Martín died in prison. It looks as if her lawyer, Urrizola, seized on her death as an opportunity to present new evidence for the defense: while it was moot for the dead woman, her mother's sentence might still be in play. Consequently, beginning in December 1611, Urrizola called defense witnesses once more.[110] This time, they were willing to pin guilt on Don Pedro and express outrage at what had happened to their female neighbors. It seems clear that María Martín's death in prison, which became public knowledge, affected their readiness to talk.

Urrizola's deponents gave statements through January 1612. The witnesses' reputations were impeccable and their testimony damning.[111] Juan de Alzate, aged seventy, said Margarita and her now dead daughter were known as good Christians and had no suspicion or sign of belonging to any evil sect, much less that of witches, until this contentious litigation from Don Pedro de Echaide. If Margarita and María Martín had ever had ancestors contaminated by witchcraft, he would have known about it.[112] Alzate asked for his point to be emphasized in the transcript: he knew there were other families in the area with a reputation for witchcraft, though he couldn't say whether or not that reputation was justified, and he did not identify them. Nevertheless, in no way were Margarita and her daughter stained by such repute. Rather, Margarita was old and very poor. Since her daughter's death, she had been supporting her four young grandchildren with great work and pain. If she had to live elsewhere, she would die of hunger and so would the children. The Echaide family had abused both Margarita and María Martín. The Echaides were greatly to blame for this situation.

Miguel de Oyeregui, Olague's woodworker, whose young son also said he had been coerced into a witchcraft confession, testified as well that Margarita and her wards quickly would die of hunger if they were forced to leave. The two widows never had a reputation as witches; in fact, they had a reputation of nobility (*hijosdalgo*) because they never paid direct taxes. When Oyeregui learned that Pedro de Echaide had assaulted the women in their own home, "and without any cause, he was shocked that a gentleman could do such a thing." Moreover, later on the day of the attack, Oyeregui got close enough to look at Doña Graciana's hands during Mass, "and there was nothing bloody about them, nor did they appear to have been touched by a weapon."[113] Again, villagers knew the importance of forensic details in legal testimony.

Every defense witness presented by Urrizola from December 1611 through January 1612 expressed criticism of Don Pedro's actions. Some also explained why they had not originally stepped in or stepped up. One female witness confirmed that Margarita and her dead daughter were known to be noble, since they did not pay direct taxes. She said that the day María Martín was singled out for attack, which was a Saturday, Echaide walked through Olague with a club under his arm, announcing in Basque, "I am going to remove the evil spirits from those who have no soul." There were hardly any people in the village at the time because they were working the fields; this female witness eventually went to María Martín's house and saw how badly beaten she was. The next day, Sunday, the same witness saw Echaide and his wife enter Margarita's house: she guessed they were entering for harmful purposes, but she "did not want to leave the house, and instead shut herself up in it." She went on to say,

> She knows well that Echaide's wife was not hurt, nor did she seem to have blood on her face or hands, and if Margarita and María Martín had been people who had the wherewithal to complain and litigate, they would have successfully punished Echaide and his wife. The way Echaide treated them was terrible, affronting honorable people, entering their houses to hit and mistreat them the way he did. There is no doubt that María Martín died in jail out of sorrow; she would have been thirty-four years old, and she left four children without any protection.[114]

This witness's comments were both empathetic and realistic. The secular court was in principle open to everyone, but money still mattered.

Two more female witnesses also expressed fear as well as outrage. One noted that because her house was closest, she could hear the Echaide couple beating Margarita on Sunday. Once the Echaide contingent left, "she snuck out of her house through a window, so she would not be seen, and then after a little while, she went into Margarita's house." She reported that Don Pedro and Doña Graciana's violence toward the two widows had stirred up the village. She opined that if the victims had had money to spend, the Echaide clan would have been chopped down themselves.[115] Finally, María de Olagüe, a widow, age forty-eight, said she heard a huge uproar on Sunday, "but this witness did not want to be seen, in order not to get on the wrong side [*venir mal*] of the Echaide." She reported that Echaide's wife said in public that Margarita and María Martín had to die, "and as if this wasn't enough, when Doña Graciana went into the street, she waved her hands and said 'everyone, everyone is a witch [here],' and this struck this witness as very wrong."[116] Everyone in Olague said that if the two victims had not been poor widows, without protection, the Echaide family never would have dared to insult them the way they did. The trial initiated by the Echaide family trails off without any further conclusion than the verdict recorded in September 1611, which sentenced Margarita de Olagüe to two years of exile. We do not know whether she was forced to leave.

The Olague trials examined here expose three crucial truths about this witch hunt. First, children were fundamental as victims and accusers. Second, local actors had a profound understanding of legal processes—even when they made foolish decisions—as well as a significant understanding of forensic evidence. Navarrese villagers offered the kind of palpable details that Logroño's inquisitors should have been seeking. Third, residents had a sense of communal responsibility during this witch hunt, which nevertheless had limits. Miguel de Imbuluzqueta's defense witnesses verified that they had heard children retract and explain their false accusations and confessions. They also confirmed that they had seen young adults stalking and monitoring child-witches. Still, as we saw in chapter 2, no one was willing to do anything about their suspicions until they were called to give testimony in court.

Then again, there were also signs of bravery. In the case of Imbuluzqueta, multiple residents of Olague were willing to explain and defend his actions in the summer of 1611. In the case of the two widows, after María Martín's death in prison, numerous deponents expressed profound indignation at what the Echaide family had done and voiced a desire for vengeance. What makes the actions of Olague's residents so telling in this regard is that nothing in secular court was necessarily secret. People did not swear oaths to keep silent in secular legal proceedings; they were free to talk as much as they liked about what they had said in court. Moreover, everyone in Olague would have known who had been called to testify. When the witnesses for Miguel and the widows deposed, the adult offenders were still alive and well and could have sought vengeance of their own. Nevertheless, the defense witnesses for Miguel and the two widows were bold in their assertions of wrongdoing.

Ultimately, the two trials from Olague are complementary, with their races to see who could file charges first, who could afford to underwrite legal investigations, and who could claim higher status in the courts. Given the social norms and familiarity with the law in Navarrese villages in the early modern period, Miguel, Margarita, and María Martín should have known the danger of publicly slandering anyone who had verbally or physically attacked them, especially if they could not immediately file charges of their own and independently finance a court case. Their legal error was akin to the ones committed—in much greater quantity, with much wider impact—by the inquisitors in Logroño, who should have realized from earlier instructions and inquisitorial culture that they could be on the wrong path in terms of ultimate objectives. The next chapter charts the ways in which legal authorities made only fitful advances to resolve the persecution throughout 1611, not least because of the inquisitors' alternating compliance and opposition.

4

COLLABORATION, OBEDIENCE, RESISTANCE

Throughout much of 1611, authorities outside Logroño began to act in ways that could have started to remedy Navarre's witch hunt. From Madrid, the inquisitor-general initiated contact with the bishop of Pamplona and learned what the latter already knew about village violence toward accused witches. The secular and episcopal justice systems in Pamplona instigated trials against village witch torturers for having exceeded the law and for attacking their neighbors. Inquisitor-General Sandoval eventually, and adamantly, ordered an inquisitor to leave on visitation with an edict of grace in March 1611: that edict allowed confessed witches to be reconciled to the church. Yet in Logroño, the inquisitors insisted for the first half of 1611 that the spiraling accusations were not their fault. After one of them finally left for Navarre, in late May 1611, the two who remained in the tribunal did their best to block the legal activities of other courts; eventually, they even denied the effectiveness of their own colleague's journey. At the same time, legal victories by maltreated witch suspects, who collaborated in order to succeed, did not translate seamlessly into punishment for their attackers, who resisted sentencing. This chapter examines these consultations and conflicts in order to understand why solutions to this witch hunt were so hit-and-miss for so long.

On December 24, 1610, practically a year to the day that the solution was first proposed, the Suprema reminded the tribunal once more about the edict of grace it wished to promulgate.[1] The inquisitors replied in February 1611 that they had not left on visitation because the inquisitor-general had not commanded it. They were, however, administering that edict to individuals who came to the tribunal, and such people were now reconciled to the church.[2] Otherwise, the inquisitors noted that they had imprisoned three or four of the master witches who were causing the most tumult in various villages, but their strategy had not worked: the Navarrese "were frenzied over the injuries to their children, their own persons, and their households." Inquisitors Becerra, Valle, and Salazar then "supplicated Your Lordship [Inquisitor-General Sandoval] with most fervent zeal to tell us as quickly as possible what to do." They noted that Spain was losing credit with other countries (*y el mucho credito que se perdera en los reynos estraños*) because it had tolerated this diabolical sect for so long. The inquisitors wrote that they had more than 1,500 suspects named in depositions. Based on what they were hearing, they expected witches to invade Logroño soon. In their letter's very last lines, they begged the inquisitor-general to provide a remedy "before that land goes even more insane [*antes esa tierra se perturba más*], and hinders the edict of grace that Your Lordship hopes to hand out."[3]

The inquisitors knew how difficult it was for villagers in the mountains to make their way to the tribunal, even in good weather. Now, they admitted that witch suspects trying to reach Logroño "were persecuted along the way, even to the point of being stoned."[4] Yet they still declined to tell Inquisitor-General Sandoval when one of them would actually go into Navarre with the edict that would permit the reconciliation of confessed and suspected witches. If pressed, they were willing to admit that the edict of grace existed, but they still declined to put it fully into action. Then, things changed—and all because the inquisitors themselves forwarded the letters of the Jesuit Hernando Solarte to the Suprema on February 14, 1611, along with their own diatribe against him.

Secret Counsel and Directions from the Top

On February 25, 1611, Inquisitor-General Sandoval wrote two letters: one to Bishop Venegas of Pamplona and the other to the inquisitors in Logroño. Neither survives, but we can guess at their contents from the ways in which Venegas and the inquisitors responded. Solarte's letters, rather than the inquisitors' tirade about them, had made an impression on the inquisitor-general. And while the inquisitors had not guessed the connection between Solarte and Bishop Venegas, the inquisitor-general did.

Sandoval and Venegas had personal connections. Sandoval had been bishop of Pamplona from 1588 to 1596 before becoming the archbishop of Toledo in 1599 and then inquisitor-general in 1608. He had sponsored Pamplona's first successful diocesan synod in many decades. Meanwhile, Venegas was not only a canon in Toledo's cathedral through 1599 but also a member of the Suprema from 1600 to 1606; he became bishop of Pamplona in 1606. Thus Sandoval and Venegas held the same bishopric and served in the highest echelons of the Spanish Inquisition. Their professional lives intersected in multiple ways. The correspondence that survives indicates that they had a high opinion of each other.

Starting in March 1611, the inquisitor-general began to use Bishop Venegas as a consultant about the witches, and Venegas's input was then funneled back to the inquisitors in Logroño, who had no idea this was happening. When Venegas replied to Sandoval on March 4, 1611, he apologized for not yet sending along what he had discovered during his own visitation of his diocese in 1609, as well as what members of religious orders had found in 1610 when he sent them into witch-infested territory. He had been profoundly ill all winter of 1610–11. He had not dared share what he knew with intermediaries because the matter was so delicate, given that it involved inquisitors.

Venegas then emphasized that he agreed with his own investigators. He was convinced that three-quarters of the witchcraft accusations and confessions were not true; it was all a matter of fraud and deception, especially where the child-witches were concerned. The inquisition's commissioners were to blame for most of it, whether they were moved by religious zeal or private motives. Venegas was also eager to pin the mess on the French: "no one knew what a witch was until the French came, who were fleeing that judge [Pierre de Lancre], who undertook trials so haphazardly and hastily, and without substance, that they took the commission away from him."[5] Venegas pointed out how impossible it seemed that so many people in Navarre, of all ages, conditions, and sexes, could have been witches for so many years without discovery before now. He promised to elaborate on what he thought should be done when he sent along his papers.

Sandoval also must have written a fairly blunt warning to the inquisitors to immediately come up with a plan for solving the witch problem because they responded with not one but two letters on March 9, 1611. Their communications are provocative in terms of tone, insofar as both letters praised Sandoval for his religious fervor.[6] Both missives also went into tremendous detail, which the inquisitor-general apparently requested, on how to stop the witches' machinations in Navarre.[7] The three inquisitors told Sandoval that they would require help from Navarre's royal viceroy in order to track down witch-fugitives. They would need a supply of preachers who could speak Basque. They requested a document from King Philip III that would allow them to confiscate the goods of suspected witches.[8] They asked for advice about different categories of child-witches, noting that Inquisitor-General Sandoval had only mentioned boys fourteen and over and girls twelve and over in his correspondence. What were they to do with the child-witches aged ten to thirteen, not to mention the youngsters under ten?

The inquisitors' letters also went into agonizing detail about how—not when—they might best apply the edict of grace. Should they go to the trouble of setting up a new tribunal in Pamplona? Should two of them go on visitation, with different responsibilities? How many notaries would they need? Becerra, Valle, and Salazar spent entire folios outlining where the akelarres were: twenty-seven in Gipuzkoa alone; more than fifty in the entire district; in the southern plain of Navarre, there were sects only starting to be discovered. They laid out timetables for their possible routes. By now, they had more than 1,800 witches in their lists. They sent the inquisitor-general a chart that itemized villages, the number of confessed witches in each village, and the number of accomplices named by those confessed witches. In Zugarramurdi, for example, the inquisitors reported that they had thirty-four confessed witches who had identified 124 additional suspects; in Lesaka, twenty-three confessants had named 230 more; in Hondarribia, four confessants had testified against 162.[9] Undoubtedly, the inquisitors included these details to underline the intensity of their labor as well as how organized they were.

Significantly, the inquisitors also tried to limit the scope of the edict of grace, writing, "since the edict of grace was conceded generally to everyone equally, it could be implemented with all the *good confessants* who asked for mercy within the time allowed, reserving the *rigor of the law* for *bad or half-hearted confessants, and negative rebels*. And reconciliation could be applied to all the rest *who were not prisoners* and who asked for mercy, *if* they made perfect confessions" [emphases mine].[10] They were attempting to maneuver the edict to apply only to people whom they deemed fit to receive it. At the same time that they were appearing to submit to Sandoval, they were also dodging his instructions.

Based upon their joint letters to the inquisitor-general, Logroño's inquisitors appeared to be operating as a collaborative unit in March 1611. But other communications tell a different story: in fact, they were furious with each other at that moment in time. The evidence to that effect, which comes from correspondence they sent as individuals to the inquisitor-general, reveals a working environment that was threatening to go off the rails.

Anger in the Tribunal: February–March 1611

Before the two exhaustive letters of March 9 ever left the Logroño tribunal, Inquisitor Becerra wrote to Inquisitor-General Sandoval on February 19, 1611, to complain about Inquisitor Salazar. Becerra told his superior that ever since his younger associate had arrived in Logroño, he had "behaved with complete ambition and arrogance." The peace of the tribunal was broken apart; the inquisitors were forced to waste time in their hearings because Salazar insisted upon having the last word in everything. Becerra noted that he had tried to correct his associate "with the greatest love and brotherly affection" but to no avail.[11]

Salazar in turn sent his own grievances to Sandoval. His letter of March 2, 1611, demonstrates all over again that he inhabited a world in which slights, status, and privileges mattered deeply. In his lengthy complaint, Salazar portrayed himself as the suffering underdog. Becerra and Valle were so united in a single opinion that they forced him to conform. When he disagreed with them, they tended not to write down his comments. When he dissented over the verdict of witch suspect María de Arburu—whom his colleagues wanted to send directly to the stake—Inquisitor Valle "swore there would be no peace" unless he changed his vote. Inquisitor Becerra stood up and screamed at him in hearings. One of the tribunal's notaries del secreto actually interrupted Salazar and began to argue with him as he was giving his opinion. Salazar's colleagues had ordered him not to invite any of the notaries to eat with him in his home, even though they did so, and his compliance with their command had not endeared him to those secretaries.[12]

The problems with the notaries did not stop there. Salazar reported that in general, those del secreto, who were responsible for taking down sworn depositions, tended to be absent from the tribunal. Salazar wanted to regularize and keep track of their departures, but Becerra told him that such measures would insult them and make it seem as if Salazar didn't trust them. Becerra had said all this in front of the secretaries; he also told them, "there has not been a moment of peace since Salazar arrived." Salazar accused Becerra of stirring up the secretaries against him. He noted how inconvenient it was not to have all four secretaries there; sometimes, the tribunal had just two, or even only one in attendance.[13] Because the secretaries were absent, he and his colleagues were idle. The tribunal had introduced a "bunch of assistant copyists" (*copia de escribientes ayudantes*) to compensate for the missing employees.

Salazar went on. Becerra, who had seniority, thought he controlled everything, from naming familiars to the production of documents, and thus every sort of business was delayed. Becerra wanted all the inquisitors to walk around Logroño with the cross on the feast day of St. Peter Martyr, when it should have been voluntary. Becerra did not want to dress properly, either. Because he was a member of the religious order of Alcántara, he wished to wear its signature cape during proceedings in the tribunal. Earlier colleagues had stopped him from doing this, but once Salazar arrived, Becerra tried to take it up again, "with obstinacy." Becerra caused scandal by not dressing like Salazar and Valle; when he also refused to wear a priest's cope on top of the cape, he set a bad example for everyone.[14] Salazar had begged him with all humility and modesty to mend his ways, to no avail.

Finally, Salazar told the inquisitor-general that his colleagues had promised that he could go on recreational jaunts that never materialized. They had pledged to take him hunting and on country trips. Then, they suddenly decided it was a bad idea not to have an inquisitor in the tribunal, given what could happen in the jail with the sick and dying, and he was stuck there, "even on feast days and time off" (*vacaciones*). Before he arrived in Logroño, Salazar had been told he could be absent for "six days or more," but such was not the case. Salazar closed his letter by affirming that his colleagues knew he was sending it and "begged Your Holiness for a remedy."[15]

The "remedy" that Becerra, Valle, and Salazar received from Inquisitor-General Sandoval has not survived, but we know he wrote a letter to the tribunal on March 11, 1611, which arrived in Logroño eleven days after its composition. Given the drama of the tribunal's reaction, it seems clear that the inquisitor-general told the inquisitors on March 11, in the strongest possible language, to start getting along. On March 22, as a group, the three inquisitors replied:

> In this Holy Office, we have received today—and have read in secrecy, in the presence of all three of us, the prosecutor, and the notaries del secreto, as Your Lordship order[ed] us to do—the letter which Your Lordship sent on March 11. We all throw ourselves at Your Lordship's feet, recognizing and respecting the mercy and great favor over our heads that Your Lordship, as such a great master, has offered us, your humble servants. We receive the just condemnation from Your Lordship's paternal breast, and offer, on our part, the proper obedience to such holy correction, in recognition of such great favor and mercy. We beg Your Lordship to pardon any reason we may have given you to be annoyed with us, and to hold us under your protection as humble chaplains and servants, who will always beg our Lord God for long life and prosperity for you.[16]

Three days later, on March 25, 1611, Salazar wrote his own personal response to Sandoval. His message is worth quoting in full:

> The letter that your most illustrious Lordship wrote on the 11th of this month, which was read by the tribunal and immediately answered, has provoked such alarm for everyone that it is impossible to describe. And this is especially so for me, who must judge myself a criminal and guilty in the matter, since I, who have greater obligations than all the rest combined to do my best to seek the approval of Your Lordship, have committed the damage that Your Lordship has brought to our attention. And [your correction] has been so just that it leaves me utterly afflicted, and pondering how I will find a way to put it right, though it seems impossible. There is no other way forward at present except to beg with tears, at Your Lordship's feet, that you deign to accept my proposal to reform. I cannot think about or remember anything else in the world. I also beg Our Lord Jesus Christ—with my continuous poor prayers and sacrifices—that He may guard and help Your Lordship to prosper in great happiness for many years, for the great benefit of His church.[17]

Salazar signed his letter with, "I kiss Your Lordship's feet. I am the least of Your Lordship's servants." Salazar was the first inquisitor ever appointed by Sandoval. He had worked for Sandoval while the latter was the bishop of Jaén from 1595 to 1598. Salazar owed Sandoval loyalty, respect, and cooperation. His grief at having offended his patron was profound.

At the same time, Sandoval took some, though not all, of Salazar's complaints seriously. On March 11, in addition to his message to the entire tribunal, the Suprema also forwarded a "list of warnings taken from the letter written by Inquisitor Salazar Frías on March 2, 1611." In that document, Logroño's inquisitors were told to stop visiting their officials in their homes and to finish the genealogies of people they wished to employ as familiars. The Suprema ordered them to get rid of the auxiliary scribes who were taking down testimony in the absence of the notaries del secreto. The Suprema also adjured Becerra to start dressing like his colleagues.[18] These orders to the tribunal could not have increased Salazar's popularity therein. What the Suprema's "list of warnings" did not address were Salazar's grievances over his votes not being appreciated, his protests that he was not treated with enough deference, and his gripes about vacations and hunting.

Marching Orders

While Sandoval was engaging in this sort of crisis intervention, he also was thinking about the inquisitors' plan (and countless questions) about carrying out the edict of grace. When he wrote to the tribunal about their concerns, on March 26, 1611, he was brusque: he shot down some of the inquisitors' suggestions and bluntly told them what they were to do. He called the witches' sect a plague. He explicitly ordered one inquisitor on visitation. He permitted that inquisitor to take only one notary with him, as well as two learned members of religious orders who spoke Basque, to act as translators.[19] No one was to set up a new or temporary inquisition tribunal in Pamplona.

Then, Sandoval laid down highly specific rules. Access to the edict of grace and its immediate implementation were crucial. To make sure that information about it circulated widely, the edict of grace had to be published in its original form everywhere, with "authentic copies" issued on the same day in Logroño, Pamplona, and some of the villages most stricken by witches.[20] The point was to guarantee "that this edict may come to the notice of everyone, and even though it was originally given for a four-month period, the Inquisitor-General hereby extends it to six months." Whether in the tribunal or anywhere else, witch suspects who came to confess their apostasies and errors should be reconciled without exception, even if they were currently imprisoned. In fact, prisoners must be notified of the edict in case they wished to take advantage of it. Those wanting to confess could come to Logroño, find the inquisitor on visitation, or locate particular commissioners who were authorized to reconcile them.[21] The only exceptions for reconciliation were people who had relapsed into the heresy of witchcraft after having previously confessed and been reconciled. For the time being, such relapsed people should not be reconciled again but neither should they be imprisoned; instead, the Suprema should be consulted as to what to do with them.

Sandoval then instructed the tribunal to write to the bishops, telling them about the edict of grace and asking them to endorse the inquisition's handling of any cases that presented themselves. The inquisitors also should advise the bishops that now would be a good time to send preachers into the witch-plagued areas to provide religious instruction. Sandoval's instructions about bishops reflected his relationship with Bishop Venegas in Pamplona. His directives are startling insofar as they suggest a collaborative project: he seemed to imagine that the inquisitor on visitation would be acting in concert with preachers giving sermons and teaching Catholic doctrine.

Sandoval echoed what he had learned from Solarte's and Venegas's letters as he provided the inquisitors with even more directions on interviews and penances. If the inquisitor on visitation or any of the tribunal's commissioners heard witchcraft confessions, they had to take care to make them "brief, paying attention only to substantial faults, such as how they went to the akelarre, and adoration of the Devil, and apostasy, without getting into questions of accomplices."[22] For boys under fourteen and girls under twelve who said they went to the akelarres, Sandoval noted that it was unclear whether they were capable of fully knowing what they were doing, on account of their age. They consequently could not be formally convicted of heresy and should be absolved as a precaution.[23] The inquisitor and his officials should explain to villagers that no one, not even a parent, "should interfere with, threaten, or punish someone else regarding a confession." Under no circumstances should local clerics prevent confessants or suspects from receiving the church sacraments; rather, they should give them the benefit of the doubt that the inquisition would absolve them as soon as they could reach them. Local clerics, including inquisition commissioners, should not obstruct episcopal or secular justice. Printed pamphlets about the November 1610 auto de fe must be confiscated, and people should be forbidden to read them.[24] Through all these mandates, Sandoval was attempting to narrow the means by which suspects multiplied: no more questions about accomplices, no more local or familial violence, no more threats that suspects could not receive the sacraments unless they confessed, and no more publicity.

Yet in the same document, Sandoval still ordered the inquisitor going on visitation to investigate the physical details behind flight to the akelarres, "in order to clarify the doubt that goes with this material, as to whether they fly bodily or not."[25] When the inquisitors as a body replied to Sandoval's long brief on April 9, 1611, they focused only on their investigations into flight: once more, they sidestepped discussion of many of the inquisitor-general's concerns.[26] They reported that Inquisitor Salazar would be the one leaving, as he was junior and Valle had visited the district two years earlier; they confirmed that they would indeed promulgate the edict of grace everywhere on the same day. Then, they began to describe the physical artifacts of witchcraft that they had collected in their tribunal, which related to the witches' ability to fly. They currently had nine pots of waters and ointments, sent to them by various inquisition commissioners as well as Franciscan friars; the inquisitors believed witches used these substances to take wing. The inquisitors also noted that one of the Franciscans had written to say he had custody of one of the dressed toads (*un sapo de los vestidos*). Such toads were the ones the child-witches guarded, which acted as diabolical guardian angels; the toads could vomit the unguent that also allowed witches to travel through the air. The inquisitors were amazed that a Christian could actually possess one of these creatures, because up to now, they had understood such toads to be demons. They told the Suprema that they had pressed the Franciscans to find more, and they "pressed confessed witches, too, and the witches made vain promises to come up with them . . . and never fulfilled their word."[27] Rather than treating the witches' failure as a sign that the toads did not exist, the inquisitors linked it to deceit, one of the Devil's chief attributes.

The fact that Logroño's inquisitors concentrated on the witches' flight to akelarres speaks volumes about their priorities. Sandoval had just laid out new boundaries for the interrogation of witch suspects, new practices—such as the admission of confessed witches to the sacraments—and new warnings about violence and coercion. The inquisitors did not respond to any of these points. They focused instead on evidence they possessed, and evidence they might eventually possess, which would prove witches really flew. While not explicitly rebellious, they concentrated on one small part of Sandoval's letter and sidestepped the rest.

Sandoval had imagined a collaborative project in which inquisitors would reconcile suspects, and preachers would instruct villagers. In yet another sign of their disinclination to follow that plan, the inquisitors continued to set themselves up against Navarre's parish clergy. In their reply to Sandoval, they told him that suspects in the field were confessing and then revoking their confessions. They blamed this phenomenon on Martín de Irissari, the parish priest of Igantzi who had told the Jesuit Solarte about the terrible suffering in Sunbilla and Lesaka. The inquisitors wrote that Irissari was threatening people who wished to confess to witchcraft: he was reminding them of the profound dishonor they would bring to "their land and lineage," and claiming the inquisition "would put permanent sambenitos on them." Irissari allegedly had written to Rome; moreover, he was attempting to persuade Bishop Venegas to order that none of the current inquisitors could hear witch trials and to make sure an inquisitor from a different tribunal would conduct the visitation.[28] Irissari's mother had been named as a witch, so the inquisitors thought all this made sense; it was another attempt to shield the guilty. Their evidence demonstrated how wicked Irissari and other Navarrese clerics were. Since Bishop Venegas was the ecclesiastical supervisor of those priests, the inquisitors were making a passive-aggressive jab in his direction.

Back to the Bishop

Venegas did have opinions about the qualifications of the current inquisitors and their employees vis-à-vis the impending visitation. On April 1, 1611, Venegas wrote once more to Inquisitor-General Sandoval. Venegas commented that Sandoval had asked for his opinion. He went on to single out the commissioners of Lesaka and Bera as having provoked village chaos. Venegas knew them; they possessed neither intelligence nor learning. He had told them to stay completely out of any witchcraft accusations that might arise—a significant assertion of episcopal authority over men who were also inquisitorial employees.

Venegas went on to comment on the abilities of the inquisitors to solve the morass. Valle couldn't be used for the impending visitation because he had made so many discoveries on his previous one in 1609. Becerra, the oldest inquisitor in the tribunal, also was "too on board in this business" (*está demasiado embarcado en este negocio*). Venegas wrote that Valle and Becerra were so devoted to proving that the witches and their deeds were true that they wouldn't be able to act with the necessary diligence. Significantly, Venegas then told the inquisitor-general that they needed "an inquisitor who will firmly resolve to finish and clarify the matter," and he pledged to help that individual in every way.[29] His use of the verb "finish" is provocative: he obviously had a sense that the witch persecution had been underway for too long.

Thus in his message of April 1611, Venegas laid out his understanding of the inquisitors' significant psychological and legal investment in the witch hunt. He thought they were already biased in their thinking; he feared they would not adjust their reasoning if they heard opposing evidence. Though he did not come out and say that two of Logroño's inquisitors had failed in their use of discretion (*discreción*), he certainly hinted at it. As Venegas well knew, given his previous positions, discretion should have been at the heart of any inquisitor's ethos and practice because inquisitors were supposed to use their judgment in a careful way. From Venegas's point of view, inquisitors Becerra and Valle were likely to fail a test of prudence. The bishop presumably did not offer an opinion on Salazar because he had not yet met him.[30]

Venegas then decided to offer evidence on the reality of fear, coercion, and violence surrounding the witchcraft accusations and confessions. Contained in his April 1, 1611 letter was an account (*relación*) of the witch hunt, which was culled from reports by Venegas's informants who had been in the field from June to December 1610.[31] In that account, Sandoval, and presumably the Suprema, would have read about Lorenzo Hualde, the parish rector and inquisition commissioner in Bera. Hualde had told his villagers that if their children, relatives, and neighbors did not confess to witchcraft, they would be taken to Logroño, burned at the stake, and have all their property confiscated, while their sambenitos would be hung forever in Bera's church. Sandoval and the Suprema would have learned about the deaths of five women, one of whom was pregnant, in five different locales. They would have read that the commissioners had been telling the inquisitors that witch suspects were confessing spontaneously, when in fact they had been tortured. For eight full folios, Sandoval and the Suprema would have learned how the witch hunt was being fomented through coercion, lies, and the conviction that children were telling the truth.

Though Logroño's inquisitors had consistently forwarded accounts of local violence to the Suprema, it is still likely that what Venegas sent to Madrid in April 1611 was shocking to read. What might also have made an impression on the inquisition hierarchy was Venegas's endorsement of the fact that lies and silences involved employees of the Logroño tribunal. A month earlier, in March 1611, Salazar had reported that crucial notaries were often physically absent. Now, Venegas was telling Sandoval and the Suprema that inquisition commissioners in the field were not relaying the true contexts for confessions. As we will see, seeds were being planted in 1611 that would come to fruition in 1613.

Notably, offering information to the inquisitor-general may not have been entirely Venegas's idea. Buried in Leg. 1679 in the AHN is a "copy of a letter from the king to a certain bishop about a good relationship with the inquisitors." Dated January 21, 1611, the letter was from King Philip III to Bishop Venegas. The king told Venegas that it was crucial for episcopal officials to have the same positive relationship with the inquisition as royal ministers enjoyed. The king declared that there was an obligation to act as a good example in such matters when opportunities arose, especially when they pertained to the service of God. The king charged and commanded Venegas

> to give a precise order to your ministers that if, at present, they have some disagreements with the inquisitors, or have some complaint about the inquisition, to tell the Suprema about it, whereupon I am certain justice and mercy [gracia] will be realized in whatever has taken place. I am especially confident because the Cardinal Archbishop of Toledo is Inquisitor-General, whose great store of integrity, justice, and good zeal is well-known. At the same time, you will charge your ministers not to pursue any case in Rome that concerns

legal jurisdiction, given the difficulties that occur when things of this nature are litigated there, and the fact that the intervention of the Inquisitor-General can solve it all. Make an effort to see that justice has its rightful place. I will be greatly served by your carrying out this command; advise me that you have received it.[32]

It is unclear how the king could have known at such an early date—January 1611—that Venegas and his staff had been conducting their own investigations into witchcraft accusations. There is no evidence that Venegas contacted the inquisitor-general before writing his letter on March 4, 1611, but his apology on that date "for not yet sending along what he had discovered" implies that he may have intended to do so after the royal command in January. Based on the king's message, it appears that Logroño's inquisitors might have been right in March 1611 when they asserted that Venegas was contemplating turning to Rome and the papacy to solve the witch problem.

Was Salazar Already Skeptical in May 1611?

By the beginning of May 1611, Inquisitor-General Sandoval and Bishop Venegas had been liaising for about six weeks, which the inquisitors in Logroño did not know. In that same period, Inquisitor Salazar was preparing to leave with the edict of grace that had been conceded sixteen months earlier. The question now is, what was Salazar's attitude before he set out? Older studies of this witch hunt argued that he had become a skeptic about the reality of witchcraft by May 1611. There are two pieces of evidence to that effect.

The first was Salazar's dissenting vote, in June 1610, on whether to send María de Arburu to the stake.[33] Arburu was seventy years old and the mother of another alleged witch, the cleric Pedro de Arburu. According to Salazar's original opinion, she was rustic, ignorant, and afraid to confess because she believed an admission would automatically condemn her. Salazar referred to her throughout his commentary in June 1610 as a negativa, which meant she persisted in denying the charges. Salazar noted too that the witnesses against her were defective: they not only contradicted each other but omitted "key facts" in their descriptions of the witches' gatherings, namely, the Devil's masses and sermons in the akelarres. The same witnesses did not always mention that María's son, Pedro, and his cousin, Juan de la Borda, assisted the Devil in his ceremonies, which the inquisitors also thought was a confirmed truth.

Furthermore, the tribunal had no witnesses who could attest that they had seen María de Arburu actually renounce Christianity. Witnesses were presuming she had done so because she was seen in the akelarres, but Salazar and his colleagues knew that people could attend akelarres without explicit apostasy, as the cases of young children proved. Finally, Salazar noted that the Devil could produce doppelgängers of his witches, and such might have happened in María's case: for example, witnesses put another accused witch, Juan de la Bastida, in diabolical gatherings on the very days he was imprisoned in the inquisition's secret cells. Salazar wrote that when witch suspects confessed openly, such defects in the evidence were treated as moot by the tribunal. But in the case of María, who was a negativa, leaping to the presumption that she had apostatized was insufficient for the death penalty. Salazar wanted her put to torture to ascertain the truth.[34]

The other skeptical-sounding testimony from Salazar came later, on March 3, 1611, when he and his colleagues voted on whether to put four witch suspects from Zubieta into the tribunal's prison.[35] The suspects had been brought to Logroño by Zubieta's mayor and village constables on order of commissioner Aranibar. Aranibar had told the tribunal in late February 1611 that he feared Zubieta's villagers would knife the suspects to death or burn them alive if he could not get them out of town.[36] When the party from Zubieta showed up in Logroño, the inquisitors asked what had happened in the village. The officials responded that four adult suspects had been put into the river and then were suspended from trees for three days. Salazar wrote that suffering from or even seeing such violence could have caused a great deal of fear, though witnesses had not mentioned the violence when they were examined. As a result—"and because of the mob by which [the witch suspects] were taken prisoner and brought here"—his opinion was that the question of their imprisonment couldn't be resolved until the circumstances of their confessions were verified and the Suprema consulted.[37]

We can glean several noteworthy points from these two pieces of evidence. In the case of María de Arburu, Salazar was willing to notice contradictions and missing details: in June 1610, he was bothered by the gaps between what was by then a template for the witches' activities and what witnesses against Arburu did not say. He also cared about intent. The witnesses against Arburu had not actually witnessed her rejection of Christianity, and she had declined to confess as much to the inquisitors. It was the combination of missing specifics, a lack of eyewitness testimony, and Arburu's refusal to disclose that was bothersome. Next, Salazar took circumstances and emotions seriously. He and his colleagues had read about the popular violence in Zubieta before the prisoners arrived, thanks to commissioner Araníbar's correspondence. Salazar was willing to imagine what that violence could have wrought: he explicitly mentioned fear, though he did not go so far as to mention the possibility of false confessions. These details mark a difference between Salazar and his colleagues, for Becerra and Valle were less concerned about evidentiary fissures and positively dismissive about terror. They wrote that the popular violence in Zubieta was irrelevant because the parents were justly outraged.[38]

Yet it is also important to note what Salazar did not do. In June 1610, during the vote on María de Arburu, he did not scoff at the Devil's mass and sermons but treated those details as proven, along with the witches' unguents. He did not challenge witches' voluntary confessions. He did not treat spectral evidence as if it made investigation impossible. He wanted María de Arburu to be tortured to determine the truth. Later, when it came to the prisoners from Zubieta, Salazar noted that there was certainly evidence against them. Making Salazar into a skeptic before he left the tribunal will not work, because his behavior and writings in the field demonstrate that a process was unfolding. It was not a straightforward one.

Developments in the Field

Salazar departed on visitation on May 22, 1611. We know he went to Pamplona and spoke with Bishop Venegas before he traveled into the mountains: he was expected to do so by the Suprema and his colleagues. Scholars now agree that Venegas undoubtedly shared his concerns with Salazar, but whether Salazar was instantly converted to the bishop's point of view is questionable.[39] We have two surviving letters from him while he was away, both written in September 1611. The letter written first explains what had happened before that date as well as his current state of mind; we can use it to grasp developments in his legal reasoning that he wished to share with his superiors.

From Hondarribia, on September 4, 1611, Salazar told the Suprema that he was writing to them about important matters. First—as per the inquisitor-general's instructions—he was publishing the edict of grace everywhere, and people were receiving it with gratitude and peace. He was reconciling everyone who came to him, even if they were from France. When he left the tribunal on May 22, the inquisitors had 338 confessions to witchcraft, of which 117 qualified for reconciliation from heresy because the rest were from children. Now, almost four months later, Salazar had reconciled 1,546 people according to the following categories: 1,199 were children under the age of fourteen (boys) and twelve (girls), who were absolved as a precaution, in accordance with the inquisitor-general's mandate. Salazar also had absolved 271 people of the heresy of witchcraft who were fourteen and older (men) and twelve and older (women), with many of them "being old and even decrepit." He had ordered 34 people to abjure a light suspicion of heresy; 42 others had revoked previous witchcraft confessions. Salazar also had seen a "countless number of children under age five," over whom he had pronounced "certain exorcisms of the Church," which he and his colleagues had agreed upon before his departure.[40]

Salazar then asked the Suprema about two teenage girls who were posing difficulties. One had confessed to witchcraft on June 23 and been reconciled, but she reappeared a month later to report tearfully that two neighbors had taken her back to the akelarre while she slept, without her consent. She had done nothing heretical while surrounded by the witches and the Devil, and she was in tremendous spiritual pain and regret over her apparent relapse. The second teenager had confessed to Salazar on July 18 and reappeared on August 3. She returned with her parents, "and with all of them continuously crying, she relayed that she had been taken back to the akelarre by the master witch who used to take her there before, without her having understood how or when she took her, and without her being able to resist."[41]

Inquisitor-General Sandoval's instructions of March 24, 1611, had specified that reconciling those who had relapsed into witchcraft was "reserved." The Suprema had to be consulted about individuals who had fallen once more into this heresy; Salazar accordingly wanted to know what the Suprema wanted to do. He had consoled the two teenagers to the best of his ability. He wrote that they had made him remember other cases in which suspects offered emotional confessions but still did not know how they were taken to the Devil's reunions. Sometimes, these individuals were even taken the night before they confessed to him, and Salazar worried whether they were evincing the right kind of contrition. All these ambiguities meant that he would delay responding to the Suprema's original instruction to investigate whether the witches truly flew.

As a sort of progress report, however, Salazar went on to tell his superiors that he had been conducting multiple experiments on ointments in pots. Out of the sixteen pots that had been turned in to him since May, he didn't believe that even one was truly from an akelarre because none of the contents had actually been poisonous or harmful in any way. He believed they were fake, and he now had a "huge suspicion" that the pots of ointments sent to the tribunal were counterfeit, too. Meanwhile, the progress of his trip was being impeded by the need to find sick and dying people who had previously confessed to inquisition commissioners but were unable to travel to him.

In Salazar's first September letter, he raised significant issues about veracity. There was the obvious problem of the substances in pots. But he also was affected by the emotions displayed by the two girls who said they had relapsed into witchcraft. He seemed to trust that their sorrow was genuine. Spiritual sadness was integral to a state of contrition, but contrition was at odds with a relapse into heresy: the pairing of authentic contrition with apostasy did not make spiritual sense. Furthermore, the teenagers had not intended to return to the Devil's flock: they never agreed to go back, and they did not know how they had been transported there. In this instance, the teenagers' display of feelings, combined with their inability to explain themselves and their apparent lack of motive, left Salazar confused and, perhaps, suspicious. Yet there were no statements of disbelief in the Devil or witches in his letter to the Suprema.

What his September 4 missive also contained was a short history on how he had treated revocations to witchcraft confessions. Salazar told the Suprema that after he had departed Logroño in May, he had sharply repelled anyone who wanted to revoke a confession, on order from his senior colleagues in the tribunal. He did not receive permission from the Suprema to receive any *revocantes* until June 28, and even after that date, the inquisition's principle of secrecy left him unable to publicize that he would welcome people who wanted to retract witchcraft confessions.[42] People feared they would be punished for having confessed falsely while under oath, which was itself a sign of heresy. Salazar concluded that because popular violence had prompted many to confess, and because many of the confessions he was hearing were lukewarm, "I now suspect that the number of revocantes will be high, even though up to now, only forty-two have spoken out."[43] Again, he was paying attention to emotional tone.

It could be tempting to read Salazar's prediction about revocantes as signaling skepticism about witchcraft confessions in general. But it's crucial to note that throughout his visitation, he continued to treat those confessions as trustworthy. (Given that confessions were the "queen of proofs" in the inquisitorial process, it would have been unthinkable for him to have discredited them outright.) For example, as we saw in chapter 2, after María de Ulibarri abjured her heresy, Salazar sentenced her to pray ten Our Fathers and ten Hail Marys every day for two months; during that time, she was to fast every Friday and confess regularly with the rector or parish priest.[44] Yet

Salazar had heard Ulibarri say out loud that her own mother's confession to witchcraft was false, that her mother committed suicide out of despair at having falsely named accomplices, and that her mother had named her as a witch despite the fact that neither of them had seen each other at the akelarres.[45] There is no evidence that Salazar reacted to the dreadful story about the mother as mitigating the guilt of the daughter, though he would remember it for years. He took what the daughter said about herself at face value.

In other examples, after Graciana de la Plaza confessed to witchcraft in front of Salazar while he was on visitation, he ordered her to abjure a light suspicion of heresy and then told her that if she fell again into any religious error, she and her goods would be treated with the full force of the law and without mercy, even if she begged for it.[46] In April 1611, Juana de Irurita, a widow, appeared before Martín de Irissari to confess to witchcraft. In October 1611, when she came to Salazar to revoke that confession, he denied that she had grounds to do so. He told her, "it wasn't believable that fear made her confess to witchcraft, because she confessed before the commissioner of Doneztebe-Santesteban without being forced to do so, and without being frightened. She was put into a state of fear [only] a single time by the residents of Zubieta." Salazar had learned months earlier about the violence in Zubieta, but he refused to extrapolate those conditions to make them applicable to this particular widow. He told Irurita that she had not been sufficiently threatened and abused in her local environment to prove that her original confession arose from terror. Salazar and his interpreters then began to press her about owning dressed toads and pots with ointments, even though his letter to the Suprema on September 4 had pointed out that all the ointments he had found so far were fraudulent.[47]

Thus Salazar's first surviving letter from the field reveals his pastoral instincts, presumptions, and efforts at obedience.[48] He treated signs of repentance very seriously and actively searched for people to reconcile. He was struck by the emotional tenor of revocations but continued to trust confessions. Not surprisingly, given the reprimand he and his colleagues had received in March 1611 from the inquisitor-general, Salazar followed the Suprema's instructions to the letter. Until that body told him he should *not* investigate the means by which witches flew, he would continue to pursue them, even if other challenges kept him from focusing on flight alone.

While on visitation, Salazar also witnessed parental rage. In his second surviving letter, written this time to his colleagues on September 28, 1611, Salazar noted that his efforts had been hampered in San Sebastián. He had only been able to absolve as a precaution a small number of children who were underage. Older people were not coming to him; although San Sebastián's officials had imprisoned fourteen adults, only one had been willing to confess to Salazar and be reconciled. He was forced to leave the other thirteen alone because they were such adamant negativos. The secular authorities found themselves very much behind in the legal process, since they had not collected proof or started trials for any of the accused.[49] When Salazar attempted to console the city's residents, "with one scream [con un grito], they said they knew that all these [jailed] witches were the ones taking their children, and hoped that I might be able to sentence them, or at the least, receive them as prisoners of the Inquisition, which is impossible, as you know." Salazar also reported that he was having trouble guaranteeing that the one woman he had reconciled would be able to live in peace and freedom, as the edict of grace promised. At the very least, her neighbors wanted to exile her. Although Salazar felt obliged to defend her, he also did not want to "force the situation in such a way that the town would become distressed from my standing up for her."[50] By the end of September 1611, then, Salazar understood that sometimes, terror and torture could produce false confessions. But he did not treat revocations as if they were valid by default, nor did he treat negativos as inevitably innocent. He would never take up either position.

Trials in the Secular Court

During Salazar's time in the field in 1611, certain villagers there were pursuing justice for having been tortured and defamed, and they were pleading their cases in the secular and episcopal legal jurisdictions. Crucially, Salazar would learn about those villagers' efforts, and there is no doubt they affected him, though it took time for him to make the effect known.

When neighbors accused neighbors in this witch hunt, a number of the maligned went to the royal secular court in Pamplona to regain their reputations and punish the men and women who had attacked them. In Elgorriaga, a husband filed a case about the treatment meted out to his wife, who had been marched in a ladder for an entire night; in that instance, the prosecutor also heard depositions from other victims, men as well as women.[51] In Arraioz, nine women filed what amounted to a class-action lawsuit against their fellow villagers: here, neighbors had afflicted suspects with torments involving ropes, chains, private imprisonment, deprivation of food, and freezing water. Plaintiffs in both prosecutions were Basque speakers and predominantly illiterate; their villages were some thirty miles away from the center of government and law in Pamplona, but they knew how to file court cases there. Far from being a foreign entity, the secular court system was familiar to Navarrese villagers in the early seventeenth century.[52]

In these secular trials, the plaintiffs produced one eyewitness after another who could attest the public abuse. In Elgorriaga, women and men had been marched in ladders through multiple villages, with crowds of boys and men shouting insults along the way. Women, including pregnant ones, had been imprisoned in the basement of the palace of Jauregizar in Arraioz for more than a week. Suspected witches confined with chains in their own houses could not attend Mass, an absence that everyone noticed.[53] When suspect Graciana de Barrenechea was taken to the house of inquisition familiar Miguel de Narbarte, she eventually was tied to a pillar outside, whereby passing neighbors could see her and adjure her to confess and ultimately, watch her die.[54] Women and men in these villages—and throughout the entire Valle de Baztan, per the witnesses—had been assailed for months.

The defendants tried to explain that they had acted on orders from inquisitorial employees. Their witnesses tried to explain that the defendants had been reacting to their communities' fear and panic over children being converted into the Devil's servants. Neither approach worked. The prosecution claimed that the defendants had slandered and assaulted the plaintiffs; the defendants needed to show they had not slandered and assaulted the plaintiffs. Instead, the defendants attempted to prove their actions were justified through inquisitorial instructions and parental terror. None of the defendants or their witnesses could demonstrate that the slander and torture had not occurred, which is why the plaintiffs won their cases.[55]

Triumphing in court meant that the plaintiffs had achieved a measure of vengeance, but their legal victory did not mean that the sentences were immediately effective. The witch torturers of Arraioz and Elgorriaga worked feverishly to evade the penalties. In Arraioz, Juan de Perochena, the village's constable, and Miguel Zuito were condemned in December 1612 to significant periods of exile for their key roles in the witches' torment. Perochena was given a six-year period of exile and was forbidden from holding the elected office of constable for ten years; Zuito was sentenced to a year of exile.[56] Exile was a terrifying penalty that could further decimate the economic and social stability of families, beyond what they had already suffered when their heads of household were imprisoned in Pamplona during trial. Perochena and Zuito's defense lawyer tried to help his clients by asking the court to give the men two months to get their family finances in order before leaving Navarre.[57] The court declined that request. Perochena and Zuito were commanded to depart within six days; they refused to go. Their trial is full of further petitions seeking to have them removed, and yet more petitions asking to let them stay.

Perochena and Zuito did not stop there. They had been commanded to leave in December 1612. In March 1613, six of their accusers filed a formal notarial document called an "act of cessation" (*acto de desistimiento*). The act communicated that a husband and wife, along with four other women who had also been part of the original prosecution, "now consented that [Perochena and Zuito] not leave to complete their sentences of exile, but wished instead that they might stay in this place, or outside the Valle de Baztan, or wherever they prefer." The group of former plaintiffs wanted no obstacle placed in their torturers' way or any penalty exacted upon them. (As a sign of the terror of this witch hunt, one of the women involved was representing her daughter as well as herself because the daughter had run to Gipuzkoa.) From this moment forward, the petitioners said they pardoned the men who had tortured them. The women asked the viceroy and his council, as well as all other judges and justices involved in their case, to suspend the order of exile in conformity with this formal "act of forgiveness" (*acto de perdón*).[58] Some of the individuals who sponsored this notarial document had been among the poorest of the accused witches in Arraioz; they had been abused to the point of death. We can only imagine what sort of pressure or bribery led them to sanction this legal document. Thankfully, it seems to have had no effect whatsoever, and presumably Perochena and Zuito eventually were forced to leave.

Meanwhile, in Elgorriaga, the village constable who managed the witch torturers and carried out abuses himself, Juan de Legasa, was originally sentenced to ten years of exile before the royal court dropped it to two, but he and his cohort also refused to depart. The trial record contains dozens if not hundreds of petitions demanding that the culprits leave, as well as counter-petitions asking to void their sentences.[59] Eventually, Legasa and his friends left, in late January 1612, but three of them, not including Legasa, eventually snuck back in. Tomás Hernale, the husband who had started the original prosecution on behalf of his wife, informed secular judges in Pamplona on April 3, 1612, about the men's transgression.

Ultimately, Legasa and his cohort were forced into obedience, with a twist. Upon being informed of their "breaking of exile" (*quebrantamiento de exilio*), which was another crime, the royal court in Pamplona ordered the assailants to depart once more. Then, the court almost immediately annulled its own directive through a peace contract.[60] That decree of amnesty,

sponsored by someone "to whom respect must be shown," ordered the viola-
tors of exile not to leave again, and stipulated that Legasa "could come [back]
to his house." The document continued, "not one of the [witch torturers], or
the wives, children, and families of their houses . . . shall treat badly, through
injurious words, Tomás Hernale or his wife, or provoke any scandal of any
kind. Rather, they shall be friends, and treat each other in conformity with
the law of God. If they do the opposite, then the decree of Navarre's royal
court will remain in effect, in all its severity. . . . The desire here . . . is to use
the mercy of God with them." When this order was read before the relevant
parties, on May 15, 1612, Legasa and his accomplices stated they "accepted
all that was contained in it, as much as they could and must by law, and they
would carry it out, because it was their determined will, as good Christians,
to have charity and love with their neighbors."[61] Ultimately, this cohort of
witch torturers submitted to a gag order. Whether their compliance resulted
in community peace is anyone's guess. When a census was taken later in
1612, Tomás Hernale, who had spearheaded the original prosecution against
the torturers of his wife and others, had left the village.[62]

Trials in the Episcopal Court

As the Arraioz and Elgorriaga trials were proceeding, Bishop Venegas's court
was prosecuting an analogous case, this time against a cleric. The episcopal
trial arose from the village of Erratzu, also in the Valle de Baztan, after residents complained that their parish priest, Miguel de Aguirre, had slandered,
imprisoned, and abused them over false accusations of witchcraft. Much like
the class-action event in Arraioz, neighbors in Erratzu came together not
only to testify but to finance the prosecution.[63] Their statements about Aguirre were incriminating. For example, Aguirre had refused to administer last
rites to a shepherd whom he had charged as a witch: nothing could have
been a greater offense against Pamplona's synodal constitutions of 1590. In
another instance, an eighty-year-old woman learned Aguirre had named her
as a witch. She went to him and begged for the sacrament of penance; he
called her an evil, wicked witch, and said he wouldn't hear her confession
until she admitted her witchcraft. After Christmas, Erratzu's constables put
her into the stocks for five months. She couldn't run away; she was too old
and had no resources.[64] One male witness told the episcopal court that his
sisters had fled to France out of fear of being accused.[65] Multiple deponents
said Aguirre threw people in and out of prison as he saw fit.[66]

Another woman in Erratzu testified that Aguirre "squeezed her, persuading her to say that she was a witch, and when she said she was not, he responded with great anger and pride, telling her she was a wicked witch, and he had more than twenty witnesses against her to have her burned, and he would make sure they burned her if she didn't say she was a witch." Aguirre then broke the woman's rosary. He knew how to invoke tropes about the inquisition to terrify his parishioners; at the same time, this victim knew how to invoke two of the seven deadly sins against him.

Aguirre also understood what clerical behavior was supposed to look like after the Council of Trent. He produced character witnesses who insisted he only treated his parishioners with loving correction. He had been horrified to learn that his flock contained witches; he cared deeply about the risk to their souls. All the witnesses against him were witches, hence their testimony was not reliable.[67] He and Erratzu's constables had sought advice from inquisition commissioner Leon de Araníbar, so it was not as if their actions were unauthorized.[68] In that respect, Aguirre echoed the excuses of the constables in the villages of Elgorriaga and Arraioz, which were also in the Valle de Baztan.

Erratzu's accused witches explained to Venegas's episcopal court that they had suffered tremendously. So severe were their dishonor and misery that sixteen villagers, including one married couple, sought restitution in not one justice system, but two. The sixteen traveled to Pamplona in November 1611 to testify against their priest before the episcopal court; while they were there, they filed charges against Erratzu's constable in the royal court as well.[69] They wished "to clear their consciences, having confessed to witchcraft when they were not witches." They testified before a royal notary that they were withdrawing their confessions: they had admitted being witches without oaths and outside the sacrament of penance.[70] In sum, Aguirre's victims were determined to fight back against his libels and attacks; they wanted him punished in every court they could enter. Summed up, their position was, "if they had to be imprisoned [by Aguirre], then he too needs to be put into the bishop's tower."[71]

While we unfortunately no longer possess at least one secular trial brought against Erratzu's constable, we do know what happened in the episcopal case against Erratzu's priest because Venegas's officials monitored Aguirre closely. Aguirre was not cooperative: he ran away after the bishop's investigation began in August 1611. Episcopal agents found so much evidence that Aguirre had bribed his defense witnesses that their notaries had to re-interview everyone; the episcopal prosecutor even suggested Aguirre should be exiled from the entire Valle de Baztan.[72] Later, Aguirre would claim to be so ill that he could not travel to Pamplona. On January 21, 1612, he was sentenced to two months of seclusion in Erratzu's parish church, as well as a one hundred ducat fine and court costs. Afterwards, he would be absolved, yet his legal machinations did not stop there. After he was transferred to the parish of Lekaroz in 1614, he financed a secular legal case on behalf of numerous Erratzu villagers who had participated in his witch persecution, and who may have been named in other lawsuits that have not survived.[73]

The Effects of What Salazar Learned

It is incontestable that Inquisitor Salazar heard about these episcopal and secular prosecutions while he was on visitation, even if the verdicts came later. In August 1611, his name appears in Erratzu's episcopal case, when he personally ordered the priest Aguirre to start admitting accused witches to the sacraments.[74] Commissioner Araníbar wrote to Salazar at the end of October 1611 and confessed his own role in Erratzu's witch hunt: he admitted that he had ordered Aguirre to imprison suspects.[75] As for the secular prosecutions of witch torturers, investigations into the calamities in Elgorriaga began by April 1611; Salazar left on visitation in late May. In Arraioz, where the prosecution of witch abusers started in May 1612, witnesses said that the Spanish Inquisition had long known what had been happening there.[76] Finally, as Salazar passed through Olague in 1611, he would have become aware of the two secular prosecutions for defamation that were in progress in that village.

Crucially, Salazar was the original conduit by which his inquisitor-colleagues became aware of prosecutions, not just investigations, against witch torturers in the secular and episcopal jurisdictions. Though his letter has not survived, he wrote to Becerra and Valle from the field about those indictments. In a massive communication to the Suprema on June 15, 1611, Becerra and Valle relayed what Salazar had told them as well as the results of their own inquiries.[77] Salazar had reported that both the bishop and the royal viceroy refused to quash the trials and punishments of villagers who had attacked their neighbors over witchcraft. He also allegedly implied that the secular jurisdiction had started its investigations at the urging of Bishop Venegas.[78] Perhaps Venegas's influence had an effect, though the extant secular trials never mention it; perhaps Becerra and Valle blamed Venegas for this unwelcome legal competition because they already were convinced he was hostile.

Becerra and Valle continued. They told the Suprema that they knew popular violence had occurred but said it had only been going on for six months, when the villagers saw "the inquisition was delayed in going on visitation with the remedy." The inquisitors' abjuration of responsibility was ironic: *they* had not put off a visitation with the edict of grace; instead, it was the fault of the entire institution. Becerra and Valle noted that after receiving Salazar's letter, they had written to Venegas and the viceroy to see if their colleague's account was correct. It was. They told the Suprema that in the ensuing letters from the bishop and the viceroy, they could see "the resolution of the justices, and the rigorous proceedings that they are carrying out against local authorities of those places, and against everyone who isn't a witch, with very serious imprisonments and difficulties."

Becerra and Valle were determined to deny the legitimacy of the efforts taking place in the secular and episcopal courts. They said their resistance to those jurisdictions was a matter of religious conviction. They told their superiors they were in great pain from seeing the Devil's promises come true, for he had assured his followers that he would carry out a lawsuit (*pleito*) in the witches' defense, whereby the witches would be liberated.[79] Becerra and Valle were utterly distressed to see witches protected and Catholics punished. From their point of view, village officials had acted against the Devil's brood with good and holy zeal, albeit somewhat recklessly. Local justices hated the witches so very much, and their pursuit of these heretics had benefitted everyone. Everyone knew that the true remedy for this nefarious sect lay in harsh punishments, even if the royal court was mistakenly proceeding with compassion.

The inquisitors had to admit that according to Navarrese law, village constables had no right to punish anyone. This was how the secular court was justifying its proceedings, in such a way that the inquisitors' hands were tied. Their tribunal could not affect what the secular court was doing; it could not issue any directives. This was the most harmful scenario the Devil could have concocted: he was blocking the efforts of the inquisition and the remedy of so many souls.[80] After Becerra and Valle had written to the viceroy, the latter had responded with some accounts of what was being proven in secular court. Becerra and Valle could see that some constables had committed great excesses, but it was from the righteous pain of seeing their children lost (*perdidos*). The inquisitors had already sent the Suprema descriptions of the mistreatment. They had been unable to remedy it, though they had tried. Still, they had information that any excesses weren't really that severe.

Becerra and Valle also wanted the Suprema to know that witch suspects who were tormented in the villages and insisted they were innocent actually admitted being witches once they were in the tribunal, thanks to the mercy of God and the admonishments they received there. All but one had confessed to remarkable things; processing their statements had been a mountain of work.[81] Moreover, in June 1611 Becerra and Valle repeated what they had first reported two months earlier. They were in possession of nine pots of witches' ointments, which they had shown to their witch prisoners: the accused had verified which ointments were for flight to the akelarres and which were poisons. The inquisitors had brought in four doctors and four apothecaries—"the most adept in this entire land"—and "in our presence, and also having gone off by themselves in a corridor that is next to the hearing room, they recognized the pots, and talked about what was contained in them." The experts said that the pots' contents were not known in either the medical or apothecary arts nor could they have been made by humans.[82]

The two inquisitors concluded by insisting that the royal secular court in Pamplona had to stop its proceedings against local justices or else the witches would be persuaded that the Devil could defend them and avenge them against the Christians. At the same time, Becerra and Valle admitted that they could not impede the secular court via censures, without provoking serious problems and sorrows. Ultimately, they left no room for collaboration or cooperation.

Becerra and Valle's long diatribe shifted in fits and starts. The inquisitors couldn't deny that they had corresponded with the viceroy and the bishop nor could they disavow what those authorities had told them. They could, however, try to mitigate the gravity of what they were learning by pointing to the "good and holy zeal" of village constables as well as their certainty that village excesses had not been so awful. From their point of view, the Devil once more was doing everything in his considerable power to undermine Catholicism, and the secular and episcopal courts were helping. The inquisitors had warned the Suprema of the dire situation in the villages; they had told their superiors about popular violence, which they had tried, and failed, to fix. The situation was not the tribunal's fault, for it had not received the support it needed. The inquisitors' hands were tied vis-à-vis the secular cases. The Suprema had to step in.

Rebellion in the Ranks

Thus while Salazar was in the field—reconciling confessants, absolving suspects, and pronouncing exorcisms—he learned firsthand about the village violence that was flooding Navarre. He communicated details about the actions of the other courts to his colleagues in Logroño. His colleagues in turn wrote to the Suprema and demanded corrective action. The Suprema did not step in; the surviving evidence suggests that Becerra, Valle, and Salazar did not attempt to interfere with the other legal jurisdictions for the rest of 1611. Though there had been interpersonal conflicts among the inquisitors in February and March 1611, from May through June of that year, the inquisitors appeared to be operating once more as a unit.[83] And yet Becerra, Valle, and their prosecutor, Isidoro San Vincente, began to send up warning signs in July that all was not right in Logroño.

On July 9, 1611, Becerra and Valle told the Suprema that Logroño had been wracked for two months with rumors about witches in the city. Many residents had seen extraordinary fires between 10:00 p.m. and 12:00 a.m. A French boy, age nine, appeared at the tribunal to beg for help: witches, including his own uncle, had persecuted him in his own land and now had followed him to Logroño. Becerra and Valle were positively indignant that French witches would have dared enter the city and carry out their wickedness with an inquisition tribunal so close by. They accordingly had arrested three Frenchmen, whom they had placed in the house of one of their familiars. The inquisitors asked the Suprema what they should do.[84]

At the same time, the tribunal's prosecutor, San Vincente, wrote his own memorandum to the inquisition leadership. San Vincente wanted the property of the witches sentenced in the 1610 auto de fe to finally be sold. He wanted the sambenitos of the convicted witches hung in their local churches. He argued that the witch trials in progress in the tribunal should continue, irrespective of the edict of grace that Salazar was administering. He asked that Salazar be told to ratify in the field any confessions or depositions that were outstanding so that they could be used once the edict of grace had expired.[85]

When the Suprema replied on July 23, 1611, its message was curt.[86] No one should be newly imprisoned while the edict of grace was being administered. If the imprisoned Frenchmen wished, they could be reconciled through the same edict. Where the current witch prosecutions were concerned, those defendants had to be offered the edict of grace too, not once, but twice. The edict should be read to them when their trials were approximately halfway over, and again before sentencing.[87]

The urgency and scope of the pleas coming from the tribunal reached a crescendo three months later. On October 3, 1611, San Vincente presented a polemic in the tribunal's defense to the inquisitors, which he begged them to forward to the Suprema. He charged Inquisitor-General Sandoval with extending the edict of grace another six months without consultation.[88] He challenged Sandoval's understanding of the witch hunt, since neither he nor the Suprema "had seen the things that [the inquisitors] have grasped and considered for the whole inquisitorial district." San Vincente denied that Salazar was being effective in the field and asserted that he had only reconciled twelve out of three hundred accused witches. He opined that numerous people who had confessed to witchcraft in Navarre had relapsed; he claimed the Devil was achieving what he had promised his disciples.

Then, in a dramatic passage, San Vincente wrote that witches in Logroño had caused the death of one of the tribunal's Basque interpreters as well as the death of that interpreter's four-year-old nephew. The wife of the jailor of the house of penitence had found the dead child with powders in his mouth. San Vincente next reported that Salazar's own housekeeper had appeared at the door of his house, "crying, full of bruises and signs [of witchcraft] on her body, which made me so sad and compassionate." San Vincente said he would refrain from divulging all the other injuries and extraordinary illnesses that agricultural workers around Logroño had suffered from the witches' harmful magic. He concluded by noting that many inquisition commissioners were threatening to quit their jobs if the edict of grace was extended.[89]

San Vincente's memo of October 1611 was an extraordinary attempt to negate an edict that the tribunal had been ordered to promulgate, which Salazar was still administering. His letter was designed to push all kinds of panic buttons. He adduced tiny numbers in terms of who had benefitted from the edict of grace and highlighted relapse instead. His comment that inquisition commissioners throughout Navarre were threatening to quit their jobs implied that the inquisition's entire infrastructure in Logroño could disintegrate. Moreover, the witches who had been in Logroño in July apparently were still there. The idea that their harmful magic was affecting lands around the tribunal was another sign that the Devil and his sect were amplifying their evil magic. Then there was the question of human deaths, for the witches had taken down not only a well-respected translator but the translator's nephew. San Vincente's description called up special poisons, secretly administered, as well as the malevolence that witches always exercised toward children. Finally, not even Inquisitor Salazar's housekeeper in Logroño was immune from the witches, for they had physically and emotionally abused her.

It seems likely that San Vincente's October polemic, as well as his colleagues', arose because of communication with Salazar himself. The two surviving letters from Salazar in the field, dated September 1611, say nothing about doubting the reality of witchcraft. Nevertheless, Salazar may have communicated troubling sentiments during an in-person conversation. San Vincente left Logroño for San Sebastian on September 11, 1611, and returned September 21.[90] Salazar was in San Sebastian at the same time. Significantly, September 1611 was the very month in which the original edict of grace, conceded for six months in March 1611, was due to expire. When San Vincente wrote to the Suprema in October 1611, he relayed that the inquisitor-general had extended the edict without consulting the tribunal. In September 1611, Salazar could well have told San Vincente that *he* wanted the edict extended and had written to the inquisitor-general accordingly.[91]

That last point seems especially likely, given that Inquisitors Becerra and Valle's enormous memo of October 5, 1611, begins with the comment, "Salazar wants the edict extended for four months." Becerra and Valle wrote that they saw no reason for such an extension because the edict only worked for "persons who appeared in the tribunal, who were making authentic confessions."[92] They repeated their prosecutor's assertion that exactly twelve people of legal age had come to Salazar to be reconciled. They told the Suprema about the deaths of the interpreter and his nephew, with the added detail that the interpreter had been an inquisition commissioner who had just discovered a new sect when the witches killed him.[93] Ideas of spiritual and mortal combat were in full force.

I have no idea how San Vincente, Becerra, and Valle decided to assert that Salazar had reconciled exactly twelve individuals with the edict of grace by early October 1611. Fatally, that trio didn't seem to know that Salazar had written to the inquisitor-general on September 4, wherein he reported that he had reconciled 271 adults so far.[94] The inquisitors in the tribunal, along with their prosecutor, were making up numbers: presumably, the Suprema and Inquisitor-General Sandoval would have noticed the discrepancy.

The correspondence from the tribunal in 1611 demonstrates that the inquisitors who remained there were highly invested in curtailing the edict of grace and asserting it was failing. Becerra and Valle pressed home the relentlessly diabolical character of the witches as Salazar's visitation and the secular and episcopal trials of witch torturers continued. They fumed over their inability to intervene in secular court; the evidence suggests they did their best to obstruct their employees from testifying in that legal jurisdiction.[95] In February 1612, the Navarrese *Cortes*, or parliament, petitioned King Philip III to stop the Logroño tribunal from "interfering in criminal cases involving inquisition familiars, or any other lay prosecutions, but rather, [the inquisitors] must leave them to the royal tribunals."[96] From our perspective, by the end of 1611, the Spanish Inquisition in Logroño was positively fractured in this witch hunt, with some of its employees working to reconcile witch suspects, while others sought to punish them. As we will see in the final chapter, that fragmentation hardened throughout 1612 and 1613, until growing evidence of misconduct slowly persuaded the inquisition's leadership to end the persecution.

5

TRANSGRESSIONS AND SOLUTIONS

The beginning of the end of Navarre's largest witch hunt started with the initiative and collaboration of certain members of the three justice systems. In 1611, Inquisitor-General Sandoval had no hesitation asking Bishop Venegas for advice, and Venegas had no qualms about giving it. Venegas went on to collect evidence that added context and details to the Suprema's impressions, and he was not willing to stop at memos: he forcefully blocked certain clerics from witch-hunting and brought a key perpetrator to trial, thereby setting an example and achieving some redress. His priorities were mirrored by the secular justices in Pamplona, who continued to prosecute witch torturers, even though a representative of the viceroy had told Inquisitor Valle in November 1609 that they would stop doing so.[1] Those trials reverberated across the villages. Meanwhile, Inquisitor Salazar formed the fourth leg of the chair while he was in the field from May 1611 to January 1612. He would always do his best to please his patron, which meant that he carried out the inquisitor-general's instructions to the letter. He also listened seriously to Venegas, rather than viewing him as a competitive enemy. Thanks to those attributes, Salazar ended up reconciling hundreds of villagers to the Catholic Church with the edict of grace, and he never attempted to interfere in the secular and episcopal prosecutions that were occurring simultaneously. By the time he returned to Logroño in early January 1612, reparative justice was making some headway in Navarre.[2]

This chapter is devoted to the period 1612–14, when inquisitors Becerra, Valle, and Salazar argued ever more forcefully about the proof they had accrued and the errors they had made. Each side accused the other of bias; each side pointed out violations of protocol. The evidence examined here features understudied as well as new archival discoveries: radically, the latter include texts that call out the crucial notaries del secreto of the tribunal as rogue agents whom the inquisitors, including Salazar, declined to control. Awareness of the notaries' delinquency undoubtedly contributed to the Suprema's decisions in 1614, which were intended to stop this witch hunt cold.

Paper Wars: Salazar's Report of March 1612

When Salazar returned to Logroño from visitation, the key question was what would happen next. The answer quickly became clear. Over the three years from 1612 to 1614, the inquisitors involved in this witch hunt conducted a paper war among themselves, aimed at the inquisition hierarchy, and Salazar fired the opening shot. When he came back to the tribunal, he did something unprecedented: he did not confer with his colleagues as he was writing up results or present them with the opportunity to vote on the cases he had covered, though he gave them access to more than five thousand folios of his notes. Instead, he only presented them with a final report, dated March 24, 1612, which he intended to send directly to the Suprema.[3]

Salazar's account began on a factual note, as if he were merely relaying the results of what he had found. He started with numbers. He had been in Navarre from May 22, 1611, to January 10, 1612. He had handled 1,802 witchcraft cases in all. He had absolved 1,384 children as a precaution; he had absolved 41 adults as a precaution who abjured a light suspicion of heresy; he had reconciled 290 adults who confessed to witchcraft. Of the 290 adults who confessed, 100 were over the age of twenty, which meant another 190 were teenage boys between the ages of fourteen and nineteen, as well as teenage girls between the ages of twelve and nineteen. Salazar also heard 6 people confess to having relapsed and listened to 81 more revoke their original confessions to witchcraft.

Salazar then took up one of the Suprema's persistent questions, which had featured in its instructions since 1609: Did the witches truly go to the Devil's akelarres? Most of the witches Salazar interviewed said they flew; occasionally, they said they went to the Devil's gatherings on the shoulders of their master witches. Almost all reported that they left their houses through "a crack, hole, window, or chimney, through which a person could not naturally go without physical risk."[4] The witches told Salazar that no one in their houses knew they were gone.[5] Most said they never encountered anyone on their way to the akelarre, or saw lights, or got wet if it was raining or snowing. Some said they were taken to the Devil's gatherings in the middle of the day, while they were in the middle of ordinary routines. One even reported that she had been kidnapped from church while a friar was preaching about Salazar's edict of grace.[6] In his March 1612 summary, Salazar combined such findings with the testimony of many other deponents who told him they had no idea how they traveled to the akelarres and found themselves there against their will. Salazar concluded that while the Devil could certainly make such things happen, it "was more easily admitted as a work of the Devil that he only tricked those people into thinking they were invisible [when] they thought they had disappeared." Being thus fooled, they really believed it, and that was how the Devil had the community "entangled in tares."[7] There was nothing particularly novel about Salazar's remark, since it expressed faith in the Devil's ability to deceive, a belief that was routine for all Christians in the early modern period.

Salazar then highlighted what he found to be some highly bizarre testimonies about what the witches did, which he clearly thought were emotionally and physically implausible. For example, certain witches told him they had lovers inside the akelarres, but never spoke to them outside the akelarres. The witches could even be married to other witches but again, never communicated with each other except in the Devil's gatherings. It was as if the witches moved to a state of absolute detachment from their partners once the akelarres ended.[8] Moreover, three women told Salazar that within two hours of having sex with the Devil, they had given birth to large toads, while a fourth said she had given birth to a toad through her mouth. Rather than confining toads to the roles of guardian angels and suppliers of poisons, these witch suspects made them the literal outcome of diabolical unions and extended the birth process to unheard of channels. Some of the witches also asserted that when they attacked statues in a local church, the statues rose up and fought back, as if they were alive.[9] Witches were expected to desecrate sacred Christian objects, but these individuals said they engaged in literal physical combat with them. Finally, the witches told Salazar about their multiple attacks on him: they had dropped poisons into his mouth while he slept and set his chair on fire while he was sitting in it. He had felt nothing.[10]

In a nod to what the Suprema always wanted to know, Salazar spent two full folios on instances of flight to the akelarre that could not be proven.[11] As for the other external acts that he also had wanted to prove, he again came up empty. Teenage girls who said they had sex with the Devil were examined by midwives and determined to be virgins.[12] Witches claimed an akelarre had happened at exactly the same moment and in the same place where two inquisition secretaries were walking, neither of whom saw or felt a thing.[13] Salazar himself examined a site where an akelarre had allegedly occurred, but the ground was undisturbed and the grass fresh.[14] A witch purportedly breast-fed a snake, but Salazar couldn't locate either the woman or the serpent.[15] None of the ointments or powders that he had examined had been real: they were all counterfeit.[16] Again, Salazar framed his experience in the field as shot through with deception.

A little more than halfway through his March 1612 summary, Salazar made clear where his trajectory was headed. The Devil was always busy in his efforts to destroy the work of God; he could make things appear other than they truly were. From Salazar's point of view, that diabolical industry and talent both produced the witch hunt and rendered the inquisitors helpless. None of the witches' activities could be proven with sensory or tangible evidence from human beings, even though such evidence had to be the basis of proof in any inquisition trial.[17] Salazar had been unable to find witnesses to witchcraft who were not witches themselves. Moreover, though the tribunal had heard from hundreds of witnesses who testified that they had seen certain individuals in the akelarre, those witnesses had not necessarily seen the witch suspects apostatize. Such had been the case with María de Arburu; such evidence was insufficient for an inquisitorial verdict.[18]

Though his colleagues had denied the severity of village abuses throughout 1611, Salazar was willing to raise them after being in the field for more than seven months. In March 1612, he noted, "the lack of confidence [only grows] from knowing the force, inducements, and wicked motives that led them to testify, given that [many] were imprisoned and assaulted and threatened so violently." It was horrifying to consider how the accused had been made to twist the truth. Salazar said such fear affected not only those actually named as witches, but all the residents of the villages, given that local justices united with fathers, mothers, or siblings to produce the confessions. Even the local clergy had become involved. To make matters worse, inquisition employees had been a party to the coercion as well: either they authorized the violence by concealing it or committed it with their own hands. It was a miracle that anyone had escaped this web of coercion.[19]

Argumentatively, Salazar moved from a lack of sensory evidence to local viciousness and forced confessions. He then took up the attempted revocation of those false confessions. When revocantes finally were allowed to appear before him, after June 28, 1611, they reinforced his awareness of violence by telling him in detail how they had been driven into their original statements. Consistently sensitive to tone and emotion, Salazar noted that out of the eighty-one revocantes whom he had heard, "some were at the point of death, and all of them always demonstrated much more peace and security in their souls in these revocations than persons I reconciled through confessions." Salazar headed off the possible protest that villagers were simply imitating each other when they sought to revoke. He had kept the hearings so secret that no one outside his portable court knew what was being said to him, hence no one outside its hearings knew there was anything to imitate. The revocantes simply wanted to repair their consciences. If only they had known they would have been welcomed, he would have seen so many more. He felt very guilty that he had repelled them at the start of his visitation; some had bravely told him that they had to revoke, even if they would be burned at the stake for having lied under oath.[20] Salazar then relayed the terrible anecdote of the mother who committed suicide by drowning because she felt so guilty for having falsely named accomplices while she was held in the Logroño tribunal.[21] Salazar's invocation of pastoral faults was thorough. The mistakes were everywhere, from the implicit or explicit endorsement of torture to the rejection of the spiritually anguished to the prohibition of the ecclesiastical sacraments.

In March 1612, Salazar ended his report with comments on what should be done. He did not regard the situation as either stable or concluded. He repeated two of the points that Bishop Venegas had made a year earlier to the inquisitor-general: three-quarters of the depositions were probably false; no one in Navarre knew what witches were until people started to talk and write about them. (Like Inquisitor-General Sandoval and Bishop Venegas, Salazar knew nothing about Navarrese traditions of witchcraft.) He asserted that no more legal edicts of any kind should be issued because any public discussion of these matters was harmful.[22] Salazar thought many more people would come to the tribunal to revoke their witchcraft confessions if they knew they "would be received kindly, without risk or condemnation." Yet he worried that he had followed so well the inquisitorial rule of secrecy that many people did not realize revocation was an option. He did not trust what the inquisition commissioners might do in the field, now that he was back in the tribunal.

In the same document, Salazar noted that inquisitors Becerra and Valle would object to it, not least because he had met with Bishop Venegas:

Given the certainty that my colleagues will challenge my opinion in this business, I wish to certify how affectionately I have asked them to look over the records of my visitation, and [copy] as much as might be useful for them. . . . And I also certify that as much as I owe to and esteem the Lord Bishop of Sigüenza [Venegas], I had no way to see him more than once in Pamplona, which was when I went through on visitation, as my colleagues expressly ordered me to do. And he might have expressed something about matters of witchcraft [when we met], but after that one meeting, I never interacted with him again in writing or in person.[23]

Inquisitorial culture dictated that inquisitors and bishops should vie with one another. Even though the inquisitor-general and his colleagues had told him to visit Venegas in Pamplona, Salazar suspected that the fact that he had done so would still leave him open to suspicion and recrimination.[24] His explicit anticipation of conflict would have reminded the Suprema once more that this tribunal was prone to infighting.

Paper Wars: The Colleagues' Responses

Where the witches were concerned, competition among Logroño's inquisitors rather than with other legal jurisdictions became the watchword in 1612 and 1613. Becerra and Valle were not silent: they too sent a letter to the Suprema, also dated March 24, 1612. They told the Suprema that Salazar had violated protocol. Instead of submitting a report that listed each of the confessed witches, the witnesses against them, and his preliminary decision about their guilt, which his colleagues would vote upon, Salazar wrote summaries about individual cases, which he handed off to Becerra and Valle to read. The two inquisitors wrote, "And once we saw them, we were astonished. To vindicate his unique vote on the witches who went to the auto de fe [in the case of María de Arburu], he now publishes such extraordinary things, which are so opposite to the depositions and confessions of a very great number of trials and witches in this tribunal. He hopes to reduce the whole matter to dreams and demonic fraud."[25] Becerra and Valle asserted that they needed to see the whole of Salazar's papers—"all the trials, proof, and confessions" —in order to respond to them. They would show the Suprema that the witches' sect was real. The Suprema should not read Salazar's memorials until that body could simultaneously read Becerra's and Valle's opinions. They wrote that Salazar had proceeded on visitation "determined to reinforce his suspicions as well as the opinion that the Lord Bishop of Sigüenza [Venegas] tries to defend, with whom our colleague has a special friendship."[26] The evidence indicates that Salazar was undergoing a slow but meaningful change in epistemology while he was in the field, in the wake of forensic evidence and human conversations, but his colleagues were convinced he had started out with a bias. They were implacable when faced with ambiguity; Bishop Venegas had told the inquisitor-general in April 1611 that Becerra and Valle were prisoners of their preconceptions.

The two documents by the three inquisitors reached Madrid on March 31, 1612. Thereafter, Becerra and Valle worked to craft a memorial of their own design, which they appear to have sent to the Suprema in late summer 1613. The only part of their document that survives is in Pamplona's AGN; it has been characterized as an appendix to the now-missing report. Sixty-five folios in length, the manuscript, signed by Becerra and Valle, is titled "Inquisition of Navarre: Notebook of Verified Acts by Witches." It is a remarkable text that deserves its own study.[27] Prefaced by a table of contents that lists thirty-two separate items—including walking to the akelarre, the Devil's mark, and diabolical sex—the notebook identifies specific witches who did particular things. It gives each witch's name and age and assigns each one a number. At the end of the manuscript, the witches are arranged by number into two lists: one is titled "Persons Who Confessed to Witchcraft and Were Reconciled in This Tribunal since September 7, 1610"; the other is labeled "Witches Reconciled during the Visitation," which could refer either to Valle's visitation in 1609 or Salazar's in 1611.[28] The first list contains 84 witches and the second, 177. At the very end of the manuscript, the confession of María de Endara is transcribed.[29]

The point of Becerra and Valle's notebook was to substantiate that the witches really did what they said they did, as opposed to Salazar's assertion that the witches were deceived. Thus when the Devil marked his witches with his claw, "they felt pain and the mark remained forever." During the day, the witches made powders and poisons in their own homes, while the Devil watched; the witches then used those substances to carry out vengeance against their enemies and to destroy crops.[30] The meat that the witches ate in the akelarres was foul—an implicit reference to human corpses. That food upset the witches' stomachs to the point that they often vomited the next day in their houses. Any of these signs or actions could have been seen by other people in those households; Becerra and Valle were thus implying that they could find eyewitnesses who were not witches, when Salazar could not.

Becerra and Valle refuted Salazar's other assertions point by point. Their witches always went to the akelarres when they were awake; they got wet when it rained and talked to each other about what happened there.[31] For example, "María de Indart, age forty . . . says that on the nights of the akelarre, she did her weaving until it was time, and then she anointed herself and went; sometimes she was in bed, and the Devil awakened her, and she got up and anointed herself."[32] María de Aldabe, age twenty-nine, confirmed the same. If any of the witches said they went to the akelarre while they slept, that occurred "when they were novice witches, when they only went to the akelarre when their masters took them, anointing them and taking them from their houses." Sometimes, the masters took them while they slept so they would not cry or make a noise and thereby wake the people who slept with them who were not witches. And "all of them, and all the youngsters [*pequeños*] confirm that even if they were taken out of their houses while asleep, they woke up on the road or as soon as they arrived at the a[k]elarre." The witches always returned wide-awake to their houses and beds.[33]

Becerra and Valle explicitly stated that they had eyewitnesses to the ake-larres who were not witches themselves. For example, María de Endara had attended an akelarre and had seen the Devil before becoming a witch: the two had a substantial conversation, in which he promised to make her even richer, on the condition that she revoke her Christianity.[34] Becerra and Valle even combed through Salazar's five thousand pages of notes to use his own evidence against him. For instance,

> Juan de Garay declared in the visitation of lord inquisitor Salazar Frías that on Saint Michael's day [September 29] of 1610, he was asleep in his house, in a place . . . where he guarded cows. And people took him from the hut—he didn't know who or how—and they carried him for a distance like a bullet, whereupon he woke up and saw many persons whom he could name, men and women, in-cluding his own father and a female first cousin. And when he saw them at that hour of the night, he made a sign of the cross and they all disappeared, and he fainted.

After Juan came to, he made his way slowly back to the hut, where he was very ill and unable to eat or drink for fifteen days. The people he identified as witches had been named as such by others, and "some of them confessed and were reconciled."[35]

For many folios, Becerra and Valle described acts that the witches committed while they were awake, which could have been seen by others and observed by non-witches. The inquisitors' aim, of course, was to overwhelm Salazar's account with counterevidence and better evidence from allegedly superior sources. For example, they took care to point out that all the witches they cited were over the age of twenty, except for five, whose ages ranged from fifteen to nineteen. They also repeatedly emphasized the witches' intentions, in order to demonstrate that the culprits knew what they were doing. For example, in the case of Miguel de Goiburu, who was burned at the stake in effigy in the 1610 auto de fe, "when he broke away from Christianity, he knew very well that he was baptized, and that on account of his baptism, he was a Christian and had the faith of Jesus Christ. Having reneged as he did, he [knew that he] thus separated himself from Christianity and the God of the Christians."[36] None of Becerra and Valle's witches was confused or uncertain, ever. When their suspects found themselves among the Devil's brood, it was always on purpose.

Witches and Jews

At the very start of this persecution, before Salazar joined the tribunal, Becerra and Valle told the Suprema that they would be focusing all their efforts not only on witches in Zugarramurdi but also on allegedly judaizing conversos in the village of Los Arcos. We have very limited evidence as to what happened in Los Arcos, although it appears that the Suprema dismissed an important case there that involved a priest.[37] Significantly, in their 1613 memorial, Becerra and Valle made many of their witches sound like crypto-Jews. For example, Graciana de Barrenechea purportedly said that her sect was better than that of the Christians.[38] Juan de Goiburu said "all the time he has been a witch, he always has believed and understood that the law and sect of the witches was better than the faith of the Christians, and that under that sect, one could be saved."[39] María Miguel "always believed and held as certain that that wicked lord was the god who would save her, and he was better than the God of the Christians."[40] When the Devil ordered his followers not to talk outside the akelarre, it was to prevent Christians from knowing who the witches were and what they did, "because if such were known, their sect would not be preserved." When witches went to church to hear Mass, and confessed and received the Eucharist, they "were doing so only out of compliance, so that no one would notice anything unusual and see that they were witches." Any Christian act they performed was feigned.[41]

With such statements, Becerra and Valle were echoing more than a century of inquisitorial tropes about Jewish converts to Christianity, even though they were writing about witches. The Spanish Inquisition was founded in 1478 because of a fear that "new Christians" were continuing to practice Mosaic Law and hence were heretics. The expulsion of Spain's Jews in 1492 was motivated by the supposed need to separate Jewish communities from converted ones, for fear of contamination. From the thirteenth century on, Christians in Europe had cast Jews as deliberately resistant to theological argument and called them "blind." By the later sixteenth century, inquisitors "knew" that Spanish and Portuguese conversos were secretive, stubborn rebels against the Christianity they had inherited or been forced to accept: this is why Becerra, Valle, and Salazar tracked Portuguese converso merchants as they moved through Navarre to southern France.[42] In the case of Becerra and Valle, they moved alleged characteristics and values from one heretical group to another. When they wrote that witches were "under the sect" of the Devil, they were echoing the phrase, "under the Law of Moses." Their expression that the Devil's religion was "better than that of Christians" echoed the comment that "the Law of Moses was better" than Christianity. From 1609 through 1613, Becerra and Valle expressed themselves as if witchcraft and Judaism were twin sects in a way that Salazar seems to have avoided, though he too was vitally concerned about the heresy of judaizing. Becerra and Valle's conviction that older witch suspects were incorrigible may also have reflected stereotypes about Jews' persistence in their faith.[43]

Salazar's Reply: Offenses in the Tribunal

Becerra and Valle showed their memorandum of October 1613 to Salazar, and he was sufficiently provoked to respond to it. What he sent to the Suprema the same month illuminates his values and what he believed the Suprema would find most telling. Obedience was at the top of the list.[44] Here, for the first time, Salazar went into detail about the ways in which the tribunal had ducked the Suprema's mandates. In March 1609, before Salazar ever arrived in Logroño, the Suprema had specifically asked Becerra and Valle to search their archive for precedents on prosecuting witchcraft, which they should then send to Madrid. In October 1613, Salazar revealed that in July 1609, his colleagues had only sent along materials that seemed to encourage witch-hunting, though they knew that their tribunal also contained much more cautious directives. Salazar had joined the Logroño tribunal on June 20, 1609; perhaps he saw what his new colleagues sent forward and then later checked the tribunal's archives for himself.

Salazar made his point that Becerra and Valle were resisting instruction even as early as 1609 by highlighting what they had ignored. For example, "on 14 December 1526, a letter from the Suprema about the sect of witches was written to the tribunal . . . and it said that through the statement and confession of suspected witches, no one should be imprisoned, nor should others be condemned on the suspects' word, until investigations are carried out." Five years later, in 1531, the Suprema had instructed the inquisitors not to trust the depositions of alleged witches if their statements could not be verified by non-witches. In 1538, the Suprema had warned that witch suspects could be mistaking dreams for reality. The 1538 letter also admonished the inquisitors not to trust the famous witch-hunting treatise, the *Malleus maleficarum*, and counseled them to conduct thorough investigations into homicides purportedly caused by witchcraft. In 1555, the Suprema told the tribunal that no witch suspect should be imprisoned without its permission. It reiterated that warning in 1595. Finally, in 1596 the Suprema had freed and imposed no penances on witch suspects who revoked their original confessions.[45] According to Salazar, by disregarding these orders and precedents, Becerra and Valle revealed their unwillingness to use their discretion where suspected witches were concerned.

Salazar then moved to actual violations of procedure with the accused. His colleagues failed to record contradictions in testimony. They pressured defendants into saying exactly what they needed to corroborate other cases. They brought suspects face-to-face to achieve confessions—something the Suprema already knew, since all three inquisitors had told them as much in July 1610. They promised repeatedly to free anyone who confessed, which saved them the time, trouble, and expense of trials. They declined to record revocations of confessions made in their presence and then ignored revocations and contradictions overheard and relayed by their prison warden.[46] They disregarded pleas to revoke made by individuals who were dying in their jails.

In yet more transgressions, Logroño's inquisitors had persuaded the tribunal's defense attorneys not to offer arguments for the accused. Sometimes, they told those attorneys that a defendant's attempt to stain (*tachar*) a prosecution witness was not likely to reveal capital enmity, which, of course, they could not have known. On other occasions, Becerra and Valle said defense witnesses would not be capable of affirming a truth that already was established.[47] Salazar was employed by the tribunal while all these errors were being perpetrated; he knew the malfeasance was ongoing. Perhaps he was too junior to raise objections in 1609–10; maybe the inquisitor-general's demand in March 1611 that the inquisitors get along silenced him. Either way, Salazar's first complaint to the inquisitor-general in early March 1611 said nothing overt about errors in inquisitorial processes nor did his report to the Suprema in March 1612.

Things had changed by late 1613. One of the most inflammatory charges to come out of Salazar's October polemic that year was the accusation that the Logroño tribunal had been complicit in the village torture of witch suspects from 1609 to 1612:

> And as for the notorious suspicion, which I've already mentioned, that the people [of Navarre] suffered such violent and wrongful humiliations from their own relatives, and even secular justice [the constables], and from inquisitorial commissioners who should have prevented the mistreatment, it now turns out that we inquisitors agreed to it. Beyond the fact that we failed to stop it, I have learned through various means that we actually encouraged it. Note the letter that we wrote to the Viceroy of Navarre, on 17 May 1611, which praised such mistreatment [of accused witches].[48]

Salazar was correct, to a degree. His colleague Valle had written to the viceroy of Navarre on May 17, 1611 to demand that investigations into the possible abuse of witch suspects must cease.[49] Valle wrote in the name of the tribunal, before Salazar left on visitation, but Salazar insisted he had never seen this particular message.[50] What is perhaps equally noteworthy is what Salazar neglected to say in 1613: namely, that over the previous four years, the inquisitors in Logroño had so little control over their commissioners and familiars that the latter acted independently and did not even bother to consult with the tribunal on what they were recommending. Commissioner Araníbar had confessed as much to Salazar when he wrote to him in October 1611 and admitted he had authorized local torture.

In 1613, Salazar stated that his colleagues were so full of hatred toward the witch sect that they were determined not to allow anyone to escape the label of witch once it had been applied. They had not acted carefully; they had not used their judgment. Instead, Salazar charged that their actions were directed toward a single outcome, to find every witch suspect guilty.[51] Salazar also contended that his associates' preconceptions had governed the advice they had sent him more than two years earlier. In late May 1611, just as he had started on visitation, he had written to the tribunal to ask whether he could hear people who wished to revoke their previous confessions and testimony. His colleagues had swiftly replied on June 6 with this directive: "The matter of people who have been reconciled by the Holy Office and now wish to ask to revoke their confessions is most serious. Those who have such nerve should be brought as prisoners to Logroño, where they will be heard according to law, in order to be punished as they deserve for wrongful revocations, impenitence, and relapse, and for having deceived the Holy Office."[52] Given the inquisitor-general's harsh reprimand in March 1611 about getting along, it's no wonder Salazar followed his colleagues' mandate about revocantes in June of that year. The situation only changed on June 28, 1611, when the Suprema told Logroño that all its inquisitors and their employees could hear revocantes.[53] From Salazar's perspective in 1613, his colleagues originally had constrained him in an imperious manner and had prevented him from using his discretion. He bemoaned the fact that he had originally obeyed them.[54] Here, his complaints about being bossed around had a much more serious foundation than his grievances about hunting and holidays in March 1611.

Salazar's polemics in 1612 and 1613 built upon each other in terms of critique. The former spoke to a lack of legal proof against witch suspects; the latter reported intentional violations of legal procedures and legal goals where those suspects were concerned. We can easily imagine the impact that Salazar's diatribes had on the inquisitor-general and the Suprema when combined with the materials from Bishop Venegas. And yet, the Logroño tribunal was rife with even more misconduct. When Salazar first complained about his colleagues in March 1611, he hinted at a strange relationship—at once overly familiar and insufficiently supervisory—between the inquisitors and their notaries. Inquisitors and notaries were dining together. The notaries frequently were absent from the tribunal, which left the inquisitors stalled in their work. In 1611, the Suprema immediately issued a memo correcting those excesses, and the matter might have ended there. What previous scholars did not fully realize, however, is that the Suprema received multiple pleas for help in 1612 from the prosecutor in the Logroño tribunal because the notaries del secreto were out of control.[55]

Gaming the System: The Notaries

Evidence of the inquisitors' continuing incompetence with their notaries in 1612 lies where no one reasonably would have thought to look for it: namely, in an inquisition dossier put together in 1619–20. That dossier's call number is AHN, Inqu., Leg. 1683, Exp. 1, and its reason for being was a visitation of the Logroño tribunal by Inquisitor Martín Carrillo y Aldrete. Carrillo was assigned to inspect the tribunal because of reports of conflicts and misbehavior there. As part of his evidence-gathering on the history of discord in the tribunal, Carrillo or his assistants lifted materials dated 1611–14 from the main inquisition dossier on this witch hunt, Leg. 1679, and put them into Leg. 1683.

It is worth recalling what the notaries del secreto were authorized to do. They were supposed to take down defense statements as well as witnesses' sworn depositions in inquisition hearings. They were absolutely adjured to observe the rule of secrecy that pertained to all inquisitorial proceedings. In sum, their job lay inside the tribunal, not outside of it. Yet nine months after the Suprema's correction of March 1611, the notaries del secreto were hardly ever in residence in Logroño. On January 19, 1612, the inquisition prosecutor, Isidoro San Vincente, wrote to Inquisitor-General Sandoval without the inquisitors' knowledge. San Vincente explained that he simply had to speak up because his conscience demanded it; he had tried gentle correction, but it had failed. He had to inform the inquisitor-general about the constant absence of the notaries del secreto from their place of employment.[56] The tribunal was supposed to have four or five such secretaries in place, but very often, only one was actually there; sometimes, the inquisitors couldn't even hold hearings because all the notaries were gone. Thus San Vincente confirmed in January 1612 that the transgressions Salazar had mentioned nine months earlier were still ongoing. The prosecutor then added this detail: the notaries' absences were not short, for they could be gone for "two, three, four, and even more months." He went on to report that the inquisitors were aware of the issue, but "did not have the resolution to fix it."[57]

It seems that the notaries del secreto were eager to leave Logroño in order to carry out genealogies of potential inquisition employees who needed to prove their purity of blood [limpieza de sangre]. Carrying out genealogical investigations was financially worthwhile, especially when the notaries were financially creative. According to San Vincente, the notaries were inflating the sums that they believed they were due from the tribunal. If the standard for interviews was four witnesses a day—for which they received two ducats—then the notaries insisted that their salary should be tripled if they interviewed twenty. On top of that sum, they were demanding five hundred maravedís from each job candidate.

San Vincente reported that the notaries were greatly overstating how much time they needed to be away, and there were no repercussions for their lengthy absences. They didn't even bother to enter their absenteeism in the book held for that purpose in the tribunal. As far as San Vincente could tell, only one absence had been recorded between 1608 and 1612; a second one allegedly had been written down, but the notaries had ripped out the leaf on which it was logged.[58] San Vincente then cast doubt on the actual work the notaries del secreto were accomplishing while they were gone. He asserted that they could not possibly be examining so many witnesses in a competent manner: they had to be taking down the barest annotations and then filling in the details later. He also was convinced that the notaries' style of interrogation was resulting in incomplete investigations: they "ran over" witnesses who wanted to offer damaging testimony about the backgrounds of various candidates. The background reports they ultimately produced, called *informaciones*, were inferior to the work of the commissioners stationed in the field.[59]

San Vincente's letter of January 19, 1612, had an immediate impact. By February 3, Inquisitor Becerra had received a personal inquiry from the inquisitor-general about the notaries; presumably the letter was directed to Becerra because he was the senior member of the tribunal. Becerra replied that whatever complaint the Suprema had received was "vastly exaggerated." While there might have been some indiscretions, Becerra had now ordered San Vincente to pull together all the genealogical reports that could have been mishandled. The tribunal would find out everything and verify the truth. All would be done with precision.[60] The Suprema was not convinced. On February 19, 1612, the council wrote to the inquisitors as a body, repeating, anonymously, San Vincente's protests.[61]

The Suprema's attempts to keep San Vincente's identity a secret were in vain. Ironically, one of the notaries del secreto had already opened the inquisitor-general's secret inquiry to Becerra from February 3, 1612, and read most of it. Given that all the evidence pointed to San Vincente—because "I have often spoken to [the notaries] about these matters"—he admitted to the tribunal that he had authored the original complaint in January.[62] When he wrote once more to the Suprema, on April 1, 1612, San Vincente described the notaries del secreto as in full revolt against him. They were adamantly protesting any possible changes in their routines. They were also creating excuses and justifications as fast as they could dream them up.

In his second missive of April 1612, San Vincente said he could prove that the notaries were double-dipping in terms of fees. By their own accounts, they had been in two locations at once or had traveled in a single day to places that were too far apart for such to be feasible. He then contested any idea that the notaries might have only left the tribunal to carry out imprisonments. That idea was ludicrous. Such had occurred exactly twice over the previous four years, and even then, the notaries were not necessarily behaving in an ethical matter. In one of the two cases, a tribunal notary named Peralta threatened to arrest a Portuguese man in Pamplona unless he was paid, and for more than a year, Peralta "had him in his power, and got many ducats." Furthermore, the idea that there was a "tradition" of the notaries being absent was absurd. All anyone had to do was to look at the quantity of genealogical reports completed by the notaries under the previous regime. When Dr. Juan Ramírez ran the tribunal in 1607 and 1608, the notaries del secreto completed eight informaciones in one year and fourteen in the other. By contrast, in 1609, they completed forty-nine, and the annual number had grown ever since. San Vincente had looked it up; no one could argue with the math. To make matters worse, the notaries were conducting the investigations for the genealogies "in their own lands." Sometimes, they neglected to include crucial information that would have disqualified the candidates, such as "having a Jew for a father."[63] While San Vincente did not come out with it explicitly, the implication was clear: the notaries were acting as patrons in their local districts for inquisitorial jobs. Who knew what sort of clients they were attracting or how many bribes they were taking?

Logroño's inquisitors must have suspected that San Vincente was writing once more to the Suprema. They wrote their own lengthy defense on April 3, two days after San Vincente's letter left the tribunal. Their letter quoted verbatim from San Vincente's letter of January 19 as they attempted to refute the claims of their own prosecutor. They ended up misrepresenting the math, explaining away their notaries' absences, and defending those notaries' fees.

In the inquisitors' version of history, the tribunal's notaries del secreto had produced 161 reports on qualifications for employment since 1606, which worked out to a mere twenty-four a year. They thereby attempted to erase the staggering increase offered by San Vincente. Furthermore, the inquisitors said their notaries used the genealogical investigations as a cover for other, more secretive errands: the notaries went out "to give a cloak and concealment to other legal business," and they were reimbursed for a portion of their costs in the genealogical work. No one in the district was paid sufficiently for inquisitorial labor; the notaries del secreto usually went out with at least a servant or a horse, which they could not do without.[64] As a result of the district's poverty and its low salaries, the inquisitors allowed their notaries to carry out certain genealogical investigations so that they could recoup what they had to spend.

The inquisitors then pointed out that their notaries del secreto had worked around the clock for two solid years in pursuit of witches, with no time off.[65] Out of "consideration for their continuous work and exhaustion, and to alleviate it," the inquisitors had given them permission at other times to leave the tribunal to pursue genealogies.[66] If the notaries had amplified the hours and days that they were working, "we have understood it to be on account of the extreme labor they have undertaken, given that they have occupied themselves all day and most of the night" with the continuous work of the tribunal. They were so expert at their job that they achieved more in one day than commissioners and familiars did in three.

Of course, any assertion that notaries had been "occupied . . . all day and most of the night" with the tribunal's work contradicted mightily the charge by San Vincente that these crucial employees were routinely absent for two, three, or four months at a time. Ignoring that discrepancy, inquisitors Becerra, Valle, and Salazar then threw their prosecutor under the proverbial bus. They had merely inherited the tradition of the notaries' departures.[67] It was the tribunal's prosecutor—meaning, San Vincente—who actually paid the notaries. The prosecutor was obliged to tell the inquisitors about any abuses so that they could be fixed. The inquisitors had always paid attention to the length of the journeys, the conditions on the ground, the workload, and the number of witnesses examined each day by their notaries. They had modified their employees' salaries accordingly and always in consultation with the prosecutor. If transgressions were still happening, it was the prosecutor's responsibility to fix it.[68]

Then, Becerra, Valle, and Salazar breezily accounted for the other critiques. They had no idea that any of their notaries' write-ups was inferior. If a notary counted nine days away as thirty-one, it was because he was "counting the same days for each party from whom he received information." Inquisitor Valle thought the recent absence of notary Currillo was actually thirteen days only . . . or perhaps it was twelve. As for the idea that there were never any notaries del secreto in the tribunal, there once was an occasion when notary Francisco Pardo was absent and then notary Currillo fell ill: the inquisitors had to make up the difference by bringing in the notary who handled the sequestration of property.[69] The notaries never left without an order from the tribunal. If, once gone, they became delayed, "it seems to us that it was not on account of greed, or a desire to defraud the tribunal from the time they should have been present, since once they returned, they achieved in one day what would have been sufficient work for two or three." Becerra, Valle, and Salazar had to admit that a year ago, Becerra had learned that there had been "an altercation between the prosecutor [San Vincente] and Francisco Pardo de la Fuente, the most senior notary, over writing down the absences in the necessary book. Pardo de la Fuente had ripped out a leaf from the book of absences because the prosecutor had made the entry in his own hand, with Pardo de la Fuente saying that it wasn't the prosecutor's business to do so but the responsibility of the oldest notary."[70] In front of San Vincente, Becerra had reprimanded the notaries for such negligence and warned them of their obligation to enter all the absences on time.

The inquisitors continued to dismiss the charges. Though they had carefully looked over the book of absences, they could not actually find any signs that a leaf had been ripped out. They possessed an administrative order (*carta acordada*) from April 1577 that stipulated that each investigation into a potential inquisition familiar should cost six reales, though that sum didn't include the written directive to carry out the work or writing down the interrogatories for the witnesses or the general, written directives that had to be given to the regular commissioners. Currently the tribunal was authorizing a cost of twelve reales for each witness, six reales for each commission that entailed an interrogatory for investigation, and four reales for writing down instructions that had to be given to the commissioners. The three inquisitors "believe[d] these prices were in conformity with the inquisition tribunal in Valladolid," which was the center of government for King Philip III.[71] Becerra, Valle, and Salazar closed their defense by praising their notaries del secreto: they were "very honorable and peaceful; good role models; well-born and noble people, and without them we couldn't have handled even one-quarter of the cases we've processed over the last four years." They then acknowledged that they would receive the correction that the inquisitor-general had given them "with all submission and humility" and promised to obey the executive order about their notaries del secreto not leaving the tribunal.

These explanations were not enough. Six weeks later, on May 17, 1612, the Suprema wrote to censure Logroño's inquisitors for having violated the executive order in the first place.[72] Each inquisitor would be fined two hundred reales, which had to be turned over immediately to the receiver of sequestered property. Henceforth, no notary del secreto would ever leave the Logroño tribunal to receive information about lower inquisition employees without permission from the Suprema. The inquisitors were ordered to pass along this information to the notaries, who henceforth would receive nothing for any accounts they might compose, and who would be punished rigorously if they disobeyed.[73] The Suprema went further. It ordered the tribunal to carry out an accounting of the relaciones completed by the notaries del secreto. Retroactively, those notaries would only receive five hundred maravedís a day for that work; to recompense their victims, their salaries would be reduced. The tribunal's receiver of sequestered property would take charge of the extra monies.

Perhaps not surprisingly, given the distance between Madrid and Logroño, the entrenchment of the notaries del secreto in their local environments, and the combative relationship among the inquisitors, nothing improved. One more letter from San Vincente survives, which he sent to the Suprema on July 13, 1612.[74] The adjectives he used to describe the tribunal are telling: "agitated," "embittered," "excessive." Officials there, including the notaries, "were wanting to avenge their personal hatreds." Things were worsening every day, and there was no hope of a remedy unless the Suprema and the inquisitor-general ordered a visitation of the tribunal itself. The notaries del secreto were still leaving; San Vincente wrote, "it would be a lesser evil if they all had concubines and received bribes." He closed by asking the inquisitor-general to "have a page write to him, once this letter has been received."

At this point, San Vincente seems to disappear from the historical record.[75] By November 3, 1612, the Suprema had agreed to lift the fines it had levied against Logroño's inquisitors, who apologized to the inquisitor-general for the "disagreements and arguments" they had with one other.[76] They wanted to reassure their superiors that their interactions were greatly improved. They had received the reprimand "with submission, and acknowledgement that it is reasonable." They found themselves "with great feeling and pain for having given Your Lordship trouble with our disagreements, which we will try to the best of our ability to stop, so that there may be the concord that Your Lordship demands."[77] A week later, on November 10, 1612, the inquisitors allowed a petition from the notaries del secreto to go forward to the Suprema. There, the notaries begged for an increase in their salaries. On five hundred maravedís a day, they had become poor and were unable to buy food for their households; they needed two ducats. The inquisitors endorsed their request.[78]

The new evidence about Logroño's notaries is stunning. It illustrates once more the potential futility of commands issued from Madrid and received elsewhere. It demonstrates another instance of the inquisitors' inability to control their own employees, even ones who worked in the same physical space. It shows that these inquisitors were willing to lie; it reflects a consistent level of neglect on their part, given that their carelessness had gone on for years. Most importantly, revelations about the notaries could have had an effect on the Suprema. Those notaries were charged with manipulating depositions about the qualifications of commissioners and familiars. If such were true, then the inquisitors could have hired individuals with what the culture viewed as dishonorable backgrounds; they would have damaged the status of their tribunal accordingly. Yet the primary responsibility of the notaries del secreto was the faithful transcription of statements spoken under oath by defendants and witnesses who were being examined by inquisitors, or by prosecution and defense attorneys. It is not a stretch to think that the Suprema might have linked the notaries' irresponsibility when away from the tribunal to the activities they performed within the tribunal. If those secretaries were willing to occlude and falsify in one situation, what was keeping them from doing the same in another? What might they have done with the depositions given in witch trials? Moreover, if they were never in place to take down testimony in the first place—for San Vincente had said they could be gone as long as four months—what might that mean? In March 1611, Salazar told the inquisitor-general that the tribunal had hired a "bunch of assistant copyists." Though the tribunal was ordered to let those not-fully-trained copyists go, could it have kept them on? How was the Suprema supposed to square San Vincente's assertion that the notaries were gone from two, three, or four months at a time with the inquisitors' insistence that the same employees had worked around the clock for two years in pursuit of the witches?

In short, the correspondence about the notaries throughout 1612 gave the inquisitor-general and the Suprema further cause to wonder about the reliability of the inquisitors' legal processes and legal documents. By October 1613, Becerra and Valle had forwarded their arguments against Salazar, and Salazar had followed with an explicit tally of the tribunal's multiple instances of noncompliance and legal lapses. At that point, the inquisition's hierarchy apparently became convinced that they needed to take drastic action.

Salazar in Madrid

By January 1614, Salazar was posted to the inquisition tribunal in Jaén, in Andalucía—a location almost as far away as possible from Logroño while still being in Spain. Presumably, the Suprema sent him there. In March 1614, that council asked Salazar to come to Madrid, where he remained until the end of August.[79] Over those five months, he consulted with the Suprema about how to resolve the witch situation in Navarre. It seems very likely that Salazar was summoned into this role because of his lengthy relationship with Inquisitor-General Sandoval. He had worked for Sandoval from 1595 to 1598, when Sandoval was the bishop of Jaén; Sandoval had put Salazar into an inquisition post to begin with, in 1609. Salazar had been willing over the previous two years to relay his tribunal's legal and supervisory failings to the Suprema. Finally, Salazar had echoed in his own memos the opinions of Bishop Venegas, now dead, about the bias of inquisitors Becerra and Valle.

The last document that Salazar handed over to the council in 1614 about the Navarrese witch hunt has never been thoroughly assessed. The text is astonishing in terms of its recognition and acceptance of the other legal jurisdictions, awareness of fault, and pastoral impulses.[80] The memorandum began by noting how urgently Navarre needed a remedy for the witch hunt; it then said, "Inquisitor Licentiate Alonso de Salazar Frías holds as appropriate the following measures." First, all the inquisition commissioners should make clear to everyone the pain and horror the inquisition has had over the "serious violent acts with which lower secular officials and relatives induced the criminals" (i.e., the confessed witches and witnesses). The commissioners should point out to everyone that these violent acts only became known because the royal court of Navarre began to punish the offenders—in other words, inquisition employees would now publicize information about the inquisition's ignorance and praise the actions of a different legal jurisdiction. Salazar's memo stipulated that no one should ever obstruct the secular court, whether by legal or extralegal means. Henceforth, the inquisition would carry out a "stern demonstration" against anyone who interfered in any way. Next, any inquisition employees who appeared to have taken part in the terror and violence should be called to the Logroño tribunal, where the appropriate punishment would occur and trials would be conducted. Here, Salazar singled out Lorenzo Hualde of Bera, along with unnamed commissioners of Echeverría and Maestu.[81] We have no evidence that such confrontations or prosecutions ever occurred, but then, all the tribunal's records were destroyed in the early nineteenth century.

Salazar was explicitly concerned about the care of souls in the witch hunt's aftermath. He consequently affirmed that the ability to revoke a witchcraft confession should be publicized widely. Priests and rectors should be warned not to prohibit parishioners from the sacraments if the latter had been victims of extrajudicial violence; assuming the priests and rectors had been in residence, the fact of abuse would be relatively easy to ascertain. Then there was the matter of legal and social redress. All the trials and investigations about witchcraft currently underway in the Logroño tribunal should be suspended and never taken up again. No witch relaxed or reconciled at the November 1610 auto de fe should have sambenitos placed in their parish churches or anywhere else: the inquisition had a precedent for omitting sambenitos in other witchcraft cases.[82] Moreover, no witch's property should be confiscated, even if the sentences at the auto de fe had said as much. For the witches who had died in the tribunal's jails, whose cases were not finished, no prosecutor should ever pursue their trials, and their heirs should not be stained with the dishonor of their relatives' imprisonment and prosecution: such news should be given to every child and relative of the prosecuted. When it came to the two clerics sentenced in the auto de fe for witchcraft— Pedro de Arburu and Juan de la Borda—Salazar insisted that any part of their sentences relating to reclusion, suspension, or exile that they had yet to complete should be lifted. In their cases, they too should not be prevented from receiving honors because of their inquisition trials.

Salazar laid out as well new processes for inquisitors and their employees to follow where witches were concerned. For people who appeared spontaneously to make a witchcraft confession about themselves or to accuse others, their statements must be written down literally and promptly, with any and all imperfections recorded. This point may have reflected the corrupt practices of the tribunal's notaries, though Salazar did not elaborate. He then recommended that any spontaneous confessions received in the Logroño tribunal should be dispatched in a kindly manner, without delay, imprisonment, or confiscation of goods. When people appeared before commissioners in the field to spontaneously confess, those inquisition employees should write down what they heard and send it on to the tribunal. The tribunal in turn would then order the commissioners to reconcile or absolve the confessants; those employees in the field would not have to consult further with anyone unless there were extraordinary circumstances that demanded it.

Significantly, Salazar ultimately seemed to favor erasing witchcraft investigations from all inquisitors' edicts of visitation, everywhere. He wrote, "once it is verified that the interrogation and clause about witches have been erased in the edicts of visitation that other inquisition tribunals publish, so too should it be erased [in such edicts] from the inquisition in Logroño, so that the tribunal is brought into conformity."[83] He ended by recommending that all the inquisition instructions on witchcraft should be gathered into a single bundle, whereupon they could be copied and always kept on hand. This "new order," or way of proceeding, should be made obvious to every inquisition employee. Never again should anyone be confused or mistaken in what to do where witches were concerned. Salazar thus implied that literally everyone attached to the Logroño tribunal had potentially or actually been in a state of error as the witch hunt proceeded, including himself.

New Instructions: 1614

When the Suprema issued its new mandates on witchcraft on August 29, 1614, its directives reflected what its members had learned about the Logroño tribunal over the previous three years. From January 1609 through the first two months of 1611, the Suprema had consistently supported the tribunal's efforts with witch suspects, even as it declined to offer additional financial help. But in its 1614 instructions, the Suprema began with a direct rebuke. It wrote that its members "had studied all the judicial reports [apuntamientos] and warnings, with your discordant opinions [vuestros pareceres en discordia]." The council continued, "this is such serious business, and [you knew] how much the cases you dispatched mattered to us, especially those of the auto de fe [of November 1610]." The Suprema had previously surveyed all the orders as well as the old and new instructions on witchcraft that the inquisition's registers contained; it also knew about the ill-treatment and violent acts that relatives, local justices, and neighbors had carried out against "some of the criminals [reos] marked with this sect." The Suprema noted that, "even without the other flaws that might be found in the trials," the council well understood the serious harm the violence had provoked, because it "obscured even further the truth that we have sought in such grueling and difficult-to-prove material, as witchcraft always has been."[84] The Suprema's insinuations here would not have been lost on any of Logroño's inquisitors. The latter had bombarded the Suprema with their own conflicts and contrary readings of the evidence. The inquisitors had ignored defects in their own proceedings and persisted in the sentences they delivered against the witch suspects in the November 1610 auto de fe. Witchcraft cases were terribly difficult to prove under the best of circumstances, even without local violence and employee misconduct. In this instance, inquisitors Becerra, Valle, and Salazar had failed in their professional, legal, and ethical obligations.

After its opening reprimand, the Suprema's recommendations did not move through a logical trajectory of topics. The document contains thirty-two separate instructions, which zigzag between areas to be investigated, actions that inquisitors in Logroño should specifically undertake, and future requirements that all inquisitors should follow.[85] Salazar's suggestion that the heresy of witchcraft be omitted from edicts of visitation was ignored:

instead, the first six points of the Suprema's list concern proving whether the witches' actions really occurred, which demonstrates both tradition and the possibility that Becerra's and Valle's October 1613 report had an impact.

Notably, in 1614, the Suprema never advanced the position that all witches' supposed activities were fantasy. Instead, it told its inquisitors to investigate the deaths of infants and adults to see if "they had been sick beforehand, or sustained an accident, or died naturally or violently; experts should be consulted." Next, inquisitors should carefully survey accused witches' houses to see the means by which they entered and left and whether anyone might have opened or closed the windows and doors. They should inquire into whether the accused "really go to their fields and meetings, and whether anyone who is not a witch saw them in their meetings during the night or day."[86] The inquisitors should then turn their attention to the deaths of livestock and talk to the owners about any possible demonic signs on the animals' bodies. As far as agricultural losses were concerned, did the damage occur in winter, when it might have hailed or snowed? Was ice a factor? If individuals thought witches had created storms, inquisitors should ask whether the time of the year could explain the event. Finally, the Suprema told its inquisitors to caution preachers, either in person or through their commissioners, to stop tying every natural disaster to witches. Storms and agricultural losses "are sent on account of our sins, or through the condition of the weather." It was a real problem when people imagined that adversities were caused only by witchcraft.

The Suprema also detailed what procedures to follow and put limits on the extrapolation of guilt. When people appeared spontaneously to confess to witchcraft, "their style, language, and contradictions should be written down exactly."[87] This point could have been a swipe at the notaries del secreto as well as recognition that the inquisitors had neglected exactly that sort of care. As of 1614, the Suprema stipulated that inquisition commissioners would only take down testimony and depositions before a notary where witch suspects were concerned. Afterwards, those employees must immediately send their materials to the tribunal; they could not investigate or take any other action until and unless the inquisitors told them to do so. Inquisitors should not imprison or condemn anyone on the word of another suspect without further inquiry. In each tribunal, the inquisitors as a body should agree upon the investigations to be undertaken and discuss their opinions, after which they should transmit their findings to the Suprema.[88] Inquisition leaders clearly were seeking to guarantee the accuracy of legal records, rein in the independence of commissioners and inquisitors, and mandate that inquisitors collaborate.

In its 1614 instructions, the Suprema was determined to ferret out coercion. People who appeared spontaneously to confess to witchcraft "shall be asked why they were moved to make such a confession, and whether they have been persuaded, frightened, or forced." If people testified against others, the inquisitors should be sure to investigate whether the witnesses had "some enmity against the accused." Inquisitors should ask men and women who appeared before them, and who were of legitimate age—fourteen for men, twelve for women—whether they had in fact gone to the akelarres, revered the Devil, and actually denied God and their own baptisms. They should be asked how many years they had apostatized. They should be quizzed as to whether they had "persisted during the day, while awake, with clear deliberation, in adoring the Devil and separating themselves from the Catholic faith that they received in baptism."[89] The inspiration for these points clearly came from Bishop Venegas's correspondence and Hernando Solarte's and Salazar's reports. The Suprema then laid out the same remedies it had placed in the edict of grace. For those confessants who said under re-interrogation that they had traveled to the akelarre while awake, but had not persevered in apostasy, inquisitors should cure their souls with absolution as a precaution, "in the way that was done with the Dutch and the Scots who come to [Spain's] ports."[90] The same absolution should be applied in general to those younger than fourteen and twelve.

In another nod to Salazar, Venegas, and Solarte, the Suprema adjured their officials to behave like shepherds with sheep. Henceforth, inquisitors as well as their employees must receive the accused with "complete softness" (*toda blandura*). They must proceed with "words of love and charity" in every imaginable encounter with witch suspects.[91] Anyone who wished to revoke a witchcraft confession should be received in such a way that fear would not prevent them from discharging their consciences. Theoretically, no commissioner or inquisitor could now verbally abuse the accused or threaten them with burning for trying to revoke; rather, revocations always must be accepted. No priest should deny the sacraments to suspects. Instead, the commissioners should inform local clerics that the Eucharist must be administered to accused and confessed witches, until the inquisition should order something different.[92] Logroño's inquisitors should verbally warn the commissioners that they must proceed with moderation and restraint and not take any steps beyond what these new instructions relayed.

Remarkably—or not, given the evidence at their disposal—the Suprema essentially nullified the inquisitorial documents created during the witch hunt. In points nineteen through thirty-two of the new instructions, the Suprema labeled as suspended *all* the testimonies and proofs of witchcraft that Becerra, Valle, and Salazar had collected: none of those writings could ever provoke a trial against anyone. As for the accused witches who had died in the tribunal's jail, the status of their cases should be left as it was at the time of their deaths, without any prosecutor ever being able to start the prosecutions once more. In these instances, unlike trials for judaizing, the inquisitors would no longer be able to prosecute the dead.

Other details of the 1614 instructions implicitly highlighted the failings of the Logroño tribunal and exacted a sort of retroactive, bureaucratic punishment on the inquisitors. For example, the Suprema told the inquisitors to go back through their records in order to clarify which testimonies and confessions had been induced by violence or were laden with other defects that should diminish their credibility. Given the quantity of documentation and the range of failings that could have been involved—inaccurate transcriptions, junior copyists, contradictions among witnesses, and so on—this would have been a daunting task. Notably, the Suprema commanded the tribunal to compile a report of all the expenses it had incurred in "verifying, discovering, and inquiring into these crimes." The inquisitors also had to come up with a list of goods that had been confiscated or sequestered, "so that the Suprema may determine and order what should be done with them."[93] The tribunal had consistently pleaded poverty from 1609 through 1613, but given what the Suprema had learned about the notaries, the question of fraud loomed large.

The Suprema was equally determined to overturn sentences and dissolve shame. Persons who had died at the stake in the 1610 auto de fe, as well as those reconciled there, would never have sambenitos placed in churches or see their goods confiscated. The council repeatedly emphasized that children or other relatives of accused, confessed, or prosecuted witches would always be eligible for honorable offices, including inquisitorial ones. The restoration of honor to the witches' families implied that they were innocent and that the inquisitors and their employees had consistently erred in their investigations.

Thus over 1612 and 1613, the leaders of the Spanish Inquisition became worried about the legitimacy of the documents produced in this witch hunt. They had all sorts of reasons to be doubtful. Ultimately, and in agreement with Salazar, the Suprema could not know for certain what had been proven where the witches were concerned. Lapses at every level of the inquisitorial process led the Suprema to cancel every aspect of the five years of investigation. Unfortunately for us, the Suprema did not tie its new instructions to specific points of information. But its mandates become that much more comprehensible when we combine evidence of local violence in the villages with allegations against the notaries, and then with Salazar's charges of procedural misconduct in the tribunal.

Toward the end of the new instructions, the Suprema took up questions of prevention and jurisdiction. Logroño's inquisitors must publicize throughout their district that no one, not even parents and relatives, should induce, threaten, or force anyone into a witchcraft confession made in the Holy Office. The tribunal should call in the commissioners at different times, in order to avoid scandal, and express to them "the rightful pain that the Inquisition, and especially the Suprema, feels toward the violence and vexations carried out by local justices, who had no jurisdiction to act in that way, and who weren't acting as justices, but as private persons." The tribunal should tell the commissioners that while punishment for those local justices should rest with the inquisition, the inquisition would not take the measures it could rightly pursue because the royal court of Navarre was now handling the cases. With that statement, the Suprema explicitly endorsed the justice being administered by Pamplona's secular court. To intensify its expression of confidence, the Suprema warned Logroño's inquisitors "[to] leave that royal court alone, as well as any other [legal] jurisdiction, so that those courts may proceed and punish these offenses without impediment."[94] At the same time, the Suprema noted that in the future, the inquisitors would exert rigorous punishment against anyone who acted violently toward witch suspects. The commissioners should understand that possibility and communicate it to their districts. Of course, the Suprema's threat applied to everyone, including inquisition employees at every level.

Yet despite its warnings, the Suprema also extended a sort of armistice when it came to local violence. If villagers confessed to parish priests or friars that they had committed atrocities against witch suspects, those clerics should advise them to appear before Logroño's inquisitors or an inquisition commissioner. The clergy should assure such penitents that "although they may have committed some excesses, at this point they will not be given any penalty or bother, because the inquisitors [will presume] that they had acted in that way out of zeal for the service of God." It was important that such people declare their sins to discharge their consciences and to restore honor to those whom they had accused and assaulted. If they ever behaved in such a vicious way again, however, the inquisition "would proceed against them as disturbers and obstructers of the correct and independent actions of the Holy Office."[95]

With such directives, the inquisition's leadership opened a route to forgiveness and community stability through the local clergy, while simultaneously publicizing that it would step in if more abuse arose. The council ultimately clarified that the Spanish Inquisition was going to take the judicial lead henceforth in matters of violence against witch suspects, though it was willing at this moment in time to allow other legal jurisdictions to operate without interference. The Suprema's directives were thus remarkably nuanced in terms of privilege and precedence.

The instructions of 1614 closed with a comment about speech. The council had "seen the difficulties that have arisen from talking and conferring [about witches], with everyone dividing into factions, and carrying out particular measures to verify what each one believed."[96] Henceforth, the Suprema ordered silence about witchcraft in the communities of Navarre.[97] Commissioners and confessors should be told that the topic only could be discussed when people were clearing their consciences. Before and after such statements, everyone "must preserve toward this crime the prudence and secrecy that pertains to all other matters of the Holy Office." Following Salazar's suggestion, the Suprema finally noted that all of the inquisition's instructions and letters on witchcraft should be collated, copied, and made available for inquisitors who might encounter other cases.

An End . . . or Not?

The resolution of this witch hunt thus occurred via multiple routes and involved many actors. The persecution unquestionably had more witches' advocates than earlier researchers realized, from the highest religious and legal authorities to lawyers who defended torture victims to villagers who testified for witch suspects. Bishop Venegas was both respectful and independent; perhaps his professional experience as an inquisitor and his standing as a higher ecclesiastic gave him the confidence to cross jurisdictional lines. He unquestionably persuaded his peers on the Suprema that he knew what he was talking about and then advised Salazar as the latter began his visitation. While in the field, Salazar gradually came to sever, in certain instances, the routine legal connection between confession and proof as he learned about local cruelties. When he wrote to the Suprema in March 1612, he stressed the difficulty of proving the witches' deeds via the human senses of sight, sound, and touch. When his colleagues responded with a report of their own, Salazar countered by divulging the tribunal's flagrant legal errors and his colleagues' presumptions. All the while, the episcopal and secular legal jurisdictions were hunting down and prosecuting witch torturers, and such actions were only possible because ordinary people knew how to deploy the higher courts.

With its new instructions of 1614, the Suprema was attempting to restore a chain of command that had come apart in this witch hunt. Its corrections came without a word of doubt about the possible reality of witchcraft. As for Salazar, in yet one more summary, he framed the problem as one of deductive versus inductive reasoning. His inquisitor-colleagues said that witchcraft really happened in Navarre; they asserted that all their witch suspects were guilty of diabolical worship. In contrast, Salazar preferred to say, "although a great deal of it may be possible, none of the papers [we have amassed] persuade as much." Salazar never said that witchcraft could never be real. Rather, he said he suspected that many of the inquisition's witch suspects in 1608–14 were not truly witches, given the Devil's ability and motives to deceive and harm the Christian community.[98] All three inquisitors started from the point that the Devil was an enemy of mankind, and never wavered from that truism. Where they differed was in their preference to move from idea to observation (Becerra and Valle) or from observation to idea (Salazar).[99]

As to whether legal actions and collaborations ever doused the village infernos produced by this persecution, the evidence is mixed. For example, a series of three notarial documents demonstrates that the economic position and social status of Sabadina de Zozaya did not shift after she was tortured over witchcraft accusations in Arraioz in 1611. Sabadina and her family were wealthy before the abuse and remained so afterwards. The last will and testament of Sabadina's husband, Tristant de Ursúa, was recorded on September 24, 1614.[100] Ursúa was described as very ill and bedridden but of sound mind and judgment. In standard language, Ursúa commended his soul to God, the Blessed Virgin Mary, and all the saints, in the hope that they would defend him in heavenly court. He wanted his body buried in the parish church. He listed two debts to be repaid from his estate. Meanwhile, he had made many small loans to others that should be collected, and he deputized friends and relatives to seek out those repayments. He then listed his current livestock: he and Sabadina owned a horse and a young colt, along with fourteen sows and one pig; they also owned some goats and forty-four sheep, one of which belonged to their son-in-law. Ursúa made Sabadina his sole heir and then formally disinherited his three daughters, who would keep their dowries and the "things he has given them." The daughters could make no further claims on his estate; Tristant named Sabadina as his executor. Such steps with heirs were routine.

By mid-October 1614, Tristant de Ursúa had died, and Juan de Zubieta, one of Ursúa's sons-in-law, appeared before notaries to record that his wife's dowry had been paid in full.[101] That dowry had consisted of 160 ducats, half to be paid in coin and half in livestock, plus a heifer and a sow. His wife had come to him with two beds. If Juan were to die prematurely, his wife's entire dowry would return to her; if his wife died, he would pay for her funeral expenses out of her dowry and return the rest to Sabadina de Zozaya, her mother. Finally, on May 17, 1615, Sabadina herself appeared before a notary in Arraioz to claim an inheritance. Sabadina relayed that she had a nephew named Antonio de Zozaya, who was a surgeon in the Indies, age thirty-six.[102] It had come to her attention that he had died in Zacatecas in New Spain, where he had left money and a household worth fourteen thousand pesos. Antonio had made his aunt Sabadina his heir, in recognition of the "good services she did for him while he was in Navarre, and what she has spent on burials and novenas . . . and [the good services] for his parents, and the daily offerings she made for them in church." Sabadina recognized that as a "woman, a widow, and being very aged, she could not go in person to Zacatecas in New Spain," and so she authorized two men there to find and convey her nephew's property to her. The terrible treatment that Sabadina suffered in 1611 seemingly had no permanent effects on her marriage, the marriageability of her daughters, or her household's wealth.

Other sources tell a different story. Some census records suggest that the witch hunt had significant effects on the populations of already small villages. For example, in June 1606, Olague had twenty-four legal households, whose owners all lived there. We know the owners were in residence because the census required the heads of household to take an oath to disclose their individual net worth, and people who were absent would have been noted: none was. Six years later, in July 1612, the census was administered once more. Olague's legal heads of household again agreed to state their wealth after taking oaths to "declare how much their houses would rent for." Yet out of the twenty-six households listed in 1612, almost one-third of those residences—eight—could be rented for only a single ducat because their owners were missing.[103]

Even more shocking were the censuses taken in Arraioz in the Valle de Baztan. In February 1607, Arraioz had twenty-eight houses, with all their owners present. In summer 1612, Arraioz had grown to thirty-six houses, but it appears that only nine owners were present: the rest "could not be found for this declaration."[104] The demographic shifts that Olague and Arraioz suffered could have been provoked by enmity, dishonor, or financial ruin over witchcraft accusations. Both villages endured significant witchhunting; both also experienced secular prosecutions for the verbal slander and physical abuse of witch suspects. The fact that so many of their citizens bolted speaks to the dysfunctional effects of this persecution.

Finally, there are signs that memories of this witch hunt remained potent for Navarre's villagers. For example, one investigator has ventured that a foundational printed text for Basque prose, titled *Gero* (1643), was the "work of a survivor who wished to amend the injury" incurred by the witch hunt decades earlier. Written by a priest named Pedro Agerre, known as Axular, *Gero* was styled as a guide for sinners. While Axular's text never mentions witchcraft, eleven of its sixty chapters are dedicated to anger, and the metaphor of burning by fire occurs everywhere. Axular wrote, "Death and life, war and peace are in the power of the tongue. . . . If you throw water on your enemy by speaking gently and sweetly, the fire will be extinguished, and hatred soothed."[105] The power of speech had not diminished thirty-five years after the witch hunt began.

As a different kind of memorial act, the significance of writing things down also demonstrates the impact of this witch persecution. In January 1616, more than a year after the formal end to the witch hunt, inquisition commissioner Leon de Araníbar wrote again to the tribunal that still employed him. He had just received the 1614 instructions. He reported that twenty-six residents of Zugarramurdi wanted their names written in a deposition that stated they had never been witches; he consequently submitted a document to Logroño that contained twenty-six revocations.[106] The text Araníbar sent no longer exists, but the fact that so many individuals insisted upon written verification of their Christian orthodoxy attests the continuing emotional, religious, and social havoc generated by this witch hunt. The poignancy of Araníbar's message was acute. The illiterate villagers' demand that their names be written down speaks to the trust that they continued to place in legal documents, even as the outcome of the witch hunt demonstrated that the Spanish Inquisition's legal processes merited a dose of skepticism.

The witch hunt that Navarre experienced from 1608 to 1614 is one of the most famous witchcraft episodes in European history, and understandably so. The sources analyzed here are intended to deepen our understanding of this witch persecution and daily life in early modern Europe in multiple ways. The persecution of witches over this six-year period should be framed as fundamentally a children's event, given that boys and girls predominated as victims and accusers, and parental terror vis-à-vis their offspring was an all-consuming factor in village violence. In this witch hunt, children fundamentally changed the lives of many adults. They both accepted and rejected the narratives of their elders; in some instances, they acted as a group for collective purposes. This persecution also raises questions as to how Navarrese villagers imagined their responsibilities toward the much younger people in their midst. In court, adults testified that they suspected other grownups of menacing youngsters into witchcraft confessions and accusations, and yet those adults never intervened while the threats were occurring. Moreover, the kinds of dangers the children reported provoke further wonder: Did children really believe they could have been clubbed to death by their neighbors, without any protection from their community? Familial and neighborly values in Navarre in the early seventeenth century were complicated, and they bewildered certain contemporaries as well. While the secular and episcopal legal jurisdictions understood fairly quickly that fears over dishonor could provoke false confessions, inside the Logroño inquisition tribunal, only

Salazar came to realize how far families would go to protect their reputations and possessions.

At the same time, Navarrese standards of honor were constantly calibrated, depending upon a shifting assessment of risk. While harmful, admission to witchcraft in a village was seen as far better than appearing before inquisitors in Logroño: ergo, it could become a parental responsibility to persuade a child or teenager into a confession, with or without violence. Yet teenagers and adults also fled their homes to avoid being accused, and husbands left wives—perhaps temporarily—over public suspicions and public torture. Grown men who were accused said they would have to go on pilgrimage to avoid their neighbors' contempt; the slur of "witch" was so severe that villagers responded with more slander, even though they knew the legal peril of doing so and died as a result. This study brings to the forefront questions of honor vis-à-vis age and gender. It illustrates self-defensive maneuvers that were embedded in community values.

This witch hunt turned life upside down. Upright women contemplated and carried out torture and murder. Five-year-olds became conduits to the spiritual world as they interacted with the Devil and found support from the Virgin Mary. Honorable men and women were imprisoned in private houses, tortured for weeks and sometimes months, and then excluded from receiving the sacraments. Children who appeared to be in bed were not really there. The Devil invaded the secret prisons and the house of penitence owned by the Spanish Inquisition to have sex with and threaten the accused; the Devil and his followers assassinated inquisitorial employees and their child relatives. This Devil and these witches inverted Catholic Christianity in every respect. The Devil demanded and rewarded apostasy and evil works; his witches no longer feared hell and proclaimed their loyalty to his congregation. The witches' confessions examined here illustrate the possible push-pull between an inquisitorial template and individual creativity. The witches' statements also exhibit a dynamism between the performance of psychic content already formed, and the development of a limited, temporary, or full-fledged witch identity while under community pressure or inquisitorial interrogation.[1]

The language of spiritual combat became a leitmotif over these six years of accusations, confessions, sentences, and retractions, even as the sources sometimes reveal social tensions at the root of denunciations. In fact, this witch hunt was a religious event with profound spiritual consequences for those involved. Accused witches of all ages and sexes spoke at length about their despair. Salazar believed the Devil intentionally produced the religious anguish he saw on his visitation in 1611; he was guilt-ridden over his initial inability to hear revocations of confessions. Bishop Venegas and Inquisitor-General Sandoval bemoaned the danger to so many souls; Inquisitors Becerra and Valle railed against the royal and episcopal courts for endangering Christianity through their prosecutions of witch torturers.

While Bishop Venegas and Inquisitor-General Sandoval promoted the idea that these witch beliefs came from printed pamphlets and the French, they, as well as Logroño's inquisitors, were wrong. All these authorities seem to have known practically nothing about Navarrese traditions of witchcraft, which always identified children as witches' favorite victims and relayed in detail the human and agricultural harm that witches could do. This witch persecution blended popular and elite ideas to produce the shocking paradigm that circulated through the auto de fe of November 1610 and moved through the villages. There was nothing top-down about the use of the courts either, which, remarkably for a frontier space, were within reach of ordinary citizens, albeit ones with some financial means. Individually or in collaboration, Navarrese villagers sought legal remedies for slander, torture, and false confessions as the witch hunt proceeded. They knew perfectly well how to use the law to recover their honor and avenge themselves on their assailants. Their legal dexterity is one of the key revelations of this book. The fact that witchcraft was always an object of interest for the three jurisdictions of secular, episcopal, and inquisitorial law should encourage scholars to look beyond single legal systems when investigating early modern witches in Catholic settings.

When it comes to the Spanish Inquisition and this witch hunt, the setting matters. While I would not go so far as to promote geographical determinism as the cause of this debacle, there is no doubt that the inquisitors in Logroño, their employees, and the people they interrogated experienced profoundly what scholars have called the "tyranny of distance."[2] The chain of command from Madrid to Logroño to Navarre fell apart in this persecution, with dire consequences. The commissioners improvised in the face of villagers' rage; the inquisitors gave up their supervisory roles and funneled messages from their employees to the Suprema without any critical assessment. Commissioners and familiars kept their recommendations and actions secret until investigations by the secular and episcopal courts forced them to divulge what they had done. Far from being an effective bureaucracy, the inquisition in this episode was fragmented and diffident, with its employees pursuing different tracks simultaneously.[3] New evidence about the tribunal's notaries just cements the impression of incompetence.

The Spanish Inquisition was one of the few state institutions to pervade all of Spain in this period. Yet it could barely achieve its own objectives or manage its own employees in this witch hunt. Its actions here demonstrate why we should emphasize "early" when we think about the early modern state.[4] Not one of the key characters in this study was demoted or fired for having gone off script; not surprisingly, given what we know about bureaucracies in this period, patronage continued to rule.[5] Licentiate Hualde, familiar Narbarte, and commissioner Aranıbar kept their inquisitorial jobs, or so the evidence indicates. Inquisitor Valle continued in the Logroño tribunal until his death in 1615.[6] Becerra became a member of the Suprema in Madrid in October 1613; he died in 1619.[7] Salazar too remained in the inquisitorial network. He was transferred to the inquisition tribunal of Murcia in 1618 and to the tribunal in Valencia the following year. In 1622, he returned to Logroño as senior inquisitor. He became the prosecutor for the Suprema in 1628, and then a member of the Suprema in 1631. He died in 1635 at age 71.[8]

As for Salazar's epistemology and priorities, straightforward categories won't work where he is concerned. On the one hand, he conducted forensic experiments while on visitation and came to the conclusion that the ointments and substances he had found were faked. He listened seriously to revocations to witchcraft and was capable of changing his mind. His balancing act between legal precedent, legal instructions, and what he was observing make him part of the intellectual crowd in the Spanish Empire that evaluated the gap between what they were trained to expect vis-à-vis what they were experiencing.[9] Moreover, his willingness to put pastoral values first, and to work with Bishop Venegas in righting a pastoral wrong, demonstrates a conjunction between inquisitorial and episcopal values that we have been told could not exist.[10]

Yet Salazar always obeyed the Suprema's instructions, and he spent years defending himself from having undermined his own inquisition tribunal in Logroño. His legal and pastoral preferences also changed depending upon the circumstances. In 1615, a new witch persecution broke out in Bizkaia. King Philip III deputized a secular judge, Licentiate Francisco de la Puente Aguero, to operate out of Bilbao, Bizkaia's major city; Licentiate Puente was supposed to investigate and punish the malefactors, and the Suprema endorsed his mission. In late 1616, a member of the Society of Jesus, Diego de Medrano, wrote from Bizkaia to ask the Suprema if it would allow accused and confessed witches to be absolved of their heresy during the sacrament of penance when that sacrament was administered by their local priests and confessors. Medrano worried that while Licentiate Puente had appropriately chastised the witches' bodies, their souls were still in danger. Bizkaians would sooner die than appear before the inquisitors in Logroño, but those accused of witchcraft were tainted with heresy and required a remedy.[11]

The Suprema sent the Jesuit's letter to Salazar and his new colleague in Logroño, Dr. Antonio de Aranda, and asked them to respond. Aranda went first. He noted that confessors and local priests in Bizkaia were often incompetent, to the point that sometimes their bishop had removed them from their benefices. Aranda advised instead that Basque-speaking members of the Society of Jesus should be sent into Bizkaia in pairs, to hear confessions and pardon suspects. The local clergy would publicize the Jesuits' presence; they would tell their parishioners that the Jesuits could absolve witches who had confessed as well as people who wished to revoke such confessions. The secular judge appointed by the king should handle the infanticides, agricultural disasters, and popular violence that had occurred. If there were witch suspects who truly had worshipped the Devil, their specific cases should be sent to Logroño's tribunal.[12]

Salazar firmly disagreed. He began by noting how many false confessions to witchcraft had been discovered over the previous years, even after the Suprema's new instructions of 1614.[13] One witch-finder after another had shown up, and they had all been liars.[14] Furthermore, though the Logroño tribunal had followed the 1614 instructions to the letter and had not interfered in any way with the proceedings of secular justice, that jurisdiction had repeatedly committed or covered up serious wrongs. In July 1616, for instance, a woman showed up in the Logroño inquisition tribunal to report that children in her village had named her and other adults as witches. After male neighbors broke down their doors, beat them, and left them for dead, the secular jurisdiction simply put the injured women on trial for witchcraft, "based solely on the words of children."[15]

As for the present situation in Bizkaia, Salazar wrote that there might be relatively little risk in allowing local priests to absolve suspected witches, *if* it could be known with absolute certainty that those suspects were truly penitent. Given previous experience, however, it was likely that many witchcraft confessions would be false, brought on by familial pressure and community violence. People confessing were always going to name others, which in turn spread infamy. Furthermore, if neighbors believed that witches were causing real physical harm in their villages, they would be enraged at seeing suspects absolved by local clerics. Most importantly, Salazar did not believe that any of Bizkaia's local priests and friars who heard witchcraft confessions would be able to maintain secrecy as to what they learned. Salazar wrapped up his extensive comments by noting, "All the old and new instructions that Your Lordship has put in place leave the knowledge and struggle against this crime [of witchcraft] to the inquisition alone, distinct from temporal justice . . . in no way do the two jurisdictions combine over it, ever, just as in these Catholic realms the ecclesiastical and secular jurisdictions never combine in any way, even though in certain cases, they happen to help each other reciprocally."[16] Only Spanish inquisitors had the training and knowledge to discern the truth.[17] Despite pleas over the spiritual risk to various Bizkaians, Salazar told the Suprema not to innovate.[18] Only Spanish inquisitors had the right kind of insight and diligence to hear and absolve heretics. Collaboration with other legal jurisdictions or even other religious figures was moot.

Clearly, Salazar had learned from history: he knew to fear a spiral of offense, dishonor, and lies where witch suspects were concerned. Yet despite having seen the episcopal and secular courts succeed in overturning village wrongs, as well as his own tribunal's judicial and pastoral debacle with witch suspects, he preferred in 1617 to elevate the inquisition's traditional legal privilege and purported legal expertise.[19] Like his superiors on the Suprema who never stopped demanding investigations into whether witchcraft confessions reflected reality, Salazar was ultimately incapable of reimagining his office or abandoning the presuppositions he inherited.

Notes

Introduction

1. Much of this narrative is indebted to Henningsen, *Witches' Advocate*, 30–34, 51–57.

2. For the history of this inquisition tribunal when it was located in Calahorra, see Reguera, *La Inquisición española*.

3. Significantly, as this witch hunt in Navarre began, a corresponding persecution, directed by Bordeaux judge Pierre De Lancre, was underway across the border in the Pays de Labourd. There is evidence that suspected witches on both sides of that border sought safety by fleeing one territory for the other. For the argument that seigneurial ties between the French lord of Urtubi-Alzate and the parish priest of Bera galvanized this witch hunt in Navarre, see Arzak, "Brujería, frontera, y poder."

4. The phrase "auto-da-fe" is Portuguese, while "auto de fe" is Castilian.

5. See the chart in Henningsen, *Witches' Advocate*, 198–200. Out of the thirty-one witches sentenced in 1610, nineteen were female and twelve were male.

6. The 1610 pamphlet by Juan Mongastón is reproduced in Fernández Nieto, *Proceso a la brujería*, 30–72. Other summaries of the auto de fe, written for an inquisitorial audience, are in the Archivo Histórico Nacional (AHN), Sección de la Inquisición (Inqu.), Libro (Lib.) 835, fols. 356r–369v and 385r–420r. Alberola, "El panfleto de don Juan de Mongastón."

7. Henningsen erred in stating that before this witch hunt, "Satanic witchcraft was completely unknown among the Basques": *Salazar Documents*, 48. See Idoate, *La brujería*.

8. Lambert, *Medieval Heresy*. Mark Pegg, in *Corruption of Angels*, has strongly argued that Catharism was a fiction.

9. Fears about witchcraft could be part of Christian religious reform. See Bailey, *Battling Demons*. Edward Peters, in *The Magician, the Witch, and the Law*, explains how the concept of the witch was derived from New Testament descriptions of the Devil, canon law, and ancient and medieval Christians' ideas about sorcery, magic, and superstition.

10. Meseguer Fernández, "El período fundacional (1478–1517)."

11. For the inquisitorial legal process, see Homza, *Spanish Inquisition*, xii–xv, xxii–xxviii.

12. Still, villainous or empathetic motives could enter into trials and sentences. For an example of a malicious prosecution, see Inquisitor-General Fernando de Valdés's pursuit of Archbishop Bartolomé de Carranza in the 1550s: Tellechea Idígoras, *Fray Bartolomé Carranza*, vol. 1. For inquisitors and counselors who tried to help prisoners on the basis of psychological evidence, see Nalle, *Mad for God*, and Homza, "How to Harass an Inquisitor-General."

13. *Maleficium* is the singular Latin noun for a specific act of harmful magic. Multiple acts of harmful magic are *maleficia*.

14. Salazar gave these details to the Suprema in a report dated March 24, 1612. AHN, Inqu., Legajo [Leg.]. 1679, image 237. See note 51 below for instructions on gaining access to the digitized images from this inquisition dossier.

15. As an example of standard procedure, Logroño's inquisitors were instructed in 1595 to go over their visitation records together and to cast votes on what should be done with each suspect. AHN, Inqu., Lib. 1254, fol. 257r.

16. The 1614 instructions are reprinted in Jiménez Montserín, *Introducción a la inquisición española*. Amelang, "Between Doubt and Discretion."

17. This conviction may not be accurate, given that there are sources that document inquisitors' involvement with witchcraft in Gipuzkoa between 1617 and 1623. Those materials are scattered throughout the first fifth of AHN, Inqu., Leg. 1679, but have not yet been studied.

18. Besides Henningsen (b. 1934), the other expert on this witch persecution was Julio Caro Baroja (1914–1995), who was trained as an anthropologist. Caro Baroja's studies of the witch hunt are essential, especially his 1969 article

"De nuevo sobre la historia de brujería," reprinted in his *Inquisición, brujería, y criptojudaismo*, 83–315. There is a hint in Henningsen's preface to *The Witches' Advocate* that he was outflanked by his Spanish colleague after Henningsen discovered Legajo 1679 and told Caro Baroja about it (xxvii–xxviii). Caro Baroja did not mention Henningsen's find or his ongoing research in "De nuevo sobre la historia de brujería."

19. In *Enlightenment on Trial*, Bianca Premo has recently corrected the notion that Spain was too backward to participate in the Enlightenment of the eighteenth century. Also see Kagan, "Prescott's Paradigm"; Hillgarth, *Mirror of Spain, 1500–1700*; and Greer, Mignolo, and Quilligan, *Rereading the Black Legend*.

20. Henningsen and Caro Baroja always portrayed Salazar as ahead of his time in his empiricism. See Henningsen, *Witches' Advocate*, 390; Henningsen, *Salazar Documents*, 82–83, 94–95; and Caro Baroja, "De nuevo sobre la brujería," 8–9. The notion of a witches' advocate has led scholars to look for them elsewhere. See Moreno, "La discrecionalidad de un inquisidor," and Alcoberro Pericay, "Los otros 'abogados de las brujas.'"

21. Julio Caro Baroja lamented the fact that Salazar's position was not recognized and emulated across Europe: see *Las brujas y su mundo*, 184–89.

22. Henningsen found Inqu. Leg. 1679, which consists of some 900 folios, or 1,800 pages, in Madrid's AHN in December 1967. He spent six years reading its contents and believed he was the first person to have studied thoroughly "all available materials": see *Witches' Advocate*, xxvii–xxviii. The problem was the inquisitorial lens through which he was gauging availability and relevancy. In addition, Henningsen accidentally made it more difficult to find his newly discovered sources because he gave titles to the documents in Leg. 1679 that they do

not possess. See *Witches' Advocate*, 452nn5 and 20, for example. For instructions on how to find the now-digitized folios of Leg. 1679, see note 51 below.

23. As a mixed crime that involved heresy and injury, witchcraft could always be investigated by the three legal jurisdictions of secular, inquisitorial, and episcopal justice: Orella Unzué, "Conflictos de jurisdicción."

24. Rochelle Rojas's recent dissertation, "Bad Christians and Hanging Toads," focuses on secular prosecutions of alleged witches in Navarre. Rojas follows Henningsen in her description of the Zugarramurdi witch hunt and briefly addresses (147–53) one of the cases examined in this study. Otherwise, her sources and my own rarely overlap. In his dissertation, Mikel Berraondo Piudo has assembled statistics for 250 cases of murder, in which aggression with a rock made up 5 percent of the total: "La violencia interpersonal en la Navarra moderna," 113. See also Davis, "Say It with Stones."

25. For a close examination of two of the prosecutions, which arose from events in Elgorriaga and Arraioz, see Homza, "When Witches Litigate."

26. Rojas argues that secular trials give her access to Navarrese villagers' perceptions of witchcraft because they reflect "local interrogation processes": "Bad Christians and Hanging Toads," 222–25. Unless the trials she deploys retain the investigations of courts of first instance, which were handled by village officials, they were not exactly local. Her prosecutions moved from local courts to the royal secular court in Pamplona, which is why they are extant. See Rojas, "Bad Christians and Hanging Toads," 41–44, and Homza, "When Witches Litigate," 247. In *Invoking the Akelarre*, Emma Wilby purports to find the voices of the accused and aims to delineate "the role that [witch] suspects played in

the creation of confessional content" (2). Wilby does not read Spanish; she relies on printed translations and the transcriptions of other researchers.

27. For the notion that we would never be able to know what actually occurred on the ground in this persecution, see Azurmendi, *Las brujas de Zugarramurdi*, 165.

28. In Margaret Murray's view, "witch" was a label constructed and applied by men in an effort to bring women under their control: see *Witch-Cult in Western Europe*. The flip side to Murray's argument was the contention that witches as devil worshippers truly existed: see Summers, *History of Witchcraft and Demonology*.

29. For this particular solution, see Trevor-Roper, *European Witch-Craze*. The controversy has not necessarily gone away, even as European historians have pushed back, hard, against the idea of European development as rational and progressive. Despite their anti-teleological efforts, European witchcraft could be viewed as "an aberration which created obvious puzzles for the post-Enlightenment thinker": Sharpe, introduction to Macfarlane, *Witchcraft in Tudor and Stuart England*, xii. As late as 2003, Michael D. Bailey had to state that witchcraft in the fifteenth century "was not a marginal, fantastical, or historically incomprehensible development": *Battling Demons*, 9.

30. The classic study here is Evans-Pritchard, *Witchcraft, Oracles and Magic*.

31. The former category would include Macfarlane, *Witchcraft in Tudor and Stuart England*, and Thomas, *Religion and the Decline of Magic*. The second category would include Midelfort, *Witch-Hunting in Southwestern Germany*, and Monter, *Witchcraft in France and Switzerland*. Also see Monter, "Historiography of European Witchcraft." With more research, Macfarlane's and Thomas's arguments

became obsolete. See Gaskill, "Witchcraft in Early Modern Kent."

32. As Monter noted in "Historiography of European Witchcraft." The multilayered approach was followed by Midelfort in *Witch-Hunting in Southwestern Germany*. See, too, Briggs, "Many Reasons Why," and Rowlands's review essay, "Telling Witchcraft Stories."

33. Midelfort, in *Witch-Hunting in Southwestern Germany*, was one of the first researchers to explore the question of elite vs. popular culture from both angles. Also see Briggs, *Witches and Neighbors*.

34. The expert on this point is Lyndal Roper: see *Witch Craze*, especially parts 3 and 4. Surprisingly, Navarrese evidence demonstrates that menopause was not a marker for suspicions of witchcraft.

35. In *Witch-Hunting in Southwestern Germany*, Midelfort writes that witch-hunting there was thoroughly dysfunctional. See also Kounine, *Imagining the Witch*, 3nn9, 10, 11.

36. An international symposium on the Spanish Inquisition occurred soon after Franco's death, with the presentations appearing in Villanueva, *La inquisición española*.

37. As examples, García Cárcel, *Orígenes de la inquisición española*; Ortega-Costa, *Proceso de la inquisición contra María de Cazalla*; Bennassar, *L'Inquisition espagnole, XV–XIX siècle*; Jiménez Montserín, *Introducción a la inquisición española*; Garcia Boix, *Colección de documentos*; Villanueva and Bonet, *Historia de la Inquisición*.

38. Martínez Millán, *La hacienda de la Inquisición (1478–1700)*. A flawed but fascinating example of trying to find patterns in prosecutions lies in Contreras and Henningsen, "Forty-Four Thousand Cases."

39. As examples, García-Arenal, *Inquisición y moriscos*; Contreras, *El Santo Oficio de la Inquisición en Galicia*; Dedieu, *L'administration de la foi*.

40. Corteguera, *Death by Effigy*; Lynn, *Between Court and Confessional*.

41. In this regard, Henningsen's intellectual trajectory is slightly puzzling. He finished his original study of Inquisitor Salazar and the witch hunt as a doctoral thesis in 1973 and defended it in 1974. He then spent the next six years preparing his dissertation for publication as *The Witches' Advocate* in 1980. In the preface to that book, he noted that the primary purpose of his investigation was "to illustrate the psychological and social reality [that] witchcraft held" for people and communities in northern Navarre: *Witches' Advocate*, xxvi. He also wrote, "During the long, drawn-out process of translating [from the Danish] and editing, which has delayed the publication of the book, it has been impossible for me to refer to most of the recent research on early modern witchcraft. This, however, does not affect the main thrust of the book, which is concerned with the demonological and heretical aspects of witchcraft, about which nothing of importance has appeared (with the exception of Norman Cohn's splendid 1975 study, *Europe's Inner Demons*)" (xxix). For comments on Henningsen's work vis-à-vis the historiography on witchcraft, see Homza, "When Witches Litigate," 245n2. Henningsen always has garnered more citations than Caro Baroja. For references to Henningsen in more general histories of European witchcraft, see Levack, *Witch-Hunt in Early Modern Europe*, 22–23, 58, 161, 223, 225; Briggs, *Witches and Neighbors*, 35–36, 124; Clark, *Thinking with Demons*, 173–74. Henningsen's account also has gone unquestioned by experts on early modern Spain: Monter, *Frontiers of Heresy*, 262–75; Pérez, *Historia de la brujería en España*, 205–35; Usunáriz Garayoa, "La caza de brujas en la Navarra moderna (siglos XVI–XVII)," 306–50.

42. Scholarship is vast on the ways in which late medieval and early modern law courts were put to use for private ends, including honor and vengeance. As examples, Taylor, *Honor and Violence*; Carroll, "Peace in the Feud"; Dyer, "Seduction by Promise"; Corteguera, "Painter Who Lost His Hat"; Kagan, *Lawsuits and Litigants*.

43. Rowlands, *Witchcraft Narratives in Germany*.

44. In 1613, two of Logroño's inquisitors compiled a report in opposition to Inquisitor Salazar. There they summarized witches' depositions in an effort to persuade the Suprema that the witches had not been dreaming as they relayed their experiences. The inquisitors' summary has been transcribed by Florencio Idoate in *Un documento*. In Act 19 of the report, the inquisitors listed "how the witches carried out vengeance and deaths and harm with poisons and powders"; the five witches the inquisitors described in this section were very angry indeed, to the point of killing their own children. See chapter 5 for a discussion of this important and neglected source. Nevertheless, in the surviving secular and episcopal trials, witch suspects were never described by either the prosecution or the defense as enraged or vengeful.

45. Again, reading only inquisitorial sources could leave a different impression. In the 1613 document composed by Inquisitors Becerra and Valle against Salazar, many of their witches were aged sixty or older. Some of the witches also described themselves as so poor that the Devil's promises helped sway them from Christianity. See Idoate, *Un documento*, 49–50.

46. Wolfgang Behringer is the most adamant proponent of connecting European witch trials to a change in climate called "The Little Ice Age": see "Weather, Hunger and Fear." Navarre,

like Castile, suffered a tremendous bout of plague in the 1590s. See MacKay, *Life in a Time of Pestilence*. Famine and crop-destroying storms were rampant in early modern Navarre, and some of the witches in this particular persecution were accused of practicing weather magic.

47. Virginia Krause and Laura Kounine argue that the identity of the witch was formed through the process of being on trial. Their stance is in opposition to Roper and Briggs, who interpret witchcraft confessions in terms of "underlying fantasies and anxieties." See Krause, *Witchcraft, Demonology, and Confession*, 106, and Kounine, *Imagining the Witch*, 6, 13, 19. In no way are my comments on the development of a sense of selfhood in early modern Navarre supposed to anticipate modern individualism.

48. My study thus pursues both routes described in "AHA Exchange: Rethinking the History of Childhood" by treating children not only as an "addition" to history but using them to assess adult values.

49. For the crucial perspective that colonial and modern archives erase as well as preserve historical "voices," see Fuentes, *Dispossessed Lives*, and Hartman, *Wayward Lives, Beautiful Experiments*. For a more optimistic slant, which parallels my own, see Premo, *Enlightenment on Trial*.

50. I should note that the Spanish Inquisition only very rarely accepted depositions from boys under fourteen or girls under twelve. The same held for the episcopal jurisdiction.

51. The call number for this inquisition dossier is AHN, Inquisición, Legajo 1679, exp. 2. The file has now been digitized, and images of its folios can be seen via the PARES web portal: http://pares.culturaydeporte.gob.es. It is crucial to note that the search process in PARES does not involve the specific

call number attached to the manuscript. The following URL currently will take readers to the manuscript: http://pares.mcu.es/ParesBusquedas20/catalogo/show/2340978.

Readers also can find the file by typing "procesos brujas"—nothing more or less—into the simple search box in PARES.

Chapter 1

1. Edward Bever has argued on the basis of neurobiology that belief in witches could actually produce harmful physical and mental results: see *Realities of Witchcraft* and "Bullying."

2. Briggs, *Witches and Neighbors*, 146–54, 237–41. I argue that in order to grasp witch-hunting in early modern Europe, we must expand our vision of the range of emotions that intersected with the law. For example, loathing and vengeance were pertinent in this specific witch hunt, but for the accusers, not the accused. Moreover, straightforward hatred was insufficient to explain the intensity of witchcraft denunciations and confessions in this persecution: given the archival evidence, parental terror and spiritual dread must be added to the mix. Significantly, while witches in western Europe generally were imagined to act out of hatred, and Logroño's inquisitors could imply that they expected witches to be enraged (see introduction, note 44), sources from the secular and episcopal jurisdictions in this witch hunt never mention that the witches were motivated by anger. For that stereotype, see Kounine and Ostling, introduction to *Emotions*.

3. Rojas, "Bad Christians and Hanging Toads," 334–39; also see 156, 158. Still, Rojas describes multiple examples of devastating punishments and outcomes for accused witches in Navarre: see 158, 229, 260, 263. For the claim that witchcraft accusations turned into mere slights without social consequences in urban areas in Aragón, see Tausiet, *Urban Magic*.

4. Rojas, "Bad Christians and Hanging Toads," 229.

5. Rojas treats this case on pages 97–103 of "Bad Christians and Hanging Toads." The case is Archivo Real y General de Navarra (AGN) 071319/16004729.

6. AGN, 071319/16004729, fol. 125r–v.

7. Archivo Diocesano de Pamplona (ADP), 434-N. 20, 1610, fol. 12r–v, where Barazarte himself testifies, and fols. 14r–v, 15r, 16v, where other witnesses describe the events of 1595.

8. Rojas suggests that Navarrese villages might have allowed banished witches to sneak back in and live peacefully with their neighbors and families: "Bad Christians and Hanging Toads," 156–58. Yet the royal court in Pamplona conducted hundreds of prosecutions for breaking sentences of exile handed down by its secular jurisdiction. In such cases, called *quebrantamiento de destierro*, the accused typically were found because they had stolen, pimped, falsified coinage, and behaved like vagabonds, among other crimes. I have never seen a breaking-of-exile trial involving an accused witch, which is not to say it was not possible. As the reader will see in chapter 4, when banished witch torturers reappeared in Elgorriaga, the family they had injured immediately turned them in. When the inquisition tribunal in Logroño exiled convicted heretics, its sentences routinely threatened to double the sentence if offenders returned before their sentences were up. Banished heretics took this possibility seriously enough to write to the tribunal to ask for permission to reenter Navarre if they had extenuating circumstances.

9. See the study by Tabernero and Usunáriz Garayoa, "*Bruja, brujo, hechicera, hechicero, sorgin.*"

10. Berraondo Piudo estimates that offenses against honor were the primary cause of murder in early modern Navarre: "La violencia interpersonal," 158–75.

Defamation could also occur through insults written on walls, and anonymous letters and libels circulated through villages and towns. See Ruiz Astiz, *La fuerza de la palabra escrita.*

11. Berraondo Piudo, "La violencia interpersonal," 162.

12. Obviously, matters of reputation were important not just socially but legally, and in the medieval period as well. See Fenster and Smail, *Fama.* In early modern Navarre, worries about honor affected every social class, and slander had an impact on the entire range of family members. See Berraondo Piudo, "La violencia interpersonal," 159.

13. As examples, see AGN, 056291 (1576–81); AGN, 309580 (1589–1600); AGN, 119711 (1583); AGN, 041511/170051884 (1615). For epithets involving "judío," see Berraondo Piudo, "La violencia interpersonal," 168–69. Agotes were an out-group specific to Navarre, whose origins are hotly debated. See Idoate, "Agotes en los valles de Roncal y Baztan"; Idoate, *Documentos sobre los agotes*; Antolini, *Los agotes.* I have not found that the term "morisco" was used as an insult in Navarre.

14. Like slurs over religious or racial ancestry, the label of "witch" could be intended to place a person in an unwanted out-group. It served as both an insult and a category, which is why witnesses sometimes spoke freely about families having or not having a public reputation as witches. See chapter 3.

15. Berraondo Piudo, "La violencia interpersonal," 162. For the impact of compounded insults, Taylor, *Honor and Violence.*

16. The exact phrasing of the insult was "picaro romero bellaco suzio y un bruxo." See AGN, 285148 (1611), fol. 9v. It is significant that one man called another a "brujo" because "bruja" was a recognized slur against women in particular, and the timing—1611—of such an epithet against a man may well reflect the larger context of the

witch hunt. See Berraondo Piudo, "La violencia interpersonal," 168. For the omnipresence of "bellaco" or "bellaca" as an insult, see Berraondo Piudo, "La violencia interpersonal," 162–63.

17. In the dozens of cases of defamation that I have seen in Pamplona's AGN, children and teenagers were never formally charged or even named as slanderers.

18. See below as well as chapter 3.

19. Nicole J. Bettlé, "Child-Witches," argues that child-witches were executed in significant numbers across Switzerland and the Holy Roman Empire. She cautions historians not to think of child-witch prosecutions as a late phenomenon, or one that was ancillary to the prosecution of adult suspects. I have never seen evidence that child-witches were formally executed in Spain by any legal jurisdiction, although two young girls later died of the illness and starvation they suffered inside Pamplona's royal jails in 1595–96 while awaiting trial on witchcraft charges. As far as I can tell, the child-witches in the persecution of 1608–14—those under age fourteen for boys, and twelve for girls—never were officially tried in any of Navarre's legal jurisdictions, but instead were treated as victims. Pierre Cameron, in "De victime à accuse," studies the execution of children for witchcraft in the canton of Bouchain in the early seventeenth century and examines possible developments that allowed children to be held legally liable for this heresy.

20. For the predominance of Basque-speakers in early modern Navarre, see Monteano Sorbet, *El iceberg Navarro.*

21. Voltmer, "Witch in the Courtroom," 97–116.

22. Voltmer, "Behind the 'Veil of Memory.'"

23. For a thoughtful evaluation of hearing subaltern voices in inquisitorial settings, see García-Arenal, "Polyphony of Voices." For García-Arenal, prison graffiti amounts to a "new landscape"

that goes beyond dialogues between persecutors and victims (65).

24. For a classic caution about historians' use of legal sources, see Kuehn, "Reading Microhistory."

25. For a basically identical process in the Spanish Empire in the eighteenth century, see Premo, *Enlightenment on Trial*, 34–38, 51–56.

26. The very variety of plaintiffs' and defendants' statements demonstrates that their vocabulary and narratives were not forced into a single mode. Rojas agrees: see "Bad Christians and Hanging Toads," 225.

27. Premo stresses the fact that illiterate litigants had to remain in charge of their cases to keep them moving forward. Her evidence demonstrates that people transcribing the litigants' cases used the litigants' voices to communicate who was in charge: *Enlightenment on Trial*, 38, 52. While Navarrese court testimony is not framed in the first-person voice, there is no doubt that the secular court system treated children as making statements that could stand alone in a legal sense. For example, the secular jurisdiction sought out thirteen-year-old girls to ratify their depositions; see chapter 2. The question of whether children possessed "agency" is fraught: see the recent forum in the *American Historical Review* 125 (2020), "Rethinking the History of Childhood." Evidence from Navarre indicates that children in this witch hunt could plan, collaborate, and initiate change with an eye to the future.

28. AGN, 069259/16009991 (1576), fol. 34r.

29. For the characteristics of Navarrese witches in the sixteenth century, see Idoate, *La brujería*. Rojas believes that the key features of Navarrese witchcraft in normal, non-panicked settings were the reputation of being a bad Christian (*mala cristiana*), having ancestors who were witches, and owning or interacting with toads: "Bad Christians and Hanging Toads," 224–55. Rojas finds that the concept of the Devil's sabbat, or akelarre, was more problematic, insofar as royal magistrates sometimes injected that idea into charges when it was not mentioned in witness testimony (255–56). Nonetheless, the sources transcribed in Idoate, *La brujería*, are packed with references to diabolical gatherings. Also see Nogal Fernández, "Las brujas de Ochagavía."

30. One account of the Devil's activities with these witches is in AHN, Inqu., Lib. 1252, fols. 402r–411r. Another is in the AGN: Caja 31404$^{\text{CO\_PS1}}$, Leg. 66, N. 15, fols. 1r–4r. On the latter, see Iribarren, "Interesante documento." Both of these accounts explicitly tied their content to what was said publicly at the auto de fe. Eloísa Navajas Twose and José Antonio Sainz Varela, in "Una relación inquisitorial sobre la brujería," give an overview of this witch persecution, describe the extant sources in the AHN, and transcribe one account of the November 1610 auto de fe.

31. AGN, Caja 31404$^{\text{CO\_PS1}}$, Leg. 66, N. 15, fol. 1r–v. The pain of the Devil's mark allegedly lasted for one to two months.

32. AHN, Inqu., Lib. 1252, fols. 403v–404r.

33. The toads did not readily give up that unguent: their witch-masters had to whip them and then step on them in order for the amphibians to vomit it. AHN, Inqu., Lib. 1252, fol. 404v. For the explicit identification of the toads as diabolical guardian angels, AGN, Caja 31404$^{\text{CO\_PS1}}$, Leg. 66, N. 15, fol. 1v.

34. AHN, Inqu., Lib. 1252, fol. 403r; AGN, Caja 31404$^{\text{CO\_PS1}}$, Leg. 66, N. 15, fol. 2v.

35. AHN, Inqu., Lib. 1252, fol. 405; AGN, Caja 31404$^{\text{CO\_PS1}}$, Leg. 66, N. 15, fol. 3r. The AHN source has many more details about sexual activity at the Devil's reunions. For an explanation of the Devil's hierarchy of servants, see Henningsen, *Witches' Advocate*, 91. The "queen" of the akelarre directed the meetings of the Devil's followers. There

was also a king of the akelarre: he led the male witches but was subordinate to the queen.

36. AHN, Inqu., Lib. 1252, fol. 406r. The account of the demonic Mass in the AGN source agrees with the AHN source but omits the idea of lesser demons as assistants. Later, when two clerics were arrested by Logroño's inquisitors for witchcraft, it was suspected that they assisted the Devil at Mass.

37. AGN, Caja 31404^{CO-PS1}, Leg. 66, N. 15, fol. 3r.

38. Clark, *Thinking with Demons*.

39. 1 Peter 5:8.

40. Inquisitors Alonso Becerra Holguín and Juan de Valle Alvarado first received information about a "great complicity of male and female witches" on January 12, 1609. Up to now, historians have not known who first informed the inquisitors about witch suspects in Zugarramurdi, but there is a clue in one of Inquisitor Valle's letters, written during his visitation in 1609. There, he states that "the first reports of the witches in Zugarramurdi were done by an esteemed notary of the Valle of Baztan": AHN, Inqu., Lib. 794, fol. 449r. One of the most important notaries and inquisition employees throughout this witch persecution was Miguel de Narbarte, royal notary and inquisition familiar, who was based in the Baztan. Unfortunately, no report by Narbarte about the original accusations appears to have survived.

41. AHN, Inqu., Leg. 1679, images 219–20. Correspondence from the Suprema to the Logroño tribunal also seems to confirm that the tribunal did not become aware of witchcraft until January 12: AHN, Inqu., Lib. 332, fol. 215v, dated January 8, 1609, in which the Suprema wrote to Logroño about issues with judaizers in the village of Los Arcos but said nothing about witchcraft.

42. Spanish theologians in this period viewed tacit demonic pacts as just as heretical as overt ones. See Homza, *Religious Authority*, chapter 6.

43. AHN, Inqu., Leg. 1679, image 220.

44. The *Canon episcopi* purportedly was written at the Council of Ancyra in 314 CE, but it actually was a ninth-century creation. Its presumed antiquity heightened its authority.

45. Spanish inquisitors by default were supposed to have both historical and forensic mentalities: Logroño's inquisitors should have been paying attention to legal precedent, while simultaneously listening to depositions and noticing clues about intent, extent, and duration. In 1613, Inquisitor Salazar would insist that his colleagues refused to notice contradictions in testimony and interpreted the evidence in only one direction; see chapter 5. But because Salazar did not join the tribunal until June 1609, we cannot presume that his critique applied to the first six months of the investigation.

46. AHN, Inqu., Leg. 1679, image 219.

47. AHN, Inqu., Leg. 1679, image 529.

48. In "Bad Christians and Hanging Toads," Rojas agrees that witchcraft beliefs were not a top-down phenomenon in Navarre; Idoate concurred in *La brujería*, and so did Caro Baroja in *World of the Witches*. Significantly, however, in 1611 Bishop Venegas of Pamplona firmly pinned the blame for witch beliefs on French influence and local sermons: AHN, Inqu., Leg. 1679, image 456.

49. AHN, Inqu., Leg. 1679, images 179–80.

50. The revocations of confessions made before Inquisitor Salazar in 1611 usually contain the original admissions to witchcraft, which often had been voiced before Inquisitor Valle in 1609, when the latter was on visitation. Those original confessions demonstrate that Valle was hearing child-witches while he was in the field and that he traveled far from Zugarramurdi and Las Cinco Villas: for example, AHN, Inqu., Leg. 1679, images 709, 802, 804, 897; AHN, Inqu., Lib. 794, fols. 444r, 445r, 447r, 449r.

51. AHN, Inqu., Leg. 1679, image 180.
52. Children were at the center of the witch persecution in Erratzu, Arraioz, Elgorriaga, Bera, Olague, and so on. See below as well as chapters 2 and 3.
53. Idoate, *La brujería*; Roper, *Witch Craze*.
54. AGN, 072902 (1613), fols. 42v, 30r, 32v, 38v–39r.
55. AGN, 096974 (1560), fols. 6r, 7v. Here is evidence of the power of insults spoken by children.
56. AGN, 012643 (1596), fol. 1r–v. The offender's family was profoundly poor: the culprit insisted she had told no one in the house about what she had done, nor had anyone else been involved. We do not have a sentence in this case.
57. AGN, 013570 (1606), fols. 1r–v, 2r–v. It is probably meaningful in terms of a sense of responsibility and guilt that María returned to her friend, carrying her dead child. It was a truly dreadful case: witnesses reported that the community had forced María's husband and mother to leave because they could not control their tongues, but María stayed behind and starved with her children in the woods: AGN, 013570 (1606), fol. 1r. Garthine Walker has noted that the discovery of dead children always involved shock, even when the searchers anticipated finding them: "Child-Killing and Emotion," 161–62. For infanticide in Navarre, see Berraondo Piudo, "Los hijos como víctimas."
58. AGN, 072902 (1613), fols. 43r, 6r, 7v, 41v, 39r.
59. AGN, 330569 (1612), fol. 3r.
60. It is not clear from the depositions how long the priest had been dead or whether the villagers were examining a corpse with flesh still on it (or merely a skeleton). Even if it were the latter, the fact that the bones were still in the coffin illustrated that witches had not carried away the remains of this alleged victim. See AGN, 330569 (1612), fol. 101r.
61. ADP C/242-N. 2 (1612), fols. 58v–59r.
62. As we will see, children in this witch hunt certainly could be influenced by adults, but they also were capable in certain circumstances of their own collective action. Events in the village of Olague bear this out most convincingly; see chapters 2 and 3. Children in this witch hunt did more than "seize on scripts offered by adults": Maza, "The Kids Aren't All Right," 1272.
63. When commissioner Leon de Aranibar wrote to the inquisitors from Zubieta in February 1611, he noted that the prisoners he was sending were carrying their beds and twelve ducats apiece: AHN, Inqu., Leg. 1679, image 1. At nearly the same time, the parish priest of Doneztebe-Santesteban was also sending two prisoners to Logroño, along with their beds: AHN, Inqu., Leg. 1679, image 183.
64. The witch hunt of 1609 in the Pays de Labourd was supervised by Bordeaux judge Pierre de Lancre. See Rolley and Machielson, "Mythmaker of the Sabbat."
65. Logroño's inquisitors knew that the Suprema had instructed their tribunal multiple times not to seize possible heretics who had not committed any crimes inside Spanish territory: AHN, Inqu., Lib. 794, fols. 458r, 461v–462v. Still, they worried about the potential harm that French witches could do and ultimately thought that they could practice mutually beneficial extraditions with French authorities: AHN, Inqu., Lib. 794, fol. 462r. By the time of the auto de fe in November 1610, two of the sentenced witches were described as "native to France," but they allegedly had practiced witchcraft in Navarre, which meant they were fair game: AHN, Inqu., Lib. 835, fol. 349v.
66. AHN, Inqu., Lib. 794, fols. 433v, 404v, 405r.
67. AHN, Inqu., Leg. 1679, image 529.
68. AHN, Inqu., Lib. 794, fol. 433r. María de Iriarte did not die until August 1610. María de Suretegui survived and was reconciled in the auto de fe of November 1610; she received a sentence of six

months' exile. See Henningsen's detailed charts in *Witches' Advocate*, 145–48, 198–200.

69. AHN, Inqu., Lib. 794, fol. 433r.

70. AHN, Inqu., Lib. 794, fol. 444r. Five of the dead came from the original ten prisoners, and the sixth was "one of the negativos, who has died without our being able to persuade him to confess sacramentally, despite many efforts."

71. See the chart in Henningsen, *Witches' Advocate*, 198–200.

72. AHN, Inqu., Lib. 794, fol. 219r, dated August 21, 1601.

73. AHN, Inqu., Lib. 794, fols. 74r–75r, dated April 2, 1607. By 1610, the inquisitors were pondering natural as well as supernatural reasons for their prisoners' sicknesses. They wrote to the Suprema, "these people are from the mountains, raised on fresh air, trained in work, and brought up with milk and different foods. When they're brought here to this land, everything is different: it alters their nature, and their illnesses may be caused by this." AHN, Inqu., Lib. 795, fol. 2r.

74. The inquisitors in Logroño called this torture technique the *garrote*, but it should not be confused with a method of strangulation. AHN, Inqu., Lib. 795, fol. 11r–v.

75. AHN, Inqu., Lib. 795, fol. 11r. It appears the clerics were tortured in early October 1610. The description of Arburu's words comes from inquisitorial correspondence to the Suprema. Notaries were always supposed to transcribe the words of those under torture. See Martin, "Tortured Testimonies."

76. AHN, Inqu., Lib. 794, fol. 445r, from a letter dated November 13, 1609. Amazingly, in 1613 Inquisitors Becerra and Valle told the Suprema that not only they and Salazar but also the translators and notaries del secreto had been testing suspects for the Devil's mark in the tribunal: Idoate, *Un documento*, 99–100. In no way were such experiments authorized by the inquisitorial hierarchy. For more managerial eccentricities on the part of the tribunal, see chapter 5.

77. AHN, Inqu., Lib. 795, fol. 8r, dated February 13, 1610.

78. AHN, Inqu., Lib. 795, fols. 8v–9r. Houses of penitence were owned or rented by inquisition tribunals; people sentenced to "perpetual prison" (which was never perpetual) lived there. Typically, such individuals worked during the day and returned to the house at night. While they were outside the house, they very often were ordered to wear sambenitos.

79. The tribunal told the Suprema that it had voted on twenty-two imprisonments for witch suspects but was authorizing only twelve. It seems likely that those twelve new arrests were in addition to the five captures that Inquisitor Valle had already carried out in 1609. AHN, Inqu., Lib. 794, fol. 433r–v.

80. Henningsen, *Witches' Advocate*, 260–61, attempts to reconstruct the identity of the sixteen additional prisoners whose cases were not finished until after the November 1610 auto de fe.

81. AHN, Inqu., Lib. 795, fol. 9r–v.

82. AHN, Inqu., Lib. 795, fol. 41r.

83. Scott, *Basque Seroras*, chapter 5; AHN, Inqu., Lib. 795, fol. 3r; Henningsen, *Witches' Advocate*, 140, 485n113. According to Henningsen, inquisitors were convinced that Juan Pérez Labayen, rector for the village of Etxalar, was the father of Endara's child. After Endara's arrest, Labayen kept traveling to Logroño—on the pretense of being a pilgrim to Santiago de Compostella— where he constantly sought information about her. Testimony from Labayen in 1619, in a different inquisitorial matter, indicates that Endara ultimately left her child in Logroño: AHN, Inqu., Leg. 1683, image 2198. Labayen said in 1619 that he and Endara were relatives.

84. Henningsen noted that the tribunal had not held an auto de fe since 1599. See *Witches' Advocate*, 182. For a

detailed description of the auto de fe, Henningsen, *Witches' Advocate*, 181–93.

85. AHN, Inqu., Lib. 795, fol. 10r.

86. Flynn, "Mimesis of the Last Judgment." Colin Rose quotes the studies of Pieter Spierenburg to the effect that the "violence and theatricality of early modern judicial punishment was not just a means for the state to inflict terror. Rather, agrarian Europeans accustomed to the sights, smells, and sounds of blood and death found the imposition of justice to be both just and enormously entertaining": *Renaissance of Violence*, 17. All of the villagers examined in this book would have been familiar with the sights, smells, and sounds of blood and death. Additionally, historians have long suspected that the sentences read at the inquisition's autos de fe could inform spectators about features of Judaism and Islam that then could be reproduced in unexpected ways. The same would have held true for witches' crimes and objectives. In sentencing, the inquisitors were also instructing. For a powerful statement that inquisitors could create the heresies they were pursuing, see García-Arenal, "Polyphony of Voices," 39–40.

87. AHN, Inqu., Lib. 835, fol. 369r–v.

88. AHN, Inqu., Leg. 1679, image 227, where the inquisitors told the Suprema in March 1611 that the auto de fe had not worked, and the Devil was actually increasing his brood.

89. AGN, 149947 (1610), fol. 4r–v.

90. AGN, 285047 (1610). The trial transcript records Catalina as having said, "ha mal encuentro[,] en que te ofendido yo para perderme a mi creatura," which in Spanish could be rendered as "what a bad encounter, how did I offend you so that my child would be lost [to the Devil]." Catalina's implication was that María was taking her child to the Devil's akelarres. Catalina's alleged words were translated from Basque into Spanish in the transcript: the Basque phrase for "ha mal encuentro" is stronger, to the effect that this encounter would be

deadly. Many thanks to Peio J. Monteano Sorbet for his linguistic help. Parents in this witch hunt always used the verb "perder" when it came to the fate of their bewitched children. See AGN, 285047 (1610), fol. 1v. Though this case was referred to Pamplona, there is no final verdict in the trial record; what exists is an account of the investigation by the court of first instance in Etxalar.

91. Rose posits that homicide in early modern Italy was invariably carried out by men: *Renaissance of Violence*, 26.

92. AGN, 072902 (1613), fols. 40r, 42v. On the gendering of homicide, see Berraondo Piudo and Segura Urra, *Odiar*, 32. Berraondo Piudo confirms that his 250 murder trials do not feature women as antagonists, though he describes cases in which women induced others to murder for them as well as actually hired assassins: "La violencia interpersonal," 92–96.

93. See chapter 3.

94. I wonder if the heightened rhetoric about the fears of vigilante justice could also speak to an impression that the villagers wanted to make, namely, that they ordinarily were thoroughly law-abiding.

95. In the statistics assembled by Berraondo Piudo, swords and knives predominated by far as modes of murder: "La violencia interpersonal," 113.

96. AGN, 072902 (1613), fol. 18r.

97. AHN, Inqu., Leg. 1679, image 481.

98. AHN, Inqu., Leg. 1679, images 1–2.

99. AGN, 41366 (1612), fols. 5r–6r, 187r, 188v.

100. On the threat of house burning in this witch persecution, see Homza, "When Witches Litigate," 260–61. There was a communal responsibility to rebuild in the Valle de Baztan if a house was burned down accidentally.

101. Kallendorf, *Sins of the Fathers*, 134–41.

102. Nalle, *God in La Mancha*, 58–59, as well as Nalle, "Inquisitors, Priests." See too Pasamar Lázaro, *Los familiares del Santo Oficio*, 27.

103. Araníbar was the abbot of the Premonstratensian monastery in Urdax, which had a seigneurial relationship with Zugarramurdi. He became an inquisition commissioner in 1609. Narbarte was a highly successful royal notary and inquisition familiar whose practice was centered in the Valle de Baztan.

104. Homza, "When Witches Litigate," 264–65.

105. Homza, "When Witches Litigate," 269. While Araníbar did not personally torture accused witches, Narbarte's own house was the setting for the death of one elderly suspect, Graciana de Barrenechea. Barrenechea's death was witnessed by dozens of residents of Arraioz. Later, a prosecutor for the secular jurisdiction threatened to file murder charges against Araníbar, though apparently such never occurred. See Homza, "When Witches Litigate," 261–64.

106. The fact that the torturers called men and women "witches" in public allowed them to be sued later for defamation. It is important to note that in these public torments, the slur of "witch" was repeated constantly. See chapter 4 and Homza, "When Witches Litigate."

107. AGN, 100796 (1612), fol. 107r.

108. AGN, 100796 (1612), fol. 20r–v.

109. For details on the women's experiences, see Homza, "When Witches Litigate," 255–57.

110. The trial that resulted from these tortures was conducted in the episcopal jurisdiction; see chapter 4.

111. ADP, C/242-N. 2 (1612), fols. 15r–16v. Aguirre's insults also occurred in public, but because he was a priest, his punishment was handled by the bishop of Pamplona; see chapter 4.

112. ADP, C/242-N. 2 (1612), fol. 39r.

113. Homza, "When Witches Litigate," 244–45.

114. Kallendorf documents two instances in which enraged characters in *comedias* hung women by their hair from trees: *Sins of the Fathers*, 135.

115. The surviving evidence does not clarify whether Araníbar and Narbarte specifically told villagers in the Baztan how to frighten witch suspects.

116. Homza, "When Witches Litigate," 269n108.

117. AGN, 100796 (1612), fol. 24r; ADP C/242-N. 2, fol. 23r.

118. See chapter 4 for details on these prosecutions and sentences.

119. Henningsen wondered whether there was a Navarrese tradition of reconciliation with witches that entailed public apologies: *Witches' Advocate*, 455n46. New sources about this witch hunt from the secular jurisdiction appear to confirm such a custom.

120. In pursuit of safety, multiple accused witches fled into Gipuzkoa, a neighboring Basque province. Such occurred with Miguel de Imbuluzqueta from Olague; see chapter 3.

121. One unsolved mystery of this witch hunt is what ultimately happened to children and teenagers who claimed they were witches and who accused others. In court, their parents never expressed any anxiety about their offspring's religious or social fate as confessed witches, even though we know that the dishonor attached to the slur of "witch" covered the entire family. It would be helpful to know whether child-witches found themselves restricted in marriage options or in economic pursuits later in life. María de Endara, the young widow who was sent to Logroño on witchcraft suspicions and arrived there pregnant, was described by a relative as still being a *muger principal* (a "leading woman") after she was released from the inquisition tribunal and returned to Etxalar in the second half of 1611: AHN, Inqu., Leg. 1683, image 2198. See the end of chapter 5 for problematic evidence on individual adults' recovery from the persecution.

122. Homza, "When Witches Litigate," 256.
123. The absence of witches in my suspects' genealogies is markedly different from what Rojas has found: "Bad Christians and Hanging Toads," 230–45.
124. I have not found any evidence as to whether child-witches were also excluded from the Eucharist. If they had explicitly rejected their baptismal vows, then they presumably were.
125. See the prosecutor's statement in the Erratzu case, ADP, C/242-N. 2, fol. 9r.
126. AGN, 100796 (1612), fol. 22r.
127. Whereas Smail, in *Consumption of Justice*, and Rose, in *Renaissance of Violence*, have found that their historical subjects used the courts as an opportunity for conflict resolution, witchcraft accusers and the accused were more interested in destruction than reconciliation. Kounine, "Witch on Trial," 231.

Chapter 2
1. AGN, 072902 (1613), fols. 40r, 51r–v.
2. Despite French king Henri IV's conversion to Catholicism in 1593, inquisitors in Navarre, as well as Pamplona's bishops, wrote (and presumably talked) as if Protestantism were still a threat within France and could potentially flow over the border. See Homza, *Spanish Inquisition*, 212–20, for primary sources that address enforcing indices of prohibited books, as well as Kamen, *Spanish Inquisition*, 108–22, and Martínez Bujanda, "Índices de libros prohibidos del siglo XVI."
3. For a spectacular example of a Navarrese priest who was convinced he had special spiritual gifts and annoyed his parish and bishop accordingly, Scott, "Wayward Priest of Atondo."
4. ADP, C/129-N. 17.
5. Christian, *Local Religion*.
6. ADP, C/192-N. 7.
7. ADP, C/415-N. 17.
8. See the essays in Porres Marijuán, *Entre el fervor y la violencia*, especially Álvarez Urcelay, "Iglesia, moralidad y justicia," and Reguera, "Violencia y clero."

9. ADP, C/684-N. 15, C/344-N. 14, C/228-N. 3, C/445-N. 6. Fermín was a member of the Basque noble family, Loyola, and was a relative of Iñigo, who founded the Society of Jesus.
10. ADP, C/445-N. 6, C/448-N. 20, C/430-N. 12.
11. ADP, C/859-N. 12.
12. For the struggle to break the Basque clergy's habit of running with and fighting bulls, see Scott, "Tridentine Reform in the Afternoon."
13. ADP, C/224-N. 14, C/279-N. 25, C/280-N. 4, C/336-N. 1, C/293-N. 10.
14. Scholarship on the Council of Trent is vast. As a sample, see O'Malley, *Trent and All That*; Ditchfield, "De-centering the Catholic Reformation"; and Ditchfield, "What's in a Title?" For an overview of religious reformation scholarship in Spain, see Homza, "Merits of Disruption and Tumult."
15. For these points, see *Canons and Decrees*, 46–48; 55–57, 105, 164–69.
16. Sandoval y Rojas became the archbishop of Toledo in 1599 as well as inquisitor-general in 1608. Earlier bishops of Pamplona in the sixteenth century had died while their synods were still in session, which meant that the latter could not be concluded formally. Sandoval y Rojas changed the order of his surnames in 1601; he had formerly been known as Rojas y Sandoval. For the sake of consistency, I use Sandoval y Rojas throughout. See Gómez Canseco, *Don Bernardo de Sandoval y Rojas*, 22.
17. The 1591 printed edition of the synodal constitutions has been digitized by the Fundación Sancho el Sabio, whose mission is to "collect, organize, conserve, and diffuse Basque culture." See *Constituciones synodales del obispado de Pamplona*. The digital version can be found at https://catalogo.sanchoelsabio .eus/Record/23184. See Scott, *Basque Seroras*, 60–64.
18. *Constituciones synodales*, fols. 64r, 65r–v, 66r–v; 67v; 68r, 69r.
19. Homza, *Religious Authority*, 126–29.

20. *Constituciones synodales*, fol. 70r–v.
21. An argument made persuasively by Celeste I. McNamara in *Bishop's Burden*.
22. Goñi Gaztambide, *Los navarros*, 281.
23. Goñi Gaztambide, *Los navarros*, 283, 286–89.
24. *Canons and Decrees*, 32, 34.
25. *Canons and Decrees*, 36, 38–39.
26. *Canons and Decrees*, 72–73, 148.
27. AHN, Inqu., Leg. 1679, images 519, 522–23.
28. For Venegas's career, see Goñi Gaztambide, *Historia de los obispos de Pamplona*, 65–177.
29. For Goñi Gaztambide, Venegas represented the culminating moment of the Counter-Reformation in Pamplona: *Historia de los obispos*, 67.
30. Goñi Gaztambide, *Historia de los obispos*, 85–86.
31. Goñi Gaztambide, *Historia de los obispos*, 136n85; and Insausti, "El primer catecismo en euskera guipuzcoano."
32. . . . *A los abbades, rectores, vicarios y demas personas eclesiasticas y seglares de nuestro obispado, hazemos saber, que por quanto en conservación de algunas cosas mandadas por el Santo Concilio de Trento . . .* (Pamplona, 1608); *Provisión acordada . . . en que prohibe el excesso de las ofrendas en missas nuevas y otras cosas . . .* (Pamplona, 1609).
33. Goñi Gaztambide, *Historia de los obispos*, 85–91.
34. Goñi Gaztambide, *Historia de los obispos*, 87, 138.
35. Goñi Gaztambide stressed the importance of Corpus Christi to Navarrese villagers: *Los navarros*, 293. The fact that the witches in this persecution could not see the Eucharist may thus have an even deeper cultural significance.
36. Goñi Gaztambide, *Historia de los obispos*, 69–83.
37. *Relación de las fiestas que el ilustrissimo señor Don Antonio Venegas de Figueroa obispo de Pamplona hizo el día del Santíssimo Sacramento, y por todo su octavario, este año de 1609* (Pamplona); *Fiestas del Corpus que el año de 1610 hizo el ilustrissimo señor Don Antonio Venegas de Figueroa, obispo de Pamplona* (Pamplona).
38. In Latin, the first letters of the seven sins spelled *saligia*, an acronym that dominated in the medieval and early modern period. See Bloomfield, *Seven Deadly Sins*.
39. For descriptions and analyses of two such texts, see Homza, *Religious Authority*, chapter 6.
40. Remarkably, the authors of Spanish witchcraft treatises sometimes highlighted the role of the clergy in superstitious practices, and asked laypeople to challenge them. See Homza, *Religious Authority*, 193–94.
41. Molina, *Exercicios espirituales*, 582–84.
42. Mata, *Parayso virginal*.
43. Jiménez, *Oraciones christianas*, 4, 54–55, 72–72, 78–79.
44. Andueza, *Manual de casados*, fols. 5r–7v, 25r.
45. Alexandra Wingate, a former undergraduate at William & Mary, studied private libraries in early modern Navarre for her honors thesis in Hispanic Studies. See Wingate, "A qué manera de libros y letras es inclinado: Las bibliotecas privadas de Navarra en los siglos XVI y XVII." W&M ScholarWorks, April 2018, https://sites.google.com/view/bibliotecasnavarras/home.
46. Provocatively, none of the evidence in this witch persecution supports the notion that ordinary Navarrese villagers did not understand or practice Catholic Christianity, despite their illiteracy in Spanish, their often-wretched parish priests, and their distance from the episcopal seat of Pamplona. The formerly popular argument about "Christianization" in early modern Europe does not work for Navarre. See Delumeau, *Catholicism Between Luther and Voltaire*, and Van Engen, "Christian Middle Ages."
47. AHN, Inqu., Leg. 1679, image 220.
48. AHN, Inqu., Lib. 332, fol. 230r.

49. AHN, Inqu., Lib. 794, fol. 433r. By December 1609, the inquisitors were even more convinced that the Devil was behind the prisoners' illnesses and deaths, given how violent their illnesses were, and how far outside ordinary medical knowledge: AHN, Inqu., Lib. 794, fol. 444r. For an anecdote about a male suspect having sex with the Devil in the same house of penitence, see Idoate, *Un documento*, 143.

50. Idoate, *Un documento*, 81, 90, 153.

51. Fernández Nieto, *Proceso a la brujería*, 31.

52. AHN, Inqu., Lib. 1252, fol. 410r. For an analogous account, though with more details, see Fernández Nieto, *Proceso a la brujería*, 45–46.

53. Fernández Nieto, *Proceso a la brujería*, 37.

54. AHN, Inqu., Lib. 1252, fols. 409v–410r. This anecdote is repeated in Fernández Nieto, *Proceso a la brujería*, where the pamphlet reported that the witch would have died had she not managed to get inside her house (51–52). The yelling of the children in anger matches Kallendorf's description of that emotion in Spanish plays: *Sins of the Fathers*, 134–35. The noise that the witches allegedly made in Bera also speaks to a recent claim that "demonology [relied] upon the sense of hearing." See Krause, *Witchcraft, Demonology, and Confession*, chapter 2.

55. AHN, Inqu., Lib. 1252, fol. 410v.

56. Fernández Nieto, *Proceso a la brujería*, 53–55.

57. AHN, Inqu., Leg. 1679, images 1–2.

58. In his later correspondence with Inquisitor-General Sandoval, Bishop Venegas noted the profound religious fervor that the witch hunt provoked: AHN, Inqu., Leg. 1679, image 458.

59. ADP, C/242-N. 2 (1612), fol. 213r.

60. ADP, C/242-N. 2 (1612), fol. 216r–v.

61. AGN, 072902 (1613), fols. 40v–41r.

62. María's comments alluded to the Devil as a liar, for he had "blinded" her to the true religion of Christianity. Her testimony points as well to the social effects of witchcraft accusations, though her claim that "her relatives had abandoned her" was at odds with this specific relative's efforts. Nevertheless, the drama of her situation was obvious.

63. AGN, 072902 (1613), fol. 45r.

64. AGN, Prot. Not., Narbarte, 1608, N. 137; 1608, N. 102.

65. AGN, Prot. Not., Narbarte, 1613, N. 1.

66. Berraondo Piudo notes that debts were a prime mover of crime, though he focuses on ones accrued through gambling: "La violencia interpersonal," 197.

67. AGN, 072902 (1613), fol. 14r.

68. At the same time, figures in the Baztan might not have had any economic motives at all for naming or abusing suspects. In Elgorriaga, where Juana de Echeverría was marched in the ladders by Juan de Legasa, her net worth and his were practically identical. A census from 1612 demonstrates that Echeverría's house that year was worth seventy ducats and could cost one and a half ducats to rent. Juan de Legasa's house was worth eighty ducats and would also fetch one and a half ducats in rent. AGN, Elgorriaga, 1612: CO_VALORACION, Leg. 23, N. 13–1, fol. 14r.

69. AHN, Inqu., Leg. 1679, image 1117.

70. See AGN, 100796 (1612), fols. 123r, 163r, 171v, for comments on María's sexual relationships.

71. See AGN, 100796 (1612), fol. 10r, for María's statement that she depended upon her neighbors' charity to survive. She could never have afforded to underwrite a lawsuit.

72. Berraondo Piudo mistakenly dates this case to 1622: "La violencia interpersonal," 168.

73. AGN, 013869 (1610), fols. 1r, 2r.

74. Claims about the life-saving powers of Navarrese women's headdresses to shield their wearers from blows are both constant in the early modern period and mysterious to modern historians, since they appear to be only towels or small blankets wrapped around the head.

75. AGN, 013869 (1610), fols. 2r–v, 3r.

76. Rojas has identified analogous semiotic links between the deficient practice of Christianity and witchcraft: "Bad Christians and Hanging Toads," chapter 4.

77. AGN, 013869 (1610), fols. 9r, 10r, 11r, 12r.

78. AGN, 013869 (1610), fol. 19r. Argonz's lawyer appealed the sentence, but it was upheld.

79. AGN, 149947 (1610), fol. 1v.

80. AHN, Inqu., Leg. 1679, image 479. These examples came from a report compiled by Hernando de Solarte, a member of the Society of Jesus who assisted Bishop Venegas.

81. Monter, *Frontiers of Heresy*, chapter 12. In 1526, the Spanish Inquisition's leadership forbade the confiscation of accused witches' property, but the Logroño tribunal succeeded in getting permission to do exactly that in 1609–10: AHN, Inqu., Lib. 835, fols. 349v–350v. The 1610 confiscation of the witches' goods was overturned in August 1614 by the Suprema; see chapter 5. For the destruction of houses by medieval inquisitions, see Givens, *Inquisition and Medieval Society*.

82. AHN, Inqu., Leg. 1679, images 1801–2.

83. AHN, Inqu., Leg. 1679, images 613–14, 626, 950, 1000.

84. The confession of Mari Martín de Legarra begins on image 795 of AHN, Inqu. Leg., 1679, and continues through image 804. Her revocation begins on image 805 and continues through image 807.

85. Sansetena's language about the Devil not pursuing sex with her sounds more desolate than thankful. AHN, Inqu., Leg. 1679, images 1097–98. For other women's invocations of physical appearance in courts, see Scott, *Basque Seroras*, 139.

86. Significantly, Elbete was in the Valle de Baztan, which was wracked by witchcraft accusations.

87. AHN, Inqu., Leg. 1679, images 1101–2.

88. AGN, 100654 (1609), fol. 7r. The slander case filed by Alduncin and her son, Pedro Huic, is contained in two separate files. AGN, 100654 has fols. 1r–7r, and then jumps to fol. 131r; AGN, 2377 (1609) has the missing folios.

89. On Navarrese hatred for the French, see Berraondo Piudo, "La violencia interpersonal," 169–71.

90. Someone could write a microhistory about the conflicts between Hualde and the residents of Bera. Besides the three secular cases involving this French cleric and his Navarrese village—AGN, 10396 (1605); AGN, 029603 (1605); and AGN, 17003740 (1605)—there are two more trials in Pamplona's ADP that involve Hualde. In 1603, he was sued in episcopal court for not repaying a loan of 120 ducats made to him and his father: ADP, C/186-N. 11. In 1614, the bishop prosecuted Hualde for smuggling money into France and trying to bribe his way out of it: ADP, C/253-N. 20.

91. AGN, Olague 1606, CO_VALORACION, Leg. 2, N. 7.

92. ADP, C/135-N. 4 (1592) concerned non-payment for shoes that had been made for Don Pedro and his servants. ADP, C/153-N. 29 (1599) detailed a conflict over rent; ADP, C/165-N. 16 (1599) arose from an incident in which Don Pedro allegedly walked out of a merchant's store in Pamplona without paying for merchandise. In ADP, C/1232-N. 31 (1612), yet another Pamplona merchant demanded payment from Don Pedro. In 1614, the same Don Pedro sued Miguel de Olague for not having paid him for funeral masses: ADP, C/253-N. 7. For the controversy over Don Pedro's successor, see ADP, C/291-N. 19. Many thanks to the ADP's archivist, Teresa de Alzugaray, for allowing me to see the index cards for Olague's episcopal cases.

93. Marimartín's own accounts of her age were variable.

94. AGN, 41366 (1611), fol. 9v. It is peculiar that the royal notary did not make Marimartín swear an oath to tell the truth, since she said she was over twelve.

95. AGN, 330569 (1612), fol. 95r.

96. AGN, 330569 (1612), fol. 95r. For an evocative study of threats, emotions, and obedience in a religious environment, see Broomhall, "Miracles and Misery."

97. AGN, 330569 (1612), fol. 96r.

98. AGN, 330569 (1612), fols. 15r, 90v–91r. In the later folios, Pedroco ratified and expanded his original deposition.

99. AGN, 330569 (1612), fols. 85v–86r.

100. Marimartín's brother accompanied them to Pamplona, along with other child-witches from Olague, when they went to testify before an inquisition commissioner. As they traveled there, he threatened them with a knife and told them not to alter their statements. See AGN, 330569 (1612), fol. 85v.

101. AGN, 330569 (1612), fol. 88v. Unfortunately, the witness who described this interview did not specify the date on which it occurred. It seems likely that Marimartín told her mother the truth before she spoke to the inquisition commissioners who visited Olague. See below.

102. As we will see in chapter 5, the inquisition notaries attached to the Logroño tribunal were suspected of violating the inquisition's rule of secrecy. It's certainly possible that the commissioners in Olague also violated the same rule. Those commissioners would have been Basque speakers who did not need translators.

103. Marimartín's testimony runs from fols. 95r–98v with the quotes in this paragraph appearing on fols. 97v–98r of AGN, 330569 (1612). Ostiz's violence toward Marimartín was not particularly unusual: see Reguera, "Violencia y clero."

104. Edward J. Behrend-Martínez agrees. See his essay, "Castigation and Abuse of Children," 261.

105. AGN, 330569 (1612), fol. 101v.

106. AGN, 41366 (1611), fols. 152v–153r.

107. ADP, C/1232-N. 38. María del Juncal Campo Guinea is the expert on marital cases in Pamplona's episcopal court: see "Los procesos por causa matrimonial," and "El matrimonio clandestine."

See, too, Behrend-Martínez, *Unfit for Marriage.*

108. A closed fist was an aggravating circumstance to an assault; it was much more serious than a slap with an open palm (*palma abierta*), though the latter was degrading. See Taylor, *Honor and Violence,* 51–52.

109. ADP, C/1232-N. 38, fol. 32r. A number of Unciti's defense witnesses claimed that María had married without a dowry, as if that fact could justify Unciti's maltreatment of her. María told the court that Unciti knew she had no dowry when he married her: ADP, C/1232-N. 38, fol. 42v. She explained to the court that her original dowry with her first husband had been spent on his debts when he died. Unciti had told her that he didn't want a dowry or anything else, only her person and her children, "and so she married [him] and brought her bed and bed clothing."

110. ADP, C/1232-N. 38, fol. 30v.

111. The theme of leaving one's house and walking alone appears constantly in secular legal cases when plaintiffs wanted to denigrate the reputation of female defendants. The fact that Navarrese female witches allegedly left their houses to fly to the Devil's gatherings calls up and reverses a social norm for female behavior.

112. Eyewitnesses in the episcopal case described Alzate asking Unciti for her bed as she was preparing to leave: ADP, C/1232-N. 38, fol. 35r.

113. Unciti may not have believed he was also ruining his daughter's life by steering her into accusations against her mother. As noted previously, child-witches did not seem to carry the same degree or duration of the stain that afflicted adults. So far, no further trace of Marimartín or her mother has come to light, though Marimartín's first cousin, María de Olagüe, daughter of Domingo de Alzate, filed an episcopal suit in 1616 for deprivation of virginity under promise of marriage, which she lost: ADP, C/679-N. 26.

114. ADP, C/1232-N. 38, fol. 53r. The date of the sentence was February 20, 1612. Money could have played another role as well in these familys' enmity, as parish priest Pedro de Ostiz (Unciti's first cousin) was sued in 1599 by María de Alzate's brother, Domingo de Alzate, over a two-hundred-ducat debt: ADP, C/153-N. 29. Navarrese villagers had very long memories, and Navarrese priests were firmly embedded in their local communities. See Álvarez Urcelay, "Iglesia, moralidad, y justicia"; Reguera, "Violencia y clero"; and Scott, *Basque Seroras*, chapters 3 and 6.

115. Perhaps not surprisingly, Juan de Unciti showed up again in secular court, at a later date, for more abusive behavior. In 1634, he was ordered to pay nine ducats in compensation to Pedro de Ostiz and María de Goecoechea of the village of Aniz. Unciti had accepted a mare from Pedro and María as a pawn, and the animal subsequently died from Unciti's treatment: AGN, 134610.

116. AHN, Inqu., Leg. 1679, images 589, 614, 626.

117. AHN, Inqu., Leg. 1679, images 805–7.

118. For Solarte's and Venegas's crucial roles in attempting to end this witch hunt, see chapter 4.

119. See comments made by Hernando de Solarte in AHN, Inqu., Leg. 1679, images 480–81.

120. AHN, Inqu., Leg. 1679, images 537–38.

121. AHN, Inqu., Leg. 1679, images 539–43.

122. AHN, Inqu., Leg. 1679, image 542. The cutting out of tongues was another sign of anger in Spanish *comedias*. See Kallendorf, *Sins of the Fathers*, 135.

123. I have no explanation as to why the commissioner declined to absolve her; he had the power to do so.

124. AHN, Inqu., Leg. 1679, images 543–46, for her first session with Salazar.

125. In the left-hand margin of AHN, Inqu., Leg. 1679, image 547, a notation points out the contradiction in Ulibarri's testimony.

126. All of Salazar's statements and questions were funneled through his two Basque

translators, Joseph de Elizondo and Thomas de Galarza, both of whom were Franciscan friars: AHN, Inqu., Leg. 1679, image 547.

127. AHN, Inqu., Leg. 1679, image 547.

128. I think Ulibarri was not only distressed about her mother's death but also quietly enraged about the ways in which inquisition employees had contributed to her mother's despondency. See below.

129. For this sequence of points, AHN, Inqu., Leg. 1679, images 548–49.

130. I am thinking here of Leon de Araníbar and Miguel de Narbarte, who recommended torture to local communities but hid their advice from the inquisitors until October 1611, when Araníbar confessed what he had done to Inquisitor Salazar; see chapter 1. Sometimes, too, Basque-speaking employees of the Logroño tribunal could overhear exonerating conversations and report them, only to have the inquisitors decline to take them seriously. As we will see in chapter 5, the tribunal's notaries del secreto—the secretaries who took down evidence—were also less than professional during the witch hunt.

131. Ulibarri said, "after daybreak, her mother appeared drowned in the river . . . where she appeared on foot, her head uncovered and facing toward heaven, and they left her body alone, as if she were a desperate woman": AHN, Inqu., Leg. 1679, image 551.

132. AHN, Inqu., Leg. 1679, image 553.

133. Ulibarri's anecdote about her mother had a profound effect on Salazar, who cited it repeatedly in documents he later prepared for the Suprema; see chapter 5.

Chapter 3

1. Monter, *Frontiers of Heresy*, 272.

2. AHN, Inqu., Lib. 329, fol. 418r. This instruction was repeated in AHN, Inqu., Lib.1254, fol. 257r.

3. AHN, Inqu., Lib. 331, fol. 246r. In 1596, the Suprema had ordered Logroño's inquisitors to always begin their

visitations at the end of January or beginning of February: AHN, Inqu., Lib. 1254, fol. 257r. Navarre's weather conditions would have made that mandate very hard to fulfill.

4. This warning came almost a full year before King Philip III ordered the expulsion of Spain's moriscos in April 1609.

5. AHN, Inqu., Lib. 332, fols. 163r–v, 168v, 186r.

6. See note 3 above.

7. AHN, Inqu., Lib. 1254, fols. 248r (1568), 251r (1575).

8. AHN, Inqu., Lib. 1254, fols. 247r (1568), 249r (1570), 256r (1590).

9. AHN, Inqu., Lib. 319, fol. 219v. For an overview of the inquisition's directions on witchcraft in Navarre in 1526, see Monter, *Frontiers of Heresy*, 259–62.

10. AHN, Inqu., Lib. 319, fol. 270v.

11. AHN, Inqu., Lib. 319, fol. 270v.

12. AHN, Inqu., Lib. 319, fol. 270v.

13. Inquisitor-General Manrique enjoyed calling such congresses. He presided over one in 1525 on the heresy of *alumbradismo*, another in 1526 over the baptism of Muslims, and yet one more in 1527 on possible heresy in Desiderius Erasmus's printed works.

14. AHN, Inqu., Lib. 1231, fols. 634r–637r. For a translation of the conference's propositions and the theologian's verdicts, see Homza, *Spanish Inquisition*, 153–63.

15. The two authors of this text were Antonio de Guevara, the royal chronicler and humanist, and a Licentiate Polaneo: AHN, Inqu., Lib. 319, fols. 348r.

16. AHN, Inqu., Lib. 319, fols. 348v–350r.

17. Monter, *Frontiers of Heresy*, chapter 12. The same cautionary outlook was present in the Roman Inquisition. See foundational work in Tedeschi, *The Prosecution of Heresy*.

18. AHN, Inqu., Lib. 322, fols. 216v–217r.

19. *Consultadores* were theologians or legal experts who were called in to consult with inquisitors over verdicts.

20. This document is preserved in AHN, Inqu., Leg. 1679, image 409.

21. Monter, *Frontiers of Heresy*, 268–69.

22. For the 1595 secular case against Intza's witches, see AGN, 071319/16004729. See fol. 112r for the girls who were suffering while incarcerated.

23. AHN, Inqu., Lib. 329, fol. 398v.

24. AHN, Inqu., Leg. 1679, images 115–19. At the top of the folio, in a different hand, the document is titled "Questions that the Council has ordered us to put to the criminals about witchcraft." It is unclear whether the Suprema's fourteen questions here reflected any information they had received previously from Logroño.

25. AHN, Inqu., Leg. 1679, images 219–20.

26. AHN, Inqu., Lib. 332, fols. 230r, 251v, 252v–253r.

27. Perhaps surprisingly, there is no evidence that suspects' wealth or poverty affected the inquisitors' willingness to imprison them during this witch hunt, despite the inquisitors' constant pleas of poverty.

28. AHN, Inqu., Lib. 332, fols. 252v–253r.

29. That eagerness to please would change in 1611; see chapter 4.

30. AHN, Inqu., Lib. 794, fol. 460r. It is not clear whether these French witch suspects had actually committed witch acts inside Navarre, as the Suprema would have required.

31. AHN, Inqu., Lib. 794, fols. 447r, 448v–449r.

32. Because the trial records no longer exist, we unfortunately cannot know what signs the witnesses used to deduce that murder had occurred.

33. AHN, Inqu., Lib. 794, fol. 440r.

34. As far as we can tell, given the destruction of so much evidence. As part of their polemic against Salazar in 1613, Inquisitors Becerra and Valle would insist to the Suprema that they declined to treat children under the age of six as culpable in witchcraft because they had no ability to consent. Idoate, *Un documento*, 52–53.

35. AHN, Inqu., Lib. 795, fol. 1r.

36. For these lapses in protocol, see the end of chapter 2 as well as chapter 5.

37. AHN, Inqu., Lib. 332, fols. 252v–253r.
38. AHN, Inqu., Lib. 333, fols. 8r–v, 37r, 45r.
39. This is further evidence that witchcraft accusations were sweeping Navarre before the November 1610 auto de fe.
40. AHN, Inqu., Lib. 333, fols. 86v–87v.
41. AHN, Inqu., Lib. 795, fols. 6r, 7v, 41r.
42. AHN, Inqu., Lib. 795, fol. 75r. Araníbar explicitly spurned vigilante justice in September 1610 but actively encouraged it in the winter of 1610–11. He would later testify in secular court that he had caved in to relentless parental pressure; see chapter 1.
43. AHN, Inqu., Lib. 795, fol. 75r.
44. AHN, Inqu., Lib. 795, fol. 9r.
45. AHN, Inqu., Lib. 795, fols. 41v–42r. In the kingdom of Aragón, inquisitors brought defendants face-to-face with accusers when it came to sodomy. See Berco, *Sexual Hierarchies, Public Status*. Berco's study illustrates that the adolescent males who were willing to complain about sodomy to inquisitors were both familiar and comfortable with the law.
46. This evidence speaks to popular conceptions of the inquisition's punishments as always resulting in death.
47. AHN, Inqu., Lib. 794, fols. 448v–449r. Regretfully, the surviving evidence does not explain who these accused dead witches might have been. An adolescent female figured prominently as a witch-finder in the Intza outbreak of accusations in 1595: AGN, 071319/16004729 (1595).
48. Oco's letter to Valle is in AHN, Inqu., Lib. 794, fol. 446r. Also see AHN, Inqu., Lib. 794, fol. 448r–v.
49. The Alduncin case is in two parts. AGN, 100654 leaps from folio 1 to folio 131; AGN, 2335 contains fols. 2–130. Statements of witnesses in this trial were taken in August 1609. The final verdict was handed down on February 13, 1610, by Dr. Oco and two colleagues: AGN, 100654, fol. 140r.

50. It is unclear but nevertheless seems likely that Bishop Venegas received copies of Solarte's two letters.
51. For these points, see AHN, Inqu., Leg. 1679, images 121–22. Solarte also relayed that two sisters, age twenty and eighteen, had relatives put knives to their throats eight times in order to make them confess: AHN, Inqu., Leg. 1679, image 123.
52. AHN, Inqu., Leg. 1679, image 123.
53. Solarte also reported that villagers built bonfires around the houses of witch suspects: AHN, Inqu., Leg. 1679, image 123. On the importance of rocks as weapons, see Berraondo Piudo, "La violencia interpersonal," 137, and Davis, "Say It with Stones."
54. AHN, Inqu., Leg. 1679, images 123–24.
55. AHN, Inqu., Leg. 1679, image 337.
56. AHN, Inqu., Leg. 1679, image 338.
57. AHN, Inqu., Leg. 1679, image 122.
58. Solarte's self-description, and the inquisitors' reaction to it, exemplify the contrast in styles of spiritual correction—one private and pastoral, the other public and castigatory—mapped out in Pastore, *Tra il vangelo e la spada*. Eventually, Salazar would merge the two models; see chapter 5.
59. Endara made a lengthy, detailed confession to Logroño's inquisitors. See Scott, *Basque Seroras*, chapter 5. Endara died on November 5, 1611: AHN, Inqu., Leg. 1683, image 2205. She was buried by Martín de Irissari.
60. They also noted that Inquisitor Valle had been startled to run into Bishop Venegas and his staff in Tolosa and San Sebastián in 1609 and to learn that the bishop was going to the same villages that Valle had just left.
61. AHN, Inqu., Leg. 1679, images 198, 200, 202.
62. AHN, Inqu., Leg. 1679, images 202–3.
63. A significant context for the inquisitors' reaction to Solarte's reports were the letters they received from three different commissioners in January and early

February 1611. On January 10, 1611, rector Hualde wrote from Bera: he reported the occurrence of vigilante justice, the witches' poisoning of cows, and a widow who had died suspected of witchcraft but declined to speak a word, even at the very end: AHN, Inqu., Leg. 1679, images 333–35. On January 31, 1611, the rector Miguel Irissari (not to be confused with rector Martín de Irissari) wrote from Doneztebe-Santesteban: he was sending along two suspects whom the inquisitors wanted to see. Parents there had experimented on their own by keeping these witch suspects up all night, whereupon they had confessed their crimes. Miguel Irissari had preached long and hard about the inquisition's desire to use mercy, and as a result, more suspects had come to him to confess: AHN, Inqu., Leg. 1679, images 183–84. Finally, Araníbar wrote to the tribunal on February 3, 1611, about vigilante justice that was happening in Legassa. There had been stabbings there, and multiple men were seriously injured: AHN, Inqu., Leg. 1679, image 493. All this correspondence emphasized the reality of witchcraft and the extent of village tumult.

64. AHN, Inqu., Leg. 1679, image 204.

65. Henningsen, *Witches' Advocate*, 225, was convinced that the inquisitors in Logroño intended to interrogate Martín de Irissari and Labayen. I find the evidence more confusing, insofar as the inquisitors in the relevant text refer to questioning "two religious" (*dos religiosos*) along with Irissari—and yet the only "religious" person in play, in terms of having taken vows, was Solarte: AHN, Inqu., Leg. 1679, image 205. There is additional inquisitorial correspondence about interviewing Irissari, which came to nothing, in AHN, Inqu., Lib. 795, fol. 152v. Henningsen reported that inquisitorial comments about interrogating Labayen are in AHN, Inqu., Leg. 1683, fol. 19v, but I have been unable to find them there.

66. AHN, Inqu., Leg. 1679, image 205.

67. AHN, Inqu., Lib. 333, fol. 27v, dated December 23, 1609. Here, the Suprema's characterization of witch suspects seems to reflect the witch stereotype, rather than the people whom Inquisitor Valle was seeing on visitation.

68. The inquisitors explained their January 1610 rejection of the proposed edict of grace in their letter of March 1611: AHN, Inqu., Leg. 1679, image 273.

69. As noted earlier in this chapter, the Suprema sent a summary to King Philip III in August 1610, in which that council noted that it had conceded an edict of grace for Navarre. The council nonetheless told the king that it feared the edict would be an insufficient remedy for the witches: AHN, Inqu., Lib. 333, fol. 86v. The Suprema's pessimistic outlook may have been rhetorical, as well as reflecting what it was hearing from Logroño.

70. The trial for slander involving Imbuluzqueta was only discovered by AGN archivists in 2014: AGN, 330569. The first testimonies occurred in May 1611; the prosecution lasted almost a year, with the verdict delivered in April 1612.

71. In Bera, the rector Hualde put as many as forty children into his own house as well for safekeeping. When he dropped his guard for even an hour, the witches snatched them: Idoate, *Un documento*, 171.

72. AGN, 330569, fol. 90v.

73. Compare AGN, 330569, fol. 15r with fol. 84v.

74. AGN, 330569, fol. 101v.

75. AGN, 330569, fols. 86v–87v.

76. The evidence indicates that Pedroco was coerced into naming his parents as witches on Maundy Thursday, which would have been March 31 in 1611. His father, Miguel, did not confront Graciana de Olague about the manipulation until May 6. Based on other examples from Olague—such as María de Alzate and her daughter, Marimartín—Miguel and his wife may have spent those five weeks

trying to ascertain how and why their son had voiced the accusation.

77. AGN, 330569, fol. 4r. The opening folios of this trial are devoted to witnesses who insisted that Miguel called Graciana a witch in public.

78. AGN, 330569, fols. 28r, 29r, 30r, 31r. Miguel couldn't find anyone to offer him bail because of his extreme poverty. He asked that he be given liberty "with a judicial caution and the pledging of goods."

79. AGN, 330569, fols. 37r, 48r. It looks as if Graciana was imprisoned for perhaps an hour in Pamplona's secular jail on July 9, 1611, before being released; she was not poor. See AGN, 330569, fol. 47r.

80. For his witnesses, see AGN, 330569, fols. 84r–104r; for Graciana's, fols. 61r–79r. Though Miguel launched his own case, his witnesses as well as Graciana's are in the same trial record.

81. Urrizola represented not only Miguel de Imbuluzqueta but also Margarita and María Martín de Olagüe, the two widows who also feature in this chapter. A study of Urrizola's legal strategies in defamation cases would be useful.

82. AGN, 330569, fol. 18r–v. For an enlightening quote on the depth of knowledge that city residents could have about one another, see Contreras, *Soto contra Riquelmes*, 57.

83. AGN, 330569, fol. 22r.

84. Thus Graciana also had a reason to hate María de Alzate. The theft had occurred when Graciana and María's father were living in Olague.

85. AGN, 330569, fols. 20v–21v.

86. AGN, 330569, fols. 38r–39r, 51r.

87. AGN, 330569, fol. 75r.

88. AGN, 330569, fols. 75r–v, 77r, 79r.

89. AGN, 330569, fols. 98r, 100r.

90. In all three legal jurisdictions, duration of acquaintance was a significant factor in the weight of testimony. In an inquisition trial, for example, a defendant who produced character witnesses of only a month's rather

than a year's acquaintance was at a disadvantage.

91. AGN, 330569, fol. 84v.

92. Because Graciana filed charges first, the direction of the entire surviving case was for her benefit, even though dozens if not hundreds of folios consisted of Miguel's defense. Royal prosecutors were not allowed to change the direction of their inquiry within a single case, no matter what they and their notaries turned up. Miguel's defense witnesses were damning for Graciana, but the fact that he did not have enough money to launch his own case meant that his efforts turned out to be moot. The next prosecution assessed in this chapter proves the same point.

93. AGN, 330569, fols. 122r, 135r, 141r, 143r, 148r.

94. AGN, 330569, fols. 148r, 150r, 151r.

95. After fol. 152r–v, AGN, 330569 is not foliated. The royal court in Pamplona allowed a special class of ultra-poor prisoners in its jails. Prisoners had to file a petition to be moved into that category, and the matter was investigated before they began to receive sustenance.

96. It seems clear that in trials for slander in the secular jurisdiction, both parties were expected to finance the taking of witness testimony, and the winner could claim the payment of costs from the loser. For an example, see AGN, 100796 (1612), fol. 198r.

97. AGN, 330992.

98. AGN, 41366. This case was only discovered by AGN archivist Miriam Etxeberría in 2018.

99. Some of the earlier witnesses contended that the two women were attacked on the same day in the same residence, but later ones asserted that the beatings occurred on a Saturday and a Sunday, with the daughter, María Martín, assaulted first. For customary living arrangements in Navarre in the seventeenth century, which involved "vertical generations," see Usunáriz

Garayoa, "Cuando la convivencia es imposible."

100. AGN, 41366, fols. 12r, 14v–15r.

101. It is perhaps significant that the only deponents who mentioned fear of Don Pedro de Echaide were female. Being willing to admit fright perhaps had something to do with gender norms.

102. In the 1613 summary on the witches that Inquisitors Becerra and Valle prepared, they attributed anger to five of the suspects they had prosecuted: Idoate, *Un documento*, 127–31. Significantly, though, even the surviving witchcraft confessions that we possess do not feature rage as a motivation. See the various confessions and revocations collected at the end of AHN, Inqu., Leg. 1679, images 553–1801. These confessions were made before inquisition commissioners any time from 1609 through 1611, and the revocations were heard by Inquisitor Salazar or inquisition commissioners when Salazar was on visitation in 1611; see chapter 4. For an example of witchcraft accusations as part of feuding, see Rojas, "Bad Christians and Hanging Toads," 260–67.

103. Some of these children also testified against Miguel de Imbuluzqueta. In both cases, they never changed their stories, but they did offer different specifics about what they saw the defendants do. Imbuluzqueta led the dances and prostrated himself before the Devil, while Margarita and María Martín carried the children to the akelarres and force-fed them grotesque food. The role of adult women as conveyers of food is a clearly gendered detail.

104. Urrizola had only a single witness to attest that Graciana de Olagüe had insulted Miguel first, so he could not pursue that track as he put together Miguel's defense.

105. AGN, 41366, fol. 48v.

106. AGN, 41366, fol. 55r–v.

107. AGN, 41366, fols. 100r, 105r, 111r, 116r.

108. AGN, 41366, fols. 112r, 114r, 118r, 122r, 128r, 129r. María Martín's own petitions asserted that she had been extremely ill and in constant need of the jail's doctor. She told the court that she would have died from hunger if the warden of the prison had not provided for her. She apparently was able to prove sufficient poverty to receive support, while Miguel de Imbuluzqueta could not.

109. AGN, 41366, fol. 163r–v.

110. Given what defense witnesses said about her inability to survive a sentence of exile, it appears that Margarita still had not left in December, despite the September verdict.

111. Urrizola's second round of testimony for the surviving widow's defense runs from fols. 184r–195r in AGN, 41366.

112. AGN, 41366, fol. 184r. Rojas asserts in "Bad Christians, Hanging Toads" that witchcraft accusations had to turn on ancestry. This particular witness seems to prove her point.

113. AGN, 41366, fol. 185r–v.

114. AGN, 41366, fol. 188v.

115. AGN, 41366, fol. 189v. The verb "to chop down" (*cortar*) seems to have been part of early modern Spain's lexicon of fervor and violence, given the frequency with which Logroño's inquisitors and Navarre's villagers employed it.

116. Doña Graciana thus defamed the entire village in a legally actionable way, though there is no evidence that Olague acted on the affront: AGN, 41366, fol. 192r.

Chapter 4

1. On that date, they wrote, "the edict of grace still isn't published, and with this message, we are returning [once more] the said letter [authorizing the edict] and information about it": AHN, Inqu., Lib. 333, fol. 126r. The Suprema's original concession of the edict of grace occurred on December 23, 1609: AHN, Lib. 333, fol. 27v.

2. AHN, Inqu., Leg. 1679, image 503. This letter is dated February 8, 1611; it was received in Madrid on February 28.

3. AHN, Inqu., Leg. 1679, images 501–4.

4. AHN, Inqu., Leg. 1679, image 503.

5. AHN, Inqu., Leg. 1679, image 328. Venegas's letter to the inquisitor-general is split up in Leg. 1679: the body runs from images 325–28, with the conclusion appearing on image 447.
6. AHN, Inqu., Leg. 1679, images 227, 275.
7. The first paragraph of the first letter, dated March 9, 1611, makes clear that Inquisitor-General Sandoval asked for specifics: AHN, Inqu., Leg. 1679, image 227.
8. This request in particular was especially bizarre, since the Suprema set the guidelines for the sequestration of suspects' goods as well as exceptions to those guidelines. Perhaps it was another way of expressing displeasure at the Suprema's lack of financial support.
9. AHN, Inqu., Leg. 1679, images 283–84.
10. AHN, Inqu., Leg. 1679, image 274.
11. Henningsen knew about this correspondence: *Witches' Advocate*, 222–23, and 505n71. I discovered it by accident in AHN, Inqu., Leg. 1683; this quote from Becerra comes from images 132–33. Leg. 1683 is formally titled "Libro de visita al tribunal de Logroño por Inquisidor Martín Carrillo y Aldrete." It contains a whopping 5,782 images; its contents are not in chronological order. Leg. 1683's materials supposedly are confined to the years 1617–20, but the dossier also holds multiple communications from 1611–14 by and about Logroño's inquisitors and the tribunal's notaries. The inquisitor conducting the visitation in 1619, Carrillo y Aldrete, must have wanted a historical assessment of dissension and malfeasance among Logroño's inquisitors. He and his team consequently moved earlier communications from inquisitors Becerra and Salazar, as well as the tribunal's prosecutor, Isidoro San Vincente, out of Leg. 1679, where they belonged, and inserted them into Leg. 1683. See chapter 5 for Leg. 1683's damning details on the notaries.
12. AHN, Inqu., Leg. 1683, images 94, 97, 98–99.
13. AHN, Inqu., Leg. 1683, images 98–99.
14. AHN, Inqu., Leg. 1683, image 101.
15. AHN, Inqu., Leg. 1683, image 103.
16. AHN, Inqu., Leg. 1683, image 140.
17. AHN, Inqu., Leg. 1683, image 110.
18. AHN, Inqu., Leg. 1683, images 104–6.
19. Given Salazar's complaints about the notaries' independence, as manifested by their absences, it may be meaningful that the inquisitor-general only authorized one to go on the new visitation in 1611. Perhaps the inquisitor-general feared the inquisitor on visitation could lose control over the notaries if there was more than one to supervise.
20. Sandoval did not explain how this process would take place. Presumably, the edict would have been printed in Pamplona or Logroño and then copies would have been carried to the villages, which lacked printing presses.
21. AHN, Inqu., Lib. 333, fol. 144r–v.
22. AHN, Inqu., Lib. 333, fol. 145r.
23. AHN, Inqu., Lib. 333, fol. 145v. The phrase Sandoval used was "dolicapaces," a Spanish translation of *doli capax* in Latin.
24. AHN, Inqu., Lib. 333, fols. 145v–146r, 147r.
25. AHN, Inqu., Lib. 333, fols. 146v–147r.
26. AHN, Inqu., Lib. 795, fols. 152r–153v.
27. AHN, Inqu., Lib. 795, fols. 152v–153r. Henningsen believed that this dressed toad was delivered to the tribunal by June 1611: *Witches' Advocate*, 220.
28. AHN, Inqu., Lib. 795, fol. 153r–v. It appears that information about Venegas's household and communications was being leaked to the Logroño tribunal, but I do not know how or by whom.
29. AHN, Inqu., Leg. 1679, images 485–87.
30. It's also possible that Venegas refrained from commenting on Salazar because he knew he was the first inquisitor named by Sandoval.
31. The memorial collated by Venegas from his investigators' findings runs from images 451–67 in AHN, Inqu., Leg. 1679.

32. AHN, Inqu., Lib. 1243, fol. 228r. Philip III's attitude about clerical petitions to Rome recalls the nightmarish scenario that his father, Philip II, presided over when the archbishop of Toledo, Bartolomé Carranza, was imprisoned by the inquisition in Spain, and Carranza's friends in Rome tried desperately to transfer his case there. Carranza was a prisoner in Spain from 1558–67, after which his trial was moved to Rome, where it lasted another nine years. Carranza abjured sixteen erroneous propositions in his writings in 1576 and died seven days later. See Tellechea Idígoras, *Fray Bartolomé Carranza*.

33. Henningsen makes much of Salazar's decision here: *Witches' Advocate*, 175–80.

34. AHN, Inqu., Leg. 1679, images 411–12. Henningsen believed Salazar voted for torture because

> this [was the witches'] only hope of survival . . . even before the sinister discoveries in Zugarramurdi were revealed to the public in all their horror, Salazar had expressed his doubts as to whether the conclusions of the Inquisition rested on solid foundations. It is hard to define exactly how skeptical Salazar had become. . . . It is obvious that Salazar had become skeptical about the premises on which his colleagues had based their conduct of the trial, but he probably realized with resignation that he could not prevent them from holding their auto de fe. The affair had reached the point of no return.

See *Witches' Advocate*, 180. Among the multiple problems with these conclusions, the tribunal did not receive permission to hold an auto de fe until October 1610, so it is unlikely that Salazar's trajectory of reasoning in June 1610 involved that outcome. The tribunal didn't have formal charges prepared against its witch suspects until September 1610.

35. Henningsen briefly described this particular evidence in *Witches' Advocate* and used it to reiterate what he viewed as the fundamental and eternal differences between Salazar and his colleagues (223). The votes of the three inquisitors are in AHN, Inqu., Leg. 1679, images 489–91.

36. Araníbar's letter about Zubieta is in AHN, Inqu., Leg. 1679, images 1–2.

37. AHN, Inqu., Leg. 1679, Image 490.

38. AHN, Inqu., Leg. 1679, images 490–91. Becerra and Valle wrote that mob action had no bearing on the substance of the Zubieta cases.

39. Henningsen, *Salazar Documents*, 28–30. Goñi Gaztambide agrees that Salazar was changing over time during his visitation: *Historia de los obispos de Pamplona*, 150.

40. AHN, Inqu., Leg. 1679, image 471.

41. AHN, Inqu., Leg. 1679, image 472.

42. Henningsen found the Suprema's June 28 letter in AHN, Inqu., Lib. 333, fols. 170v–171r: *Witches' Advocate*, 222, 252.

43. AHN, Inqu., Leg. 1679, image 473.

44. AHN, Inqu., Leg. 1679, image 558.

45. AHN, Inqu., Leg. 1679, image 553. See chapter 2 for an assessment of this distressing episode.

46. AHN, Inqu., Leg. 1679, image 1658. In October 1611, Graciana called commissioner Araníbar to her village of Lekaroz in order to revoke her confession. She was sick and believed she was going to die; she wanted to discharge her conscience. She had never been a witch, but children had named her as such: AHN, Inqu., Leg. 1679, image 1659.

47. AHN, Inqu., Leg. 1679, images 1684–1685.

48. For an overview of Salazar's legal priorities, see Homza, "Expert Lawyer."

49. Salazar's direct quote is "quedando los alcaldes muy atras a donde hallarse sin probanza ni processo contra ninguna dellas," which seems to imply that he expected the secular justices in San Sebastián to put the accused witches on trial.

50. The quotes from Salazar about this experience are in AHN, Inqu., Lib. 795, fol. 203r–v.

51. Henningsen briefly summarizes the Elgorriaga case in *Witches' Advocate*, 220–21.

52. Azurmendi, *Las brujas de Zugarramurdi*, 31–49, asserts that Basque villagers in this epoch would have found the secular legal system to be alien, a point contradicted by the following works: Scott, *Basque Seroras*; Homza, "When Witches Litigate"; Pimoulier, "Entre el luto y la supervivencia"; Behrend-Martínez, *Unfit for Marriage*; Barahona, *Sex Crimes, Honour, and the Law*; Dyer, "Heresy and Dishonor"; Monteano Sorbet, *Los navarros ante el hambre*.

53. Rojas argues that the label of "witch" in early modern Navarre was inextricably tied to the defective practice of Christianity: "Bad Christians and Hanging Toads," chapter 4.

54. Homza, "When Witches Litigate," 261–64.

55. The inquisition's legal system cared about the intentions behind the facts, though it also had no compunction in deducing motives from actions, since outward, visible works were read as signs of religious belief in early modern Catholic culture. In contrast, Navarre's secular court cared about facts and much less about motives, though defendants tried to excuse their actions by referring to intentions.

56. AGN, 072902 (1613), fol. 201r for Perochena and fol. 204r for Zuito.

57. AGN, 072902 (1613), fol. 104r.

58. AGN, Prot. Not. Simon de Asco, caja 15045/7, #89: "Auto de desistimiento hecho por Juan de Aldico y su muger y consortes, vezinos de Arraioz, en favor de Juan Perochena y Miguel Zuito, vezinos del mismo lugar. 14 marzo 1613." Cummins notes that while complainants could be empowered through the courts, they also could come under significant pressure from the offenders and their allies: "Forgiving Crimes," 260.

59. While they were in jail and on trial, their defense lawyer had noted that they were "very much lost and destroyed with the imprisonment, and the costs and expenses they have suffered": AGN, 100796 (1612), fol. 170r.

60. AGN, Prot. Not. Miguel de Narbarte, caja 15028/2, 1612, #61. Formal peace contracts for early modern Spain generally have not been studied, though dozens exist in the AGN's notarial records. For peace-making efforts in Castile, see Taylor, *Honor and Violence*, 57–59, 81–83. See also Palmer, "Piety and Social Distinction"; Janson, "'Pro bono pacis'"; Wray, "Instruments of Concord." Cummins writes that in early modern Naples, "true reconciliation" required the erasure of the original injury, rather than just ending hostilities. He comments that such agreements "were in form and practice religious; the debates over remission and forgiveness mirror discussions of confession": "Forgiving Crimes," 261–64.

61. AGN, Prot. Not. Miguel de Narbarte, caja 15028/2, 1612, #61, fols. 1v–2r.

62. Hernale was recorded as "absent" (*ausente*): AGN, Elgorriaga, CO_ VALORACION, Leg. 23, N. 13–1, fol. 14v.

63. ADP, C/242-N. 2, fol. 211v, where the neighbors said, "although the prosecutor is in charge, they [the residents of Erratzu] are the ones who are following the case and making investigations into it, and they contributed money toward the trial." On fol. 218v, the court record reports that residents of Erratzu had carried out an allotment among themselves to collect money for the trial's expenses and had come up with 120 ducats. The residents' language here—equating their imprisonment with what needed to happen to their rector—echoes the egalitarian economic and social status of legal residents of the Valle de Baztan.

64. ADP, C/242-N. 2, fols. 15v, 17r.

65. Midelfort has cautioned us to only use the term "witch panic" for more severe

circumstances in which suspects fled: "Witch Craze?," 24. The evidence from this witch hunt meets that criterion.

66. ADP, C/242-N. 2, fols. 29r, 32r, 45r.
67. ADP, C/242-N. 2, fol. 97r.
68. ADP, C/242-N. 2, fol. 64v.
69. For example, the married couple from Erratzu, Pedro Etxegarai and Margarita Etxegarai (she was also known as Margarita de Zubipunta) started a secular prosecution against Juan Iturralde, Pedro de Inda, and other residents of Erratzu "over injuries through accusations of witchcraft": AGN, 225559, now missing.
70. ADP, C/242-N. 2, fols. 271r–273r.
71. ADP, C/242-N. 2, fol. 211v.
72. ADP, C/242-N. 2, fols. 48r, 101r.
73. AGN, Prot. Not. Simon Asco, Caja 15045/8, #47. Dated May 3, 1614, this notarial document is an attempt to recover money owed to Aguirre for having undertaken a legal case on behalf of forty-five people in Erratzu—all male—"on account of certain imprisonments and accusations." The text does not say when the legal case began or what its outcome was. Thirty men owed Aguirre one ducat apiece; one person owed him five and a half reales; and fourteen owed him seven reales each. In the last category was the constable of Erratzu in 1611, Juan Iturralde, who supervised the imprisonments of witch suspects on Aguirre's orders.
74. ADP, C/242-N. 2. For Salazar's interactions with Aguirre, see the unnumbered text appearing between fols. 58r–59r, as well as fol. 60r. Erratzu witnesses for the episcopal prosecution against Aguirre also said they had spoken with Salazar: fols. 215r and 271r–v.
75. As in his earlier correspondence with the tribunal, even in October 1611 Araníbar attempted to duck full responsibility for village violence. He told Salazar that he indeed had given Aguirre authorization to carry out imprisonments, "as were happening in all the other places"—

whereby Araníbar neglected to admit that he had given the same instructions in all the other places. Moreover, he wrote that notary Martín de Elizondo had told him that when Elizondo was in Logroño, Inquisitor Becerra had told him that imprisoning the "master witches" was good: AHN, Inqu., Leg. 1679, image 417. I doubt Becerra ever gave such an order, because Araníbar would have referred to it in his many letters to the tribunal about village violence, as well as his testimony in secular court. Furthermore, if such an authorization from Becerra had been widely known, we would expect mentions of it to occur in the correspondence of other inquisition commissioners too, such as Lorenzo Hualde. Araníbar's larger point in his October 1611 letter to Salazar was to ask if he could testify in episcopal court, despite his immunity as an inquisition familiar. Some people in the bishop's entourage thought that if Araníbar testified that he had given Aguirre the order, one of the charges would be dropped: AHN, Inqu., Leg. 1679, images 417–18. Clearly, some people within the episcopal hierarchy wanted Aguirre cleared of the charges, and Araníbar sided with them, but Salazar did not. In the narrative Salazar wrote in October 1613, he commented on the horrors of the Erratzu witch hunt; see chapter 5.
76. AGN, 072902 (1613), fols. 50v–51r, 53v.
77. Becerra and Valle's letter runs from fols. 157r–160r in AHN, Inqu., Lib. 795.
78. AHN, Inqu., Lib. 795, fol. 157r.
79. AHN, Inqu., Lib. 795, fol. 157r.
80. AHN, Inqu., Lib. 795, fol. 157r.
81. AHN, Inqu., Lib. 795, fol. 158r–v.
82. AHN, Inqu., Lib. 795, fol. 159r. Of course, the inquisitor-general and the Suprema could have compared Becerra and Valle's assertions about the pots and ointments in June to Salazar's comments in September. There was obvious disagreement among the inquisitors on the ointments' authenticity.

83. We have no idea whether Inquisitor Salazar shared his colleagues' opinions about the other jurisdictions' cases in May–June 1611, as there is no extant evidence to tell us where he stood on the matter.

84. AHN, Inqu., Leg. 1679, images 213–14.

85. See the description of San Vincente's July 1611 communication in Henningsen, *Witches' Advocate*, 266–68.

86. AHN, Inqu., Leg. 1679, image 217.

87. Henningsen, *Witches' Advocate*, 268–69.

88. The inquisitor-general had originally extended the edict of grace for four to six months in his communication of March 24, 1611, which meant it should have ended in September 1611. See below for the possible links among Salazar in the field, another extension of the edict, and the tribunal's rage. For Henningsen's appraisal of San Vincente's October missive, see *Witches' Advocate*, 272–74.

89. AHN, Inqu., Lib. 795, fols. 208r–209r.

90. AHN, Inqu., Leg. 1683, image 206. The detail about San Vincente's trip was recorded in the tribunal's book of absences for its employees; see chapter 5 for the controversies that book generated. See also Henningsen, *Witches' Advocate*, 270.

91. Henningsen hypothesizes that information about the renewed edict of grace had reached the tribunal by the time San Vincente returned on September 21, 1611: *Witches' Advocate*, 271.

92. AHN, Inqu., Lib. 795, fol. 205r: "all of them have confessed, giving signs of their repentance with many tears." On the performativity of repentance, see Johnson, "Feeling Certainty, Performing Sincerity." Significantly, the inquisition employees who heard confessions and revocations to witchcraft from May to December 1611 occasionally commented on whether the people confessing were able to cry. See, for example, AHN, Inqu., Leg. 1679, image 1035, where a confessing witch "said all this with pain and obvious repentance, and without

tears, though she tried to show she was crying." The question of whether witches were unable to cry has never been investigated for early modern Spain.

93. AHN, Inqu., Lib. 795, fols. 205v–206r.

94. Henningsen agrees that Salazar sent this letter directly to Sandoval, but he also believes that Salazar's September 4 letter eventually was read by the inquisitors in the tribunal: *Witches' Advocate*, 253, 271.

95. Logroño's inquisitors were behaving according to professional norms when they attempted to block their employees from testifying in other legal jurisdictions.

96. I believe this royal petition was prompted by the Logroño tribunal's attempts to obstruct secular court proceedings against inquisition familiar Miguel de Narbarte, whom the royal prosecutor wanted to prosecute for the death of Graciana de Barrenechea. For this petition, see AGN, *Sección de Negocios Eclesiásticos*, Leg. 2, Carpeta 14, cited in Iribarren, "Interesante document," 427. Also see Homza, "When Witches Litigate," 261–64, and 264n114. Given his sense of legal privilege, it is entirely possible that Salazar endorsed or recommended that the tribunal try to prevent secular court testimony by inquisition employees.

Chapter 5

1. The difficulty here lies in not knowing whether complaints were brought to Pamplona's secular court in 1610 that it declined to pursue.

2. The justice pursued by Bishop Venegas and Pamplona's royal court was a mixture of the retributive and restorative. Those who had injured others had to suffer; at the same time, these legal jurisdictions sought to bring peace to village communities.

3. AHN Inqu., Leg. 1679, images 237–69 for Salazar's entire report.

4. AHN, Inqu., Leg. 1679, image 238.

5. Only one of Salazar's interviewees, an eighty-year-old man named Juan de Saldis, reported that his wife knew he was gone. Saldis, "of very good character and speech, said his wife very often realized he had been gone, and asked him where he had been when he returned to bed because he was so cold." Salazar could not interview the wife because she had been dead for years: AHN, Inqu., Leg. 1679, image 238.

6. AHN, Inqu., Leg. 1679, images 240–41.

7. AHN, Inqu., Leg. 1679, image 241.

8. As another sign of his obedience, Salazar's comments in this regard reflected the Suprema's original questionnaire for the tribunal, which it had forwarded to the tribunal in March 1609.

9. The witch suspects who voiced these details were expanding, through their own creativity, the paradigm of witchcraft that Salazar and his colleagues thought they would hear: AHN, Inqu., Leg. 1679, images 242–43.

10. AHN, Inqu., Leg. 1679, image 244.

11. AHN, Inqu., Leg. 1679, images 250–51.

12. AHN, Inqu., Leg. 1679, image 249.

13. AHN, Inqu., Leg. 1679, image 250.

14. AHN, Inqu., Leg. 1679, image 252.

15. AHN, Inqu., Leg. 1679, images 253–54. The anecdote about breastfeeding a snake is a phenomenal expansion of Eve's experience with the serpent in the Book of Genesis.

16. AHN, Inqu., Leg. 1679, image 255.

17. For intellectual conflicts over witchcraft that affected the Roman Inquisition, Duni, "Doubting Witchcraft," as well as Tedeschi, "Question of Magic."

18. The lack of actual witnesses to apostasy was what had prompted Salazar's dissenting vote on María de Arburu in June 1610. In the March 1612 report, Salazar wrote that the witches in Navarre were allegedly so widespread and active that it would have been impossible to cover up their activities if their works had really happened. Here, he seems to have been paraphrasing or

quoting Venegas, since Venegas wrote the same thing to the inquisitor-general in March 1611. AHN, Inqu., Leg. 1679, image 259.

19. AHN, Inqu., Leg. 1679, images 259–60.

20. AHN, Inqu., Leg. 1679, image 261.

21. AHN, Inqu., Leg. 1679, image 262.

22. AHN, Inqu., Leg. 1679, images 266–67.

23. AHN, Inqu., Leg. 1679, image 269.

24. Salazar had worked for and interacted with bishops from 1588 to 1609. His familiarity with Tridentine episcopal values is an important context for his interactions with Bishop Venegas: AHN, Inqu., Lib. 2220, N. 2, fols. 1v–2r.

25. AHN, Inqu., Leg. 1679, images 329–33. It is fascinating to contemplate how Becerra and Valle engaged in "mythologies of coherence" with Salazar, just as modern scholars have. See Skinner, "Meaning and Understanding."

26. Salazar made two marginal notations on their letter. Becerra and Valle had accused him of not caring about expenses, but he had been obliged to take along so many personnel. As for their point that he should have listed witnesses against suspects, he protested that such was impossible, given that he had upwards of four thousand deponents. AHN, Inqu., Leg. 1679, image 329.

27. Idoate, Un documento. Though available to Henningsen, he did not use this text in Witches' Advocate.

28. Salazar's visitation records are referred to in Idoate, Un documento, 77.

29. For an appraisal of Endara's confession, in which she pinned the blame for her diabolical conversion on the local serora, Catelina de Sopalde, see Scott, Basque Seroras, chapter 5.

30. In accordance with wider European stereotypes, inquisitors Becerra and Valle stressed that their witch suspects were furious.

31. Idoate, Un documento, 42.

32. Idoate, Un documento, 55. Indart revoked her confession before Salazar in 1611.

33. Idoate, Un documento, 57.

34. Idoate, *Un documento*, 70–71. With this anecdote, Becerra and Valle were admitting by default that María de Arburu, whose case had caused so much trouble with Salazar's dissenting vote, might have been present in the akelarre without rejecting her Christianity. They did not comment on their contradiction.

35. Idoate, *Un documento*, 77.

36. Idoate, *Un documento*, 95.

37. AHN, Inqu., Lib. 332, fol. 215v; Lib. 794, fols. 387–88v.

38. Idoate, *Un documento*, 68.

39. Idoate, *Un documento*, 96.

40. Idoate, *Un documento*, 97.

41. Idoate, *Un documento*, 93–94.

42. Significantly, in September 1609 the Suprema gave the tribunal permission to prosecute suspected judaizers if they crossed into Navarre, even if they had not practiced Jewish rites in Spain: AHN, Inqu., Lib. 333, fols. 1v–2r.

43. The scholarship on medieval Europeans' attitudes toward Jews and Judaism is massive, as is the literature on early modern Spain and its Jewish converts to Christianity. As a sample, see Cohen, *The Friars and the Jews*; Cohen, *Living Letters of the Law*; Kamen, *Spanish Inquisition*; Bodian, *Dying in the Law of Moses*; Ray, *After Expulsion*; Nirenberg, *Anti-Judaism*.

44. AHN, Inqu., Leg. 1679, images 341–60 for Salazar's entire memorial of October 1613.

45. AHN, Inqu., Leg. 1679, images 341–45.

46. AHN, Inqu., Leg. 1679, images 345–46, 349.

47. AHN Inqu., Leg. 1679, image 348.

48. AHN Inqu., Leg. 1679, image 348.

49. For references to the correspondence sent from the tribunal to Pamplona's viceroy on May 17, 1611, which had no effect, see AHN Inqu., Lib. 795, fol. 157r–v.

50. AHN, Inqu., Leg. 1679, image 348. Salazar left on visitation on May 22; perhaps he was not in the tribunal when the letter was composed. Clearly inquisitors could send correspondence without consulting one another.

51. In 1613, Salazar thereby concurred with Bishop Venegas's comments in spring 1611 about biases.

52. AHN, Inqu., Leg. 1679, image 347. Salazar's summary of his colleagues' June 1611 letter appears in his own later report of October 1613.

53. Unfortunately, the surviving evidence does not explain why the Suprema altered its earlier mandate and allowed Salazar and the tribunal to hear revocantes.

54. AHN, Inqu., Leg. 1679, image 347.

55. Henningsen found some of the correspondence in Leg. 1683 about the notaries, but not all of it; he did not explore deeply what he discovered. See *Witches' Advocate*, 308.

56. Remarkably, San Vincente had written independently to Inquisitor-General Sandoval in March 1611—after Sandoval's general rebuke of the tribunal—to offer to work as one of the notaries del secreto: AHN, Inqu., Leg. 1679, image 5.

57. AHN, Inqu., Leg. 1683, image 118.

58. AHN, Inqu., Leg. 1683, image 120.

59. AHN, Inqu., Leg. 1683, image 121.

60. AHN, Inqu., Leg. 1683, images 146–47.

61. AHN, Inqu., Lib. 333, fols. 265v–266r.

62. Though Becerra ultimately had to tell Inquisitor-General Sandoval that the letter had been opened by others, he did his very best to diminish that breach in privacy by attributing it to his colleagues, Valle and Salazar: AHN, Inqu., Leg. 1683, image 146. Sandoval learned the truth—that a notary had opened the letter—when San Vincente wrote again on April 1, 1612.

63. AHN, Inqu., Leg. 1683, images 226, 228–29.

64. AHN, Inqu., Leg. 1683, images 173–74.

65. The inquisitor-general had already been told by Salazar in March 1611 that the notaries were frequently absent.

66. Apparently taking down genealogies was less laborious than writing down witness testimony, perhaps because the notaries

could set their own schedules and work in their home districts.

67. AHN, Inqu., Leg. 1683, images 174–75.

68. AHN, Inqu., Leg. 1683, image 176.

69. AHN, Inqu., Leg. 1683, images 177–78.

70. AHN, Inqu., Leg. 1683, image 179.

71. AHN, Inqu., Leg. 1683, image 180.

72. Significantly, the Suprema did not exempt Salazar from the fine, even though he had been away from the tribunal for most of 1611.

73. AHN, Inqu., Leg. 1683, image 182.

74. AHN, Inqu., Leg. 1683, images 114–15.

75. Henningsen says that San Vincente explicitly requested a transfer from Logroño, but I cannot locate the source in his references. See *Witches' Advocate*, 312.

76. AHN, Inqu., Leg. 1683, image 152.

77. AHN, Inqu., Leg. 1683, image 153.

78. AHN, Inqu., Leg. 1683, image 136.

79. AHN, Inqu., Leg. 1679, image 371.

80. AHN, Inqu., Leg. 1679, images 393–96. Image 393 contains the title, "Lo que convenia proveer en el remedio deste negocio de la secta de brujas," which translates as "What is advisable to provide as a remedy in this business about the witches' sect." Image 396 contains the line "the last document we gave to the Consejo [Suprema], 1614." Henningsen paraphrased the contents of this text and noted that it was radical but did not evaluate its propositions: *Witches' Advocate*, 366–70.

81. AHN, Inqu., Leg. 1679, image 393. The commissioner of Maestu, Philipe Diez, had spurned any pastoral care for the mother of María de Ulibarri, who subsequently committed suicide. See chapter 2.

82. AHN, Inqu., Leg. 1679, image 394.

83. AHN, Inqu., Leg. 1679, images 395–96.

84. The Suprema's new instructions of August 1614 run from images 397–403 in AHN, Inqu., Leg. 1679. All the quotes in this paragraph come from image 397.

85. My account here revises Amelang, "Between Doubt and Discretion."

86. AHN, Inqu., Leg. 1679, image 398.

87. AHN, Inqu., Leg. 1679, image 398.

88. AHN, Inqu., Leg. 1679, image 401.

89. AHN, Inqu., Leg. 1679, images 398, 400.

90. AHN, Inqu., Leg. 1679, image 399.

91. AHN, Inqu., Leg. 1679, image 399.

92. AHN, Inqu., Leg. 1679, image 403.

93. AHN, Inqu., Leg. 1679, image 402.

94. AHN, Inqu., Leg. 1679, image 402.

95. AHN, Inqu., Leg. 1679, images 402–3.

96. AHN, Inqu., Leg. 1679, image 403.

97. For an analogous command of silence over questions of judaizing in Murcia, see Contreras, *Soto contra Riquelmes*, 284–86.

98. AHN, Inqu., Leg. 1679, image 380, for this particular passage.

99. I treat this point at greater length in Homza, "Local Knowledge and Catholic Reform."

100. AGN, Prot. Not. Miguel/Sancho Narbarte, Caja 15029, #2, document 224. Miguel de Narbarte's son, Sancho, took over his father's notarial practice.

101. AGN, Prot. Not. Miguel/Sancho Narbarte, Caja 15029, #2, document 225.

102. AGN, Prot. Not. Miguel/Sancho Narbarte, Caja 15029, #3, document 2.

103. AGN, Olague, CO_VALORACION, Leg. 2, N. 7–1, for 1606; AGN, Olague, CO_VALORACION, Leg. 2, N. 8–1, for 1612.

104. For the census in Arraioz in 1612, see AGN, Arraioz, CO_VALORACION, Leg. 5, N. 15–1, fol. 14v. Significantly, however, the missing owners in Arraioz had different values assigned to their homes, unlike the absent owners in Olague.

105. Azurmendi, *Las brujas*, 167–75 for the discussion of *Gero*, with the quote appearing on 175.

106. Azurmendi, *Las brujas*, 171. Azurmendi did not cite the source for this evidence, but it lies in AHN, Inqu., Leg. 1679, image 32.

Epilogue

1. García-Arenal, "Polyphony of Voices," explores the ways in which inquisition defendants in Palermo's prison

radicalized their religious identities as a result of their incarceration.

2. That phrase is used by Restall and Fernández-Armesto, *Conquistadors*. For a fascinating consideration of the effect of distance on Philip II's government, see Parker, *Grand Strategy of Philip II*, 47–76.

3. Though the Suprema restored a chain of command with its new instructions of 1614, none of the surviving evidence indicates that the new protocol was easy to implement. Salazar himself commented in 1617 on the lengthy and time-consuming processes of communicating and enforcing the new mandates vis-à-vis the tribunal's employees: AHN, Inqu., Leg. 1679, image 32. In *Between Court and Confessional*, Lynn examines the many ways in which an inquisitor's job could go off the rails.

4. Recent scholars have noted, "On the one hand, the [Spanish] monarchy was capable of mobilizing sufficient forces to establish dominance through the use of violence; on the other, its legal culture and political practices obviated both the inclination and the ability to create an administration of its own capable of effectively controlling the territory." Though the context for this quote is Spain's creation of a global empire, its implications are also relevant for the internal history of the peninsula. See Ruíz Ibáñez and Sabatini, "Monarchy as Conquest," 503. See as well the review essay by Price, "Versailles Revisited."

5. The study of patronage in early modern Europe is vast. As a foundational work, see Kettering, *Patrons, Brokers, and Clients*.

6. Henningsen, *Witches' Advocate*, 385.

7. Henningsen, *Witches' Advocate*, 359, 385.

8. Henningsen, *Witches' Advocate*, 385–86.

9. Bleichmar et al., *Science in the Spanish and Portuguese Empires*; Portuondo, *Secret Science*; Barrera-Osorio, *Experiencing Nature*. For more evidence of forensic efforts in this witch hunt, see AHN, Inqu., Leg. 1679, images 1033–36.

10. Pastore, *Il vangelo e la spada*. For other challenges to Pastore's argument, see Lynn, *Between Court and Confessional*, chapter 1, as well as Homza, "Webs of Conversation and Discernment."

11. AHN, Inqu., Leg. 1679, images 21–22. None of the materials in Leg. 1679 that relate to the later witch hunt in Bizkaia has been studied by historians.

12. AHN, Inqu., Leg. 1679, images 29–31.

13. AHN, Inqu., Leg. 1679, images 32–33.

14. AHN, Inqu., Leg. 1679, image 33.

15. AHN, Inqu., Leg. 1679, image 35.

16. AHN, Inqu., Leg. 1679, image 40.

17. For another example of an inquisitor who touted his ability to discern, see Lynn, *Between Court and Confessional*, chapter 4, on Juan Adam de la Parra.

18. AHN, Inqu., Leg. 1679, image 40. On image 37, Salazar noted that the remedy proposed by the Jesuit Medrano should be postponed.

19. As it turns out, in this particular instance, Salazar's superiors compromised. In 1617, they declined to extend the authority to absolve Bizkaia's witch suspects to the Jesuit order. But they nevertheless gave "inquisition commissioners, local priests, and local confessors approved by the bishop's representative" the power to absolve those suspects in Bizkaia for a single year: AHN, Inqu., Leg. 1679, image 45.

Bibliography

Archives
Archivo Diocesano de Pamplona
Archivo Histórico Nacional, Madrid

Archivo Real y General de Navarra,
  Pamplona

Primary Printed Sources
Andueza, Ignacio de. *Manual de casados con
  un tratado del Santíssimo Sacramento.*
  Pamplona, 1618.
*Constituciones synodales del obispado de
  Pamplona.* Pamplona, 1591.
Idoate, Florencio. *Un documento de la
  inquisición sobre brujería en Navarra.*
  Pamplona: Editorial Aranzadi,
  1972.
Jiménez, Matías. *Oraciones christianas sobre
  los evangelios de los domingos de advento.*
  Pamplona, 1618.

Mata, Juan de la, O. P. *Parayso virginal de
  discursos predicables en las fiestas de la
  siempre Virgen María, con doze pláticas
  para los primeros domingos del mes.*
  Pamplona, 1630.
Molino, Antonio. *Exercicios espirituales.*
  Pamplona, 1618.
Mongastón, Juan. *Relación del auto de fe.* 1610.
  Transcribed in Manuel Fernández Nieto,
  *Proceso a la brujería: en torno al auto de
  fe de los brujos de Zugarramurdi*, 30–72.
  Madrid: Tecnos, 1989.

Secondary Printed Sources
Alberola, Eva Lara. "El panfleto de don Juan
  de Mongastón sobre las brujas de
  Zugarramurdi (Auto de fe de Logroño
  de 1610), editado en 1611: ¿Documento
  histórico o literatura?" *Revista del
  Instituto de Lengua y Cultura Españolas* 33
  (2017): 259–82.
Alcoberro Pericay, Agustí. "Los otros 'abogados
  de las brujas': El debate sobre la caza de

brujas en Cataluña." *Revista internacional
  de estudios vascos* 9 (2012): 92–115.
Álvarez Urcelay, Milagros. "Iglesia, moralidad
  y justicia en Guipúzcoa, siglos XVI–
  XVIII." In *Entre el fervor y la violencia:
  Estudios sobre los vascos y la Iglesia (siglos
  XVI–XVIII)*, edited by Rosario Porres
  Marijuán, 99–130. Bilbao: Universidad
  de País Vasco, 2015.

Amelang, James. "Between Doubt and Discretion: Revising the Rules for Prosecuting Spanish Witches." In *Making, Using, and Resisting the Law in European History*, edited by Günther Lottes, Eero Medijainen, and Jón Viðar Sigurðssen, 77–92. Pisa: Plus, 2008.

American Historical Review Exchange: "Rethinking the History of Childhood." *American Historical Review* 125 (2020): 1260–1322.

Antolini, Paola. *Los agotes: Historia de una exclusion*. Baztan Valle: Ediciones Istmo, 1989.

Arizcun Cela, Alejandro. *Economía y sociedad en un valle pirenaico del antiguo régimen: Baztán 1600–1841*. Pamplona: Institución Principe de Viana, 1988.

Arzak, Juan Ignacio Paul. "Brujería, frontera, y poder." *Bilduma* 13 (1999): 170–90.

Azurmendi, Mikel. *Las brujas de Zugarramurdi*. Pamplona: Editorial Almuzara, 2013.

Bailey, Michael D. *Battling Demons: Witchcraft, Heresy, and Reform in the Late Middle Ages*. University Park: Penn State University Press, 2003.

———. "From Sorcery to Witchcraft: Clerical Conceptions of Magic in the Later Middle Ages." *Speculum* 76 (2001): 960–90.

Barahona, Renato. *Sex Crimes, Honour, and the Law in Early Modern Spain: Vizcaya, 1528–1753*. Toronto: University of Toronto Press, 2003.

Barrera-Osorio, Antonio. *Experiencing Nature: The Spanish-American Empire and the Early Scientific Revolution*. Austin: University of Texas Press, 2010.

Behrend-Martínez, Edward. "The Castigation and Abuse of Children in Early Modern Spain." In *The Formation of the Child in Early Modern Spain*, edited by Grace E. Coolidge, 249–72. Abingdon: Routledge, 2016.

———. *Unfit for Marriage: Impotent Spouses on Trial in the Basque Region of Spain, 1650–1750*. Reno: University of Nevada Press, 2007.

Behringer, Wolfgang. "Weather, Hunger and Fear: Origins of the European Witch-Hunts in Climate, Society and Mentality." *German History* 13 (1995): 1-27.

Bennassar, Bartolomé, ed. *L'Inquisition espagnole, XV–XIX siècle*. Paris: Hachette, 1979.

Berco, Cristian. *Sexual Hierarchies, Public Status: Men, Sodomy, and Society in Spain's Golden Age*. Toronto: University of Toronto Press, 2006.

Berraondo Piudo, Mikel. "Los hijos como víctimas: El infanticidio en Navarra (siglos XVI–XVII)." *Memoria y Civilización* 16 (2013): 55–82.

———. "La violencia interpersonal en la Navarra moderna (siglos XVI–XVII)." PhD diss., Universidad de Navarra, 2012.

Berraondo Piudo, Mikel, and Félix Segura Urra. *Odiar: Violencia y Justicia, siglos XIII–XVI*. Pamplona: Editorial EGN, 2012.

Bettlé, Nicole. "Child-Witches." In *The Routledge History of Witchcraft*, edited by Johannes Dillinger, 233–43. London: Routledge, 2020.

Bever, Edward. "Bullying, the Neurobiology of Emotional Aggression, and the Experience of Witchcraft." In *Emotions in the History of Witchcraft*, edited by Laura Kounine and Michael Ostling, 193–212. London: Palgrave Macmillan, 2016.

———. *The Realities of Witchcraft and Popular Magic in Early Modern Europe: Culture, Cognition, and Everyday Life*. London: Palgrave Macmillan, 2008.

Bleichmar, Daniela, Paula De Vos, Kristin Huffine, and Kevin Sheehan, eds. *Science in the Spanish and Portuguese Empires, 1500–1800*. Palo Alto: Stanford University Press, 2008.

Bloomfield, Morton W. *The Seven Deadly Sins: An Introduction to the History of a Religious Concept, with Special Reference to Medieval English Literature*. East Lansing: Michigan State College Press, 1952.

Bodian, Miriam. *Dying in the Law of Moses: Crypto-Jewish Martyrdom in the Iberian World*. Bloomington: Indiana University Press, 2007.

Briggs, Robin. "Many Reasons Why: Witchcraft and the Problem of Multiple Explanations." In *Witchcraft in Early Modern Europe: Studies in Culture and Beliefs*, edited by Jonathan Barry, Marianne Hester, and Gareth Roberts, 49–63. Cambridge: Cambridge University Press, 1996.

——. *Witches and Neighbors: The Social and Cultural Context of European Witchcraft*. New York: Viking, 1996.

Broomhall, Susan. "Miracles and Misery: Nuns' Narratives of Psychic and Spiritual Violence in Sixteenth-Century France." In *Violence and Emotions in Early Modern Europe*, edited by Susan Broomhall and Sarah Finn, 97–110. New York: Taylor & Francis, 2015.

Cameron, Pierre. "De victime à accusé: La criminalisation de l'enfant sorcier en Europe (fin XVIᵉ siècle—début XVIIᵉ siècle)." *Histoire sociale/Social History* 95 (2014): 515–46.

Campo Guinea, María del Juncal. "El matrimonio clandestino: Procesos ante el Tribunal Eclesiástico en el Archivo Diocesano de Pamplona (siglos XVI–XVII)." *Príncipe de Viana* 65 (2004): 205–22.

——. "Los procesos por causa matrimonial ante el tribunal eclesiástico de Pamplona en los siglos XVI y XVII." *Príncipe de Viana* 55 (1994): 377–90.

Canons and Decrees of the Council of Trent. Translated by Rev. H. J. Schroeder, O. P. Rockford, IL: TAN Books and Publishers, 1978.

Caro Baroja, Julio. "De nuevo sobre la historia de brujería." *Príncipe de Viana* 30 (1969): 265–328.

——. *Inquisición, brujería, y criptojudaismo*. Barcelona: Ariel, 1970.

——. *The World of the Witches*. Chicago: University of Chicago Press, 1961.

Carroll, Stuart. "The Peace in the Feud in Sixteenth- and Seventeenth-Century France." *Past and Present* 178 (2003): 74–115.

Christian, William A., Jr. *Local Religion in Sixteenth-Century Spain*. Princeton: Princeton University Press, 1981.

Clark, Stuart. *Thinking with Demons: The Idea of Witchcraft in Early Modern Europe*. Oxford: Clarendon Press, 1997.

Cohen, Jeremy. *The Friars and the Jews: The Evolution of Medieval Anti-Judaism*. Ithaca: Cornell University Press, 1982.

——. *Living Letters of the Law: Ideas of the Jew in Medieval Christianity*. Berkeley: University of California Press, 1999.

Contreras, Jaime. *El Santo Oficio de la Inquisición en Galicia, 1560–1700*. Madrid: Ediciones AKAL, 1982.

——. *Soto contra Riquelmes: Regidores, inquisidores, y criptojudíos*. 2nd ed. Madrid: Siglo XXI de España Editores, S.A., 2013.

Contreras, Jaime, and Gustav Henningsen. "Forty-Four Thousand Cases of the Spanish Inquisition (1540–1700): Analysis of a Historical Data Bank." In *The Inquisition in Early Modern Europe: Studies on Sources and Methods*, ed. Gustav Henningsen and John A. Tedeschi, 100–129. DeKalb: Northern Illinois University Press, 1986.

Corteguera, Luís R. *Death by Effigy: A Case from the Mexican Inquisition*. Philadelphia: University of Pennsylvania Press, 2012.

——. "The Painter Who Lost His Hat: Artisans and Justice in Early Modern Barcelona." *Sixteenth Century Journal* 29 (1998): 1023–42.

Cummins, Stephen. "Forgiving Crimes in Early Modern Naples." In *Cultures of Conflict Resolution in Early Modern Europe*, edited by Stephen Cummins and Laura Kounine, 255–79. Farnham, Surrey: Ashgate, 2016.

Davis, Robert C. "Say It with Stones: The Language of Rock-Throwing in Early Modern Italy." *Ludica* 10 (2004): 113–27.

Dedieu, Jean-Pierre. *L'adminstracion de la foi: l'Inquisition de Tolède, XVI–XVIII siècle.* Madrid: Casa de Velázquez, 1989.

Delumeau, Jean. *Catholicism Between Luther and Voltaire: A New View of the Counter-Reformation.* London: Westminster John Knox, 1987.

Ditchfield, Simon. "De-centering the Catholic Reformation: Papacy and Peoples in the Early Modern World." *Archiv für Reformationsgeschichte* 101 (2010): 186–208.

———. "What's in a Title? Writing a History of the Counter-Reformation for the Post-Colonial Age." *Archiv für Reformationsgeschichte* 108 (2017): 255–63.

Duni, Matteo. "Doubting Witchcraft: Theologians, Jurists, and Inquisitors During the Fifteenth and Sixteenth Centuries." *Studies in Church History* 52 (2016): 203–31.

Dyer, Abigail. "Heresy and Dishonor: Sexual Crimes Before the Courts of Early Modern Spain." PhD diss. Columbia University, 2000.

———. "Seduction by Promise of Marriage: Law, Sex, and Culture in Seventeenth-Century Spain." *Sixteenth Century Journal* 34 (2003): 439–55.

Evans-Pritchard, E. E. *Witchcraft, Oracles and Magic Among the Azande.* Oxford: Clarendon Press, 1937.

Fenster, Thelma, and Daniel Lord Smail. *Fama: The Politics of Talk and Reputation in Medieval Europe.* Ithaca: Cornell University Press, 2003.

Fernández de Pinedo, Kike, and Xabi Orsoa de Alda. "'Brujas' euskaldunes alavesas en el proceso inquisitorial de Logroño (1609–1614)." *Fontes Linguae Vasconum* 109 (2018): 419–41.

Fernández Nieto, Manuel. *Proceso a la brujería: En torno al auto de fe de los brujos de Zugarramurdi, Logroño 1610.* Madrid: Tecnos, 1989.

Flynn, Maureen. "Mimesis of the Last Judgment: The Spanish *Auto de Fe.*" *Sixteenth Century Journal* 22 (1991): 281–97.

Fuentes, Marisa. *Dispossessed Lives: Enslaved Women, Violence, and the Archive.* Philadelphia: University of Pennsylvania Press, 2018.

García-Arenal, Mercedes. *Inquisición y moriscos: Los procesos del tribunal de Cuenca.* Madrid: Siglo XXI de España Editores, S.A., 1978.

———. "A Polyphony of Voices: Trials and Graffiti of the Prisons of the Inquisition in Palermo." *Quaderni Storici* 157 (2018): 39–70.

Garcia Boix, Rafael. *Colección de documentos para la historia de la inquisición de Córdoba.* Córdoba: Monte de Piedad y Caja de Ahorros, 1982.

García Cárcel, Ricardo. *Orígenes de la inquisición española: El tribunal de Valencia, 1478–1530.* Barcelona: Ediciones Península, 1976.

Gaskill, Malcolm. "Witchcraft in Early Modern Kent: Stereotypes and the Background to Accusations." In *Witchcraft in Early Modern Europe: Studies in Culture and Beliefs*, edited by Jonathan Barry, Marianne Hester, and Gareth Roberts, 257–87. Cambridge: Cambridge University Press, 1996.

Givens, James B. *Inquisition and Medieval Society: Power, Discipline, and Resistance in Languedoc.* Ithaca: Cornell University Press, 1997.

Gómez Canseco, Luís María. *Don Bernardo de Sandoval y Rojas: Dichos, escritos, y una vida en verso.* Huelva: Universidad de Huelva, 2017.

Goñi Gaztambide, José. *Historia de los obispos de Pamplona, s. xvii.* Vol. 5. Pamplona: Ediciones Universidad de Navarra, 1987.

———. *Los navarros en el Concilio de Trento y la reforma tridentina en la diocesis de Pamplona.* Pamplona: Imprenta diocesana, 1947.

———. "El tratado 'De superstitionibus' de Martín Andosilla." *Cuadernos de etnología y etnografía Navarra* 3 (1971): 249–322.

Greer, Margaret, Walter Mignolo, and Maureen Quilligan. *Rereading the Black Legend: The Discourses of Religious and*

Racial Difference in the Renaissance Empires. Chicago: University of Chicago Press, 2007.

Hartman, Saidiya. *Wayward Lives, Beautiful Experiments: Intimate Histories of Riotous Black Girls, Troublesome Women, and Queer Radicals*. New York: W. W. Norton, 2019.

Henningsen, Gustav. *The Salazar Documents*. Leiden: Brill, 2004.

———. *The Witches' Advocate*. Reno: University of Nevada Press, 1980.

Hillgarth, J. N. *The Mirror of Spain, 1500–1700: The Formation of a Myth*. Ann Arbor: University of Michigan Press, 2000.

Homza, Lu Ann. "How to Harass an Inquisitor-General: The Polyphonic Law of Friar Francisco Ortíz." In *A Renaissance of Conflicts: Visions and Revisions of Law and Society in Italy and Spain*, edited by John A. Marino and Thomas Kuehn, 297–334. Toronto: University of Toronto Press, 2004.

———. "Local Knowledge and Catholic Reform in Early Modern Spain." In *Reforming Reformation*, edited by Thomas F. Mayer, 81–102. Farnham, Surrey: Ashgate, 2012.

———. "The Merits of Disruption and Tumult: New Scholarship on Spain in the Reformation." *Archiv für Reformationsgeschichte/Archive for Reformation History* 100 (2009): 212–28.

———. "A Reluctant Demonologist and Perceptive Lawyer: Alonso de Salazar Frías, Spanish Inquisitor." In *The Science of Demons: Early Modern Authors Facing Witchcraft and the Devil*, edited by Jan Machielson, 299–312. Abingdon: Routledge, 2020.

———. *The Spanish Inquisition, 1478–1614: An Anthology of Sources*. Indianapolis, IN: Hackett, 2006.

———. "Webs of Conversation and Discernment: Searching for Spiritual Accompaniment in Sixteenth-Century Spain." *Catholic Historical Review* 106 (2020): 227–55.

———. "When Witches Litigate: New Sources from Early Modern Navarre." *Journal of Modern History* 91 (2019): 245–75.

Idoate, Florencio. "Agotes en los valles de Roncal y Baztan." *Príncipe de Viana* (1948): 489–513.

———. *La brujería en Navarra y sus documentos*. Pamplona: Diputación Foral de Navarra, 1978.

———. *Documentos sobre los agotes y grupos afines en Navarra*. Pamplona: Institución Príncipe de Viana, 1973.

Insausti, Sebastián. "El primer catecismo en euskera guipuzcoano." *Boletín de la Real Sociedad Vasca Amigos del País* 14 (1958): 78–83.

Iribarren, José María. "Interesante documento acerca del probado en el auto de fe celebrado en Logroño el año 1610 contra las brujas de Zugarramurdi." *Príncipe de Viana* 17 (1944): 422–27.

Janson, Katherine L. "'Pro bono pacis': Crime, Conflict, and Dispute Resolution; The Evidence of Notarial Peace Contracts in Late Medieval Florence." *Speculum* 88 (2013): 427–56.

Jiménez Montserín, Miguel. *Introducción a la inquisición española: Documentos básicos para el estudio del Santo Oficio*. Madrid: Editora Nacional, 1980.

Johnson, Paul Michael. "Feeling Certainty, Performing Sincerity: The Hermeneutics of Truth in Inquisitorial and Theatrical Practice." In *The Quest for Certainty in Early Modern Europe: From Inquisition to Inquiry, 1550–1700*, edited by Barbara Fuchs and Mercedes García-Arenal, 50–79. Toronto: University of Toronto Press, 2020.

Kagan, Richard L. *Lawsuits and Litigants in Castile, 1500–1700*. Chapel Hill: University of North Carolina Press, 1981.

———. "Prescott's Paradigm: American Historical Scholarship and the Decline of Spain." *American Historical Review* 101 (1996): 423–66.

Kallendorf, Hilaire. *Sins of the Fathers: Moral Economies in Early Modern Spain*. Toronto: University of Toronto Press, 2013.

Kamen, Henry. *The Spanish Inquisition: A Historical Revision*. New Haven: Yale University Press, 1997.

Kettering, Sharon. *Patrons, Brokers, and Clients in Seventeenth-Century France*. Oxford: Oxford University Press, 1986.

Kounine, Laura. *Imagining the Witch: Emotions, Gender, and Selfhood in Early Modern Germany*. Oxford: Oxford University Press, 2018.

———. "The Witch on Trial: Narratives of Conflict and Community in Early Modern Germany." In *Cultures of Conflict Resolution in Early Modern Europe*, edited by Stephen Cummins and Laura Kounine, 229–54. Farnham, Surrey: Ashgate, 2016.

Kounine, Laura, and Michael Ostling, eds. *Emotions in the History of Witchcraft*. London: Palgrave Macmillan, 2016.

Krause, Virginia. *Witchcraft, Demonology, and Confession in Early Modern France*. New York: Cambridge University Press, 2015.

Kuehn, Thomas. "Reading Microhistory: The Example of *Giovanni and Lusanna*." *Journal of Modern History* 61 (1989): 512–34.

Lambert, Malcolm. *Medieval Heresy: Popular Movements from the Gregorian Reform to the Reformation*. 3rd ed. Oxford: Wiley-Blackwell, 2002.

Levack, Brian P. *The Witch-Hunt in Early Modern Europe*. London: Longman, 1995.

Lynn, Kimberly. *Between Court and Confessional: The Politics of Spanish Inquisitors*. Cambridge: Cambridge University Press, 2013.

Macfarlane, Alan. *Witchcraft in Tudor and Stuart England: A Comparative Study*. New York: Harper & Row, 1970.

MacKay, Ruth. *Life in a Time of Pestilence: The Great Castilian Plague of 1596–1601*. Cambridge: Cambridge University Press, 2019.

Maltby, William S. *The Black Legend in England: The Development of Anti-Spanish Sentiment, 1558–1660*. Durham: Duke University Press, 1971.

Martin, John J. "Tortured Testimonies." *Acta histriae* 19 (2011): 375–92.

Martínez Bujanda, Jesús. "Índices de libros prohibidos del siglo XVI." In *Historia de la Inquisición en España y América*, vol. 3, edited by Joaquín Pérez Villanueva and Bartolomé Escandell Bonet, 773–828. Madrid: BAE, 2000.

Martínez Millán, José. *La hacienda de la Inquisición (1478–1700)*. Madrid: CSIC, 1984.

Maza, Sarah. "The Kids Aren't All Right: Historians and the Problem of Childhood." *AHR* Exchange: "Rethinking the History of Childhood." *American Historical Review* 125 (2020): 1261–85.

McNamara, Celeste I. *The Bishop's Burden: Reforming the Catholic Church in Early Modern Italy*. Washington, DC: Catholic University Press, 2020.

Meseguer Fernández, Juan. "El period fundacional (1478-1517)." In *Historia de la Inquisición en España y América*, vol. 1, edited by Joaquín Pérez Villanueva and Bartolomé Escandell Bonet, 381–70. Madrid: BAE, 1984.

Midelfort, H. C. Erik. "Witch Craze? Beyond the Legends of Panic." *Magic, Ritual, and Witchcraft* 6 (2011): 11–33.

———. *Witch-Hunting in Southwestern Germany, 1562–1684: The Intellectual and Social Foundations*. Palo Alto: Stanford University Press, 1972.

Monteano Sorbet, Peio J. *El iceberg Navarro: Euskera y castellano en la Navarra del siglo XVI*. Pamplona: Pamiela, 2017.

———. *Los navarros ante el hambre, la peste, la guerra, y la fiscalidad: Siglos XV y XVI*. Pamplona: Universidad Pública de Navarra, 1999.

Monter, E. William. *Frontiers of Heresy: The Spanish Inquisition from the Basque Lands to Sicily*. Cambridge: Cambridge University Press, 1990.

———. "The Historiography of European Witchcraft: Progress and Prospects." *Journal of Interdisciplinary History* 2 (1972): 435–51.

————. *Witchcraft in France and Switzerland: The Borderlands During the Reformation.* Ithaca: Cornell University Press, 1976.

Moreno, Doris. "La discrecionalidad de un inquisidor: Francisco Vaca, ¿El primer abogado de las brujas?" In *Akelarre: La caza de brujas en el Pirineo (siglos XIII–XIX): Homenaje al Professor Gustav Henningsen, RIEV* Extra 9 (2012): 202–14.

Murray, Margaret Alice. *The Witch-Cult in Western Europe: A Study in Anthropology.* Oxford: Clarendon Press, 1921.

Nalle, Sara T. *God in La Mancha.* Baltimore: Johns Hopkins University Press, 1992.

————. "Inquisitors, Priests, and the People During the Catholic Reformation." *Sixteenth Century Journal* 18 (1987): 557–87.

————. *Mad for God: Bartolomé Sanchez, the Secret Messiah of Cardenete.* Charlottesville: University Press of Virginia, 2001.

Navajas Twose, Eloísa, and José Antonio Sáinz Varela. "Una relación inquisitorial sobre la brujería." *Huarte de San Juan: Geografía e Historia* 17 (2010): 347–71.

Nirenberg, David. *Anti-Judaism: The Western Tradition.* New York: W. W. Norton, 2014.

Nogal Fernández, Rocío de la. "Las brujas de Ochagavía y sus documentos (1539–1540)." *Huarte de San Juan: Geografía e Historia* 17 (2010): 373–85.

O'Malley, John W. *Trent and All That: Renaming Catholicism in the Early Modern Era.* Cambridge: Harvard University Press, 2000.

Orella Unzué, José Luis de. "Conflictos de jurisdicción en el tema de la Brujería Vasca (1450–1530)." *RIEV* 31 (1986): 797–816.

Ortega-Costa, Milagros. *Proceso de la inquisición contra María de Cazalla.* Madrid: FUE, 1978.

Palmer, James. "Piety and Social Distinction in Late Medieval Roman Peacemaking." *Speculum* 89 (2014): 974–1004.

Parker, Geoffrey. *The Grand Strategy of Philip II.* New Haven: Yale University Press, 1998.

Pasamar Lázaro, José Enrique. *Los familiares del Santo Oficio en el distrito de Aragón.* Zaragoza: Instituto "Fernando el Católico," 1999.

Pastore, Stefania. *Il vangelo e la spada: L'inquisizione di Castiglia e suoi critici (1468–1598).* Rome: Storia e Letteratura, 2003.

Pegg, Mark. *The Corruption of Angels: The Great Inquisition of 1245–1246.* Princeton: Princeton University Press, 2001.

Pérez, Joseph. *Historia de la brujería en España.* Madrid: Espasa, 2010.

Pérez Villanueva, Joaquín, ed. *La inquisición española: Nueva visión, nuevos horizontes.* Madrid: Signo Veintiuno, 1978.

Pérez Villanueva, Joaquín, and Bartolomé Escandell Bonet. *Historia de la Inquisición en España y América.* Madrid: BAE, 2000.

Peters, Edward. *The Magician, the Witch, and the Law.* Philadelphia: University of Pennsylvania Press, 1978.

Pimoulier, Amaia. "Entre el luto y la supervivencia: Viudas y viudedad en la Navarra moderna (siglos XVI y XVII)." PhD diss., Universidad de Navarra, 2010.

Porres Marijuán, Rosario, ed. *Entre el fervor y la violencia: Estudios sobre los vascos y la Iglesia (siglos xvi-xviii).* Bilbao: Universidad del País Vasco, 2015.

Portuondo, María M. *Secret Science: Spanish Cosmography and the New World.* Chicago: University of Chicago Press, 2009.

Premo, Bianca. *The Enlightenment on Trial: Ordinary Litigants and Colonialism in the Spanish Empire.* New York: Oxford University Press, 2017.

Price, Munro. "Versailles Revisited: New Work on the Old Regime." *The Historical Journal* 46 (2003): 437–47.

Ray, Jonathan. *After Expulsion: 1492 and the Making of Sephardic Jewry.* New York: New York University Press, 2013.

Reguera, Iñaki. *La Inquisición española en el País Vasco (el Tribunal de Calahorra, 1513–1570).* San Sebastián: Editorial Txertoa, 1984.

———. "Violencia y clero en la sociedad vasca de la edad moderna." In *Entre el fervor y la violencia: Estudios sobre los vascos y la Iglesia (siglos XVI–XVIII)*, edited by Rosario Porres Marijuán, 131–86. Bilbao: Universidad de País Vasco, 2015.

Restall, Matthew, and Felipe Fernández-Armesto. *The Conquistadors: A Very Short Introduction*. Oxford: Oxford University Press, 2012.

Rojas, Rochelle. "Bad Christians and Hanging Toads: Witch Trials in Early Modern Spain, 1525–1675." PhD diss., Duke University, 2016.

Rolley, Thibaut Maus de, and Jan Machielson. "The Mythmaker of the Sabbat: Pierre de Lancre's *Tableau de l'inconstance des mauvais anges et demons*." In *The Science of Demons: Early Modern Authors Facing Witchcraft and the Devil*, edited by Jan Machielson, 283–98. Abingdon: Routledge, 2020.

Roper, Lyndal. "'Evil Imaginings and Fantasies': Child-Witches and the End of the Witch-Craze." *Past & Present* 167 (2000): 107–39.

———. *Oedipus and the Devil: Witchcraft, Religion, and Sexuality in Early Modern Europe*. London: Routledge, 1994.

———. *Witch Craze: Terror and Fantasy in Baroque Germany*. New Haven: Yale University Press, 2004.

Rose, Colin. *A Renaissance of Violence: Homicide in Early Modern Italy*. Cambridge: Cambridge University Press, 2019.

Rowlands, Alison. "Telling Witchcraft Stories: New Perspectives on Witchcraft and Witches in the Early Modern Period." *Gender and History* 10 (1998): 294–302.

———. *Witchcraft Narratives in Germany: Rothenburg, 1561–1652*. Manchester: Manchester University Press, 2003.

Ruíz Astiz, Javier. *La fuerza de la palabra escrita: Amenazas e injurias en la Navarra del Antiguo Régimen*. Pamplona: EUNSA, 2012.

Ruíz Ibáñez, José Javier and Gaetano Sabatini. "Monarchy as Conquest: Violence, Social Opportunity and Political Stability in the Establishment of the Hispanic Monarchy." *The Journal of Modern History* 81 (2009): 501–36.

Scott, Amanda L. *The Basque Seroras: Local Religion, Power, and Gender in Northern Iberia*. Ithaca: Cornell University Press, 2020.

———. "Tridentine Reform in the Afternoon: Bullfighting and the Basque Clergy." *Renaissance Quarterly* 73 (2020): 489–526.

———. "The Wayward Priest of Atondo: Clerical Misbehavior, Local Community, and the Limits of Tridentine Reform." *Sixteenth Century Journal* 47 (2016): 75–98.

Skinner, Quentin. "Meaning and Understanding in the History of Ideas." *History and Theory* 8 (1969): 3–53.

Smail, Daniel Lord. *The Consumption of Justice: Emotions, Publicity, and Legal Culture in Marseilles, 1264–1423*. Ithaca: Cornell University Press, 2003.

———. "Hatred as a Social Institution in Late-Medieval Society." *Speculum* 76 (2001): 90–126.

Summers, Montague. *A History of Witchcraft and Demonology*. New York: A. A. Knopf, 1926.

Tabernero, Cristina, and Jesús M. Usunáriz Garayoa. "*Bruja, brujo, hechicera, hechicero, sorgin como insultos en la Navarra del siglos XVI–XVII*." In *Modelos de vida y cultura en Navarra (siglos XVI y XVII). Antología de textos*, edited Mariela Insúa, 381–429. Pamplona: Servicio de Publicaciones de la Universidad de Navarra, 2016.

Tausiet, María. *Urban Magic in Early Modern Spain: Abracadabra Omnipotens*. London: Palgrave Macmillan, 2014.

Taylor, Scott K. *Honor and Violence in Golden-Age Spain*. New Haven: Yale University Press, 2008.

Tedeschi, John. *The Prosecution of Heresy: Collected Studies on the Inquisition in Early Modern Italy*. Binghamton: SUNY, 1991.

———. "The Question of Magic and Witchcraft in Two Unpublished Inquisitorial Manuals of the Seventeenth Century." *Proceedings of the American Philosophical Association* 131 (1987): 92–111.

Tellechea Idígoras, José Ignacio. *Fray Bartolomé Carranza: Documentos Históricos*. 2 vols. Madrid: Real Academia de Historia, 1962.

———. "La visita 'ad limina' del Obispo de Pamplona, Don Bernardo Rojas y Sandoval (1594)." *Revista Española de Derecho Canónico* 21 (1966): 591–617.

Thomas, Keith. *Religion and the Decline of Magic: Studies of Popular Beliefs in Sixteenth and Seventeenth Century England*. New York: Charles Scribner's Sons, 1971.

Trevor-Roper, Hugh R. *The European Witch-Craze of the Sixteenth and Seventeenth Centuries and Other Essays*. New York: Harper & Row, 1969.

Usunáriz Garayoa, Jesús M. "La caza de brujas en la Navarra moderna (siglos XVI–XVII)." *Akelarre: La caza de brujas en el Pirineo (siglos XIII–XIX): Homenaje al profesor Gustav Henningsen. RIEV Extra 9* (2012): 306–50.

———. "Cuando la convivencia es imposible: Los pleitos de discordia entre padres e hijos (Navarra, siglos XVI–XVII)." In *Padres e hijos en España y el mundo hispánico, siglos XVI y XVIII*, edited by Jesús M. Usunáriz Garayoa and Rocío

García Bourrellier, 207–44. Madrid: Visor Libros, 2008.

Van Engen, John. "The Christian Middle Ages as a Historiographical Problem." *American Historical Review* 91 (1986): 519–52.

Voltmer, Rita. "Behind the 'Veil of Memory': About the Limitations of Narratives." *Magic, Ritual, and Witchcraft* 5 (2010): 96–102.

———. "The Witch in the Courtroom: Torture and the Representations of Emotion." In *Emotions in the History of Witchcraft*, edited by Laura Kounine and Michael Ostling, 97–116. London: Palgrave Macmillan, 2016.

Walker, Garthine. "Child-Killing and Emotion in Early Modern England and Wales." In *Death, Emotion and Childhood in Premodern Europe*, edited by Katie Barclay, Kimberly Reynolds, and Ciara Rawnsley, 151–72. London: Palgrave Macmillan, 2016.

Wingate, Alexandra. "A qué manera de libros y letras es inclinado: Las bibliotecas privadas de Navarra en los siglos XVI y XVII." W&M ScholarWorks, April 2018. https://sites.google.com/view /bibliotecasnavarras/home.

Wray, Shona Kelly. "Instruments of Concord: Making Peace and Settling Disputes Through a Notary in the City and Contado of Late Medieval Bologna." *Journal of Social History* 42 (2009): 733–60.

Index

books, 61
    See also printed materials
Borda, Juan de la, 36, 38, 41, 97, 135, 174
bribery
    confessions and, 6, 12, 69, 105, 143
    notaries and, 168
Briggs, Robin, 195n47
Burga, María de (or Barrenchea), 99
burning at the stake, 2, 5, 41, 47, 66, 134,
    157, 161

Calvin, John, 3
Cameron, Pierre, 197n19
cannibalism, 26–27, 31, 34–35, 81, 159
Canon *episcopi* (canon law text), 28, 199n44
Caracoechea, Pedro de, 43
Carcastillo, 52
Caro Baroja, Julio, 8, 11, 192n18,
    192nn20–21
Carranza, Bartolomé de, 216n32
Carrillo y Aldrete, Martín, 166, 215n11
Carthage, Council of, 2
Castellano, María, 42
catechisms, 56, 59
Catharism, 3
Catholicism, 205n46
    inversion of, 27, 56–58, 186
    orthodoxy, 2–3, 58
    religious environment, 51–54
    religious reform, 54–56
census registers, 8–9
Charles V, Holy Roman Emperor, 54
child accusers, 6, 29–31, 67, 69–70, 72–77,
    185
    believability of, 32, 97, 105, 189
    child-witches as, 34–35 (*see also*
        child-witches)
    family pressure on, 109–13
    slander prosecutions and, 12, 21–23,
        100, 111–13
    testimony of, 31
children
    abducted by witches, 6, 34, 45, 63–64,
        68–69, 109
    centrality to witch persecution, 120,
        200n52

community responsibilities for, 12–13,
        31–35, 68–69, 120, 185
    deaths of, 32–33, 92, 200n57
    education of, 56
    illegitimate, 67–68
    as victims of witches, 6, 21–22, 24–25,
        29–31, 33–35, 82, 120, 185–87,
        197n19, 210n34
    See also teenagers
child-witches
    absolved, 138, 140–41
    activities of, 2, 25–26, 31
    coerced into confessions, 102–4, 107,
        118
    Eucharist and, 204n124
    execution of, 197n19
    inquisitorial investigation of, 38, 40
    outcomes for, 203n121, 208n113
    self-identification as, 74–76
    visions of Virgin Mary at akelarres, 58,
        60, 62, 186
Chiperena, Juan Miguel, 49
Christian faith, renounced. *See* apostasy
clergy. *See* bishops; priests
coercion
    accusations and confessions made
        under, 6, 28, 73–74, 85, 102–4,
        107, 118, 133–34, 156
    family pressure, 12–13, 70, 107, 186,
        189
    prevention of, 177, 179
commissioners (*comisarios*), 44–45, 75, 80,
        88, 150, 187
    1614 instructions and, 176–77
    episcopal and secular justice and, 131
    local torture and, 164, 179
    witchcraft accusations and, 125, 133
complicity, 93, 96–97
comprobación, 95
confessions, 2, 45, 48
    1614 instructions on, 176
    bribery and, 6, 12, 69, 105, 143
    children and teenagers, 30
    credibility of, 178
    family pressure and, 12–13, 70, 107,
        186, 189

gender (*continued*)
    fear and, 214n101
    insults and, 21
    witchcraft accusations and, 42
    witch-hunting and, 10, 12
    of witch suspects, 21, 39, 191n5
    See also women
genealogical investigations, 166–69,
    221n66
Germany, 7, 12, 30, 194n35
Gero (1643), 183
Gipuzkoa, 6, 91, 101, 114, 126, 143, 203n120
Goecoechea, María de, 209n115
Goiburu, Juan de, 161
Goiburu, Miguel de, 161
Goizueta, 71

haeresis, 2
harmful magic *(maleficium)*, 5, 24–27,
    33–34, 150, 192n13
hatred, 67, 71–72, 164, 171, 183, 196n2,
    213n84
Hell, 61, 186
Henningsen, Gustav, 8, 11, 18, 191n7,
    192n18, 192n20, 192n22,
    194n41, 201n80, 201n83,
    203n119, 212n65, 215n11, 215n27,
    216nn34–35, 219n91, 219n94,
    220n27, 221n55, 222n80
Henri IV, King, 204n2
heresy, 2–3, 33–34
    absolution for, 48–49
    boundaries of, 58
    congresses on, 210n13
    inquisitors and, 17
    relapse into, 130, 138–39
    See also witchcraft
Hernale, Tomás, 143–44
homicide, 42, 76, 94, 163, 193n24, 196n10,
    202nn91–92, 202n95
Hondarribia, 126, 137
honor and dishonor, 13, 185–86
    confessions and, 70, 102–3, 107, 132,
    185–86
    false accusations and, 145

    family and, 22, 72, 75
    female behavior and, 77–78
    importance of, 197n12
    inquisition tribunals and, 105
    murder and, 196n10
    restoration of, 178–80
    slander and, 87, 116
    social ruin and, 48–49
    tribunals and, 36
houses of penitence, 201n78
Hualde, Lorenzo, 64, 71, 102, 133–34, 173,
    188, 207n90, 212n63, 212n71,
    218n75

Ibáñes, Juan, 81–82
Idoate, Florencio, 195n44, 220n27
Igantzi, 30, 132
Ignatius of Loyola, 59
illiteracy, 10–11, 13, 15, 24, 141, 183, 198n27,
    205n46
Imbuluzqueta, Miguel de, 44, 109–17,
    120–21, 214n103, 214n108
Imbuluzqueta, Pedroco, 74, 109–13, 120
imprisonment, 5, 45, 176
    expenses, 35–36, 217n59
    perpetual prison, 5, 201n78
    poverty and, 39, 210n27, 213n78,
    213n95
    private, 48, 99, 186
    sickness and death, 20, 36–37, 40, 62,
    115, 118, 120, 201n73, 206n49
    for slander, 113–15, 118
    of witch suspects, 124, 201n79
Inda, Juan de, 31
Inda, Pedro de, 218n69
Indart, María de, 70, 160, 220n32
Indart, Pedro de, 34
infanticide, 32–33, 76
    See also deaths
inheritances, 182
inquisitor-general, 54, 89, 98, 107
    See also Sandoval y Rojas, Bernardino
    de
inquisitorial justice system
    expenses in, 35–36

punishments (*continued*)
> *See also* auto de fe; banishment; burning at the stake; confiscation of goods and property; exile

Ramírez, Juan, 168
rape, 67
reconciliation
> confession and penance, 2, 4–5, 7, 17, 37–38, 40–41, 70, 82–84, 90, 188
> edict of grace and, 108–9, 123–24, 130, 137–38, 141, 151
> repentance and, 90

religious dissidents, 52
religious errors, 2, 5, 58
> *See also* heresy

religious pariahs, 48–49
remorse, 78–79
reparative justice, 153
repentance, 81, 90, 140, 219n92
reputation, 197n12, 197n14
> women and, 46, 69, 77–78, 208n111
> *See also* honor and dishonor

restorative justice, 219n2
retributive justice, 219n2
revocations of confessions, 28, 30, 78–79, 216n46, 218n75
> 1614 instructions on, 177
> absolution and, 102
> by children, 120
> child-witches, 199n50
> Devil and, 107
> fear and, 139–40, 157
> parish priests and, 132
> publicity about, 173
> punishment for, 165
> secular jurisdiction and, 92
> Suprema and, 163, 221n53
> written documentation of, 183

Rojas, Rochelle, 193n24, 193n26, 196n3, 196n8, 198n29, 199n48, 207n76, 214n112, 217n53
Roper, Lyndal, 195n47
Rose, Colin, 202n86
royal secular court (in Pamplona), 17, 141
> prosecution of witch torturers, 179

records of children's testimony, 31
slander cases, 20–21, 100–101, 110, 116–21
types of justice, 219n2
> *See also* secular justice system

sacraments, 58, 177
> *See also* Eucharist; penance

saints, veneration of, 57–58
Salazar Frías, Alonso de (Inquisitor)
> 1614 instructions and, 177
> career, 188
> confessions and, 70, 78–79, 82–84
> conflicts in tribunal, 13, 127–29, 154–65, 220n26
> edict of grace and, 108–9, 151, 153
> end of witch hunt and, 172–75
> epistemology and priorities, 159, 188–90
> evidence and, 199n45
> legal jurisdiction and, 100, 216n49
> notaries and, 166
> obedience, 140, 162, 188, 220n8
> report of March 1612, 154–58
> Sandoval and, 124, 173
> skepticism and empiricism, 6–7, 135–37, 179–81, 192n20, 216n34
> Solarte and, 106–8
> Ulibarri and, 209n133
> Venegas and, 215n30, 220n18, 220n24
> verification of witch activities, 95–97
> village violence and, 148–51, 186
> visitation in 1611, 6, 137–48
> witch investigations, 29, 38, 41, 58

Salcedo (Inquisitor), 88
Saldis, Juan de, 220n5
Sales Tirapu, Don José Luis, 18
saligia, 205n38
salvation, 56
sambenitos, 5, 88, 132, 134, 174, 178, 201n78
Sanchigorena, Pierre de, 66
Sandoval y Rojas, Bernardino de
> career and name change, 204n16
> directions to inquisitors, 123–35
> edict of grace and, 123–24, 130, 149–51
> notaries and, 166, 221n62